EU Legislation

Editor-in-Chief

Glenn Robinson

Second edition August 2011

First edition 2010

Published ISBN 9781 4453 8062 9

(Previous ISBN: 9780 7517 9348 2)

British Library Cataloguing-in-Publication Data
A catalogue record for this book is available
from the British Library

Published by
BPP Learning Media Ltd
BPP House, Aldine Place
London W12 8AA
www.bpp.com/learningmedia

Printed in the United Kingdom

Your learning materials, published by BPP
Learning Media Ltd, are printed on paper
sourced from sustainable, managed forests.

Contents

Table of Contents

THE EUROPEAN COMMUNITIES ACT 1972

Part I General Provisions

1 Short title and interpretation.

(1)   This Act may be cited as the European Communities Act 1972.

(2)   In this Act . . .

"the Communities" means the European Economic Community, the European Coal and Steel Community and the European Atomic Energy Community;

"the Treaties" or the EU Treaties] means, subject to subsection (3) below, the pre-accession treaties, that is to say, those described in Part I of Schedule 1 to this Act, taken with—

(a)   the treaty relating to the accession of the United Kingdom to the European Economic Community and to the European Atomic Energy Community, signed at Brussels on the 22nd January 1972; and

(b)   the decision, of the same date, of the Council of the European Communities relating to the accession of the United Kingdom to the European Coal and Steel Community; and

(c)   the treaty relating to the accession of the Hellenic Republic to the European Economic Community and to the European Atomic Energy Community, signed at Athens on 28th May 1979; and

(d)   the decision, of 24th May 1979, of the Council relating to the accession of the Hellenic Republic to the European Coal and Steel Community; and

(e)   the decisions of the Council of 7th May 1985, 24th June 1988, 31st October 1994, 29th September 2000 and 7th June 2007 on the Communities' system of own resources; and

(g)   the treaty relating to the accession of the Kingdom of Spain and the Portuguese Republic to the European Economic Community and to the European Atomic Energy Community, signed at Lisbon and Madrid on 12th June 1985; and

(h)   the decision, of 11th June 1985, of the Council relating to the accession of the Kingdom of Spain and the Portuguese Republic to the European Coal and Steel Community; and

(j)   the following provisions of the Single European Act signed at Luxembourg and The Hague on 17th and 28th February 1986, namely Title II (amendment of the treaties establishing the Communities) and, so far as they relate to any of the Communities or any Community institution, the preamble and Titles I (common provisions) and IV (general and final provisions); and

(k)   Titles II, III and IV of the Treaty on European Union signed at Maastricht on 7th February 1992, together with the other provisions of the Treaty so far as they relate to those Titles, and the Protocols adopted at Maastricht on that date and annexed to the Treaty establishing the European Community with the exception of the Protocol on Social Policy on page 117 of Cm 1934; and

(l)   the decision, of 1st February 1993, of the Council amending the Act concerning the election of the representatives of the European Parliament by direct universal suffrage annexed to Council Decision 76/787/ECSC, EEC, Euratom of 20th September 1976; and

(m)   the Agreement on the European Economic Area signed at Oporto on 2nd May 1992 together with the Protocol adjusting that Agreement signed at Brussels on 17th March 1993; and

(n)   the treaty concerning the accession of the Kingdom of Norway, the Republic of Austria, the Republic of Finland and the Kingdom of Sweden to the European Union, signed at Corfu on 24th June 1994; and

(o)   the following provisions of the Treaty signed at Amsterdam on 2nd October 1997 amending the Treaty on European Union, the Treaties establishing the European Communities and certain related Acts—

    (i)   Articles 2 to 9,

    (ii)   Article 12, and

    (iii)   the other provisions of the Treaty so far as they relate to those Articles,

    and the Protocols adopted on that occasion other than the Protocol on Article J.7 of the Treaty on European Union; and

(p)   the following provisions of the Treaty signed at Nice on 26th February 2001 amending the Treaty on European Union, the Treaties establishing the European Communities and certain related Acts—

    (i)   Articles 2 to 10, and

    (ii)   the other provisions of the Treaty so far as they relate to those Articles,

    and the Protocols adopted on that occasion; and

(q)   the treaty concerning the accession of the Czech Republic, the Republic of Estonia, the Republic of Cyprus, the Republic of Latvia, the Republic of Lithuania, the Republic of Hungary, the Republic of Malta, the Republic of Poland, the Republic of Slovenia and the Slovak Republic to the European Union, signed at Athens on 16th April 2003; and

(r)   the treaty concerning the accession of the Republic of Bulgaria and Romania to the European Union, signed at Luxembourg on 25th April 2005; and

(s)   the Treaty of Lisbon Amending the Treaty on European Union and the Treaty Establishing the European Community signed at Lisbon on 13th December 2007 (together with its Annex and protocols), excluding any provision that relates to, or in so far as it relates to or could be applied in relation to, the Common Foreign and Security Policy;

and any other treaty entered into by the EU (except in so far as it relates to, or could be applied in relation to, the Common Foreign and Security Policy) , with or without any of the member States, or entered into, as a treaty ancillary to any of the Treaties, by the United Kingdom;

and any expression defined in Schedule 1 to this Act has the meaning there given to it.

(3)   If Her Majesty by Order in Council declares that a treaty specified in the Order is to be regarded as one of the EU Treaties] as herein defined, the Order shall be conclusive that it is to be so regarded; but a treaty entered into by the United Kingdom after the 22nd January 1972, other than a pre-accession treaty to which the United Kingdom accedes on terms settled on or before that date, shall not be so regarded unless it is so specified, nor be so specified unless a draft of the Order in Council has been approved by resolution of each House of Parliament.

(4)   For purposes of subsections (2) and (3) above, "treaty" includes any international agreement, and any protocol or annex to a treaty or international agreement.

2 General implementation of Treaties.

(1)   All such rights, powers, liabilities, obligations and restrictions from time to time created or arising by or under the Treaties, and all such remedies and procedures from time to time provided for by or under the Treaties, as in accordance with the Treaties are without further enactment to be given legal effect or used in the United Kingdom shall be recognised and available in law, and be enforced, allowed and followed accordingly; and the expression ["enforceable EU right"] and similar expressions shall be read as referring to one to which this subsection applies.

(2)   Subject to Schedule 2 to this Act, at any time after its passing Her Majesty may by Order in Council, and any designated Minister or department may by order, rules, regulations or scheme] , make provision—

(a)   for the purpose of implementing any [EU obligation] of the United Kingdom, or enabling any such obligation to be implemented, or of enabling any rights enjoyed or to be enjoyed by the United Kingdom under or by virtue of the Treaties to be exercised; or

(b)   for the purpose of dealing with matters arising out of or related to any such obligation or rights or the coming into force, or the operation from time to time, of subsection (1) above;

and in the exercise of any statutory power or duty, including any power to give directions or to legislate by means of orders, rules, regulations or other subordinate instrument, the person entrusted with the power or duty may have regard to the [objects of the EU] and to any such obligation or rights as aforesaid.

In this subsection "designated Minister or department" means such Minister of the Crown or government department as may from time to time be designated by Order in Council in relation to any matter or for any purpose, but subject to such restrictions or conditions (if any) as may be specified by the Order in Council.

(3)   There shall be charged on and issued out of the Consolidated Fund or, if so determined by the Treasury, the National Loans Fund the amounts required to meet any [EU obligation] to make payments to [the EU or a member State] , or any EU obligation in respect of contributions to the capital or reserves of the European Investment Bank or in respect of loans to the Bank, or to redeem any notes or obligations issued or created in respect of any such EU obligation and, except as otherwise provided by or under any enactment,—

(a)   any other expenses incurred under or by virtue of the Treaties or this Act by any Minister of the Crown or government department may be paid out of moneys provided by Parliament; and

(b)   any sums received under or by virtue of the Treaties or this Act by any Minister of the Crown or government department, save for such sums as may be required for disbursements permitted by any other enactment, shall be paid into the Consolidated Fund or, if so determined by the Treasury, the National Loans Fund.

(4)   The provision that may be made under subsection (2) above includes, subject to Schedule 2 to this Act, any such provision (of any such extent) as might be made by Act of Parliament, and any enactment passed or to be passed, other than one contained in this part of this Act, shall be construed and have effect subject to the foregoing provisions of this section; but, except as may be provided by any Act passed after this Act, Schedule 2 shall have effect in connection with the powers conferred by this and the following sections of this Act to make Orders in Council [or orders, rules, regulations or schemes] .

(5)   . . .and the references in that subsection to a Minister of the Crown or government department and to a statutory power or duty shall include a Minister or department of the Government of Northern Ireland and a power or duty arising under or by virtue of an Act of the Parliament of Northern Ireland.

(6)   A law passed by the legislature of any of the Channel Islands or of the Isle of Man, or a colonial Law (within the meaning of the Colonial Laws Validity Act 1865) passed or made for Gibraltar, if expressed to be passed or made in the implementation of the Treaties and of the obligations of the United Kingdom thereunder, shall not be void or inoperative by reason of any inconsistency with or repugnancy to an Act of Parliament, passed or to be passed, that extends to the Island or Gibraltar or any provision having the force and effect of an Act there (but not including this section), nor by reason of its having some operation outside the Island or Gibraltar; and any such Act or provision that extends to the Island or Gibraltar shall be construed and have effect subject to the provisions of any such law.

3 Decisions on, and proof of, Treaties and [EU instruments] etc.

(1)   For the purposes of all legal proceedings any question as to the meaning or effect of any of the Treaties, or as to the validity, meaning or effect of any [EU instrument] , shall be treated as a question of law (and, if not referred to the European Court, be for determination as such in accordance with the principles laid down by and any relevant [decision of [the European Court]]).

(2)   Judicial notice shall be taken of the Treaties, of the [Official Journal of the European Union] and of any decision of, or expression of opinion by, the [the European Court] on any such question as aforesaid; and the Official Journal shall be admissible as evidence of any instrument or other act thereby communicated of [the EU] or of any [EU institution] .

(3)   Evidence of any instrument issued by a [EU institution] , including any judgment or order of [the European Court] , or of any document in the custody of a EU institution , or any entry in or extract from such a document, may be given in any legal proceedings by production of a copy certified as a true copy by an official of that institution; and any document purporting to be such a copy shall be received in evidence without proof of the official position or handwriting of the person signing the certificate.

(4)   Evidence of any [EU instrument] may also be given in any legal proceedings—

(a)   by production of a copy purporting to be printed by the Queen's Printer;

(b)   where the instrument is in the custody of a government department (including a department of the Government of Northern Ireland), by production of a copy certified on behalf of the department to be a true copy by an officer of the department generally or specially authorised so to do;

and any document purporting to be such a copy as is mentioned in paragraph (b) above of an instrument in the custody of a department shall be received in evidence without proof of the official position or handwriting of the person signing the certificate, or of his authority to do so, or of the document being in the custody of the department.

(5)   In any legal proceedings in Scotland evidence of any matter given in a manner authorised by this section shall be sufficient evidence of it.

Part II Amendment of Law

4 General provision for repeal and amendment.

(1)   The enactments mentioned in Schedule 3 to this Act (being enactments that are superseded or to be superseded by reason of [EU obligations] and of the provision made by this Act in relation thereto or are not compatible with EU obligations) are hereby repealed, to the extent specified in column 3 of the Schedule, with effect from the entry date or other date mentioned in the Schedule; and in the enactments mentioned in Schedule 4 to this Act there shall, subject to any transitional provision there included, be made the amendments provided for by that Schedule.

(2) Where in any Part of Schedule 3 to this Act it is provided that repeals made by that Part are to take effect from a date appointed by order, the orders shall be made by statutory instrument, and an order may appoint different dates for the repeal of different provisions to take effect, or for the repeal of the same provision to take effect for different purposes; and an order appointing a date for a repeal to take effect may include transitional and other supplementary provisions arising out of that repeal, including provisions adapting the operation of other enactments included for repeal but not yet repealed by that Schedule, and may amend or revoke any such provisions included in a previous order.

(3) Where any of the following sections of this Act, or any paragraph of Schedule 4 to this Act, affects or is construed as one with an Act or Part of an Act similar in purpose to provisions having effect only in Northern Ireland, then—

   (a) unless otherwise provided by Act of the Parliament of Northern Ireland, the Governor of Northern Ireland may by Order in Council make provision corresponding to any made by the section or paragraph, and amend or revoke any provision so made; and

   (b) . . . .

(4) Where Schedule 3 or 4 to this Act provides for the repeal or amendment of an enactment that extends or is capable of being extended to any of the Channel Islands or the Isle of Man, the repeal or amendment shall in like manner extend or be capable of being extended thereto.

5 Customs duties.

(1) Subject to subsection (2) below, on and after the relevant date there shall be charged, levied, collected and paid on goods imported into the United Kingdom such [EU customs duty] , if any, as is for the time being applicable in accordance with the Treaties or, if the goods are not within the common customs tariff of the [EU] and the duties chargeable are not otherwise fixed by any directly applicable [EU provision] , such duty of customs, if any, as the Treasury, on the recommendation of the Secretary of State, may by order specify.

   For this purpose "the relevant date", in relation to any goods, is the date on and after which the duties of customs that may be charged thereon are no longer affected under the Treaties by any temporary provision made on or with reference to the accession of the United Kingdom to the Communities.

(2) Where as regards goods imported into the United Kingdom provision may, in accordance with the Treaties, be made in derogation of the common customs tariff or of the exclusion of customs duties as between member States, the Treasury may by order make such provision as to the customs duties chargeable on the goods, or as to exempting the goods from any customs duty, as the Treasury may on the recommendation of the Secretary of State determine.

6 The common agricultural policy.

(3) Sections 5 and 7 of the Agriculture Act 1957 (which make provision for the support of arrangements under section 1 of that Act for providing guaranteed prices or assured markets) shall apply in relation to any [EU arrangements] for or related to the regulation of the market for any agricultural produce as if references, in whatever terms, to payments made by virtue of section 1 were references to payments made by virtue of the EU arrangements by or on behalf of [the relevant Minister and as if for every reference in section 5 to the Minister there were substituted a reference to the relevant Minister.]

(4) Agricultural levies of the [EU] , so far as they are charged on goods exported from the United Kingdom or shipped as stores, shall be paid to and recoverable by [the relevant Minister]; and the power of [the relevantMinister] to make orders under section 5 of the Agriculture Act 1957, as extended by this section, shall include power to make such provision supplementary to any directly applicable [EU provision] as [the relevant Minister considers] necessary for securing the payment of any agricultural levies so charged,

including provision for the making of declarations or the giving of other information in respect of goods exported, shipped as stores, or otherwise dealt with.

(5) Except as otherwise provided by or under any enactment, agricultural levies of the [EU] , so far as they are charged on goods imported into the United Kingdom, shall be levied, collected and paid, and the proceeds shall be dealt with, as if they were [EU customs duties] , and in relation to those levies the following enactments shall apply as they would apply in relation to EU customs duties , that is to say:—

    (a) the Customs and Excise Management Act 1979 (as for the time being amended by any later Act) and any other statutory provisions for the time being in force relating generally to customs or excise duties on imported goods; and]

    (b) sections 1, 3, 4, 5, 6 (including Schedule 1), 7, 8, 9, 12, 13, 15, 17 and 18 of the Customs and Excise Duties (General Reliefs) Act 1979 but so that—

        (i) any references in sections 1, 3 and 4 to the Secretary of State shall include the Ministers; and

        (ii) the reference in section 15 to an application for an authorisation under regulations made under section 2 of that Act shall be read as a reference to an application for an authorisation under regulations made under section 2(2) of this Act;

        and, if, in connection with any such [EU arrangements] as aforesaid, the Commissioners of Customs and Excise are charged with the performance, on behalf of the Board or otherwise, of any duties in relation to the payment of refunds or allowances on goods exported or to be exported from the United Kingdom, then in relation to any such refund or allowance [section 133 (except subsection (3) and the reference to that subsection in subsection (2) and section 159 of the Customs and Excise Management Act 1979 shall apply as they apply in relation to a drawback of excise duties], and other provisions of that Act shall have effect accordingly.

(6) The enactments applied by subsection (5)(a) above shall apply subject to such exceptions and modifications, if any, as the Commissioners of Customs and Excise may by regulations prescribe, and shall be taken to include section 10 of the Finance Act 1901 (which relates to changes in customs import duties in their effect on contracts), but shall not include [section 126 of the Customs and Excise Management Act 1979] (charge of duty on manufactured or composite articles).

(7) . . . .

(8) Expressions used in this section shall be construed as if contained in Part I of the Agriculture Act 1957; and in this section "agricultural levy" shall include any tax not being a customs duty, but of equivalent effect, that may be chargeable in accordance with any such [EU arrangements] as aforesaid, and "statutory provision" includes any provision having effect by virtue of any enactment and, in subsection (2), any enactment of the Parliament of Northern Ireland or provision having effect by virtue of such an enactment.

11 EU offences].

(1) A person who, in sworn evidence before the [the European Court] , makes any statement which he knows to be false or does not believe to be true shall, whether he is a British subject or not, be guilty of an offence and may be proceeded against and punished—

    (a) in England and Wales as for an offence against section 1(1) of the Perjury Act 1911; or

    (b) in Scotland as for an offence against [section 44(1) of the Criminal Law (Consolidation) (Scotland) Act 1995]; or

(c)   in Northern Ireland as for an offence against [Article 3(1) of the Perjury (Northern Ireland) Order 1979].

Where a report is made as to any such offence under the authority of the the European Court then a bill of indictment for the offence may, [in England or Wales or] in Northern Ireland, be preferred as in a case where a prosecution is ordered under [section 9 of the Perjury Act 1911 or][Article 13 of the Perjury (Northern Ireland) Order 1979], but the report shall not be given in evidence on a person's trial for the offence.

(2)   Where a person (whether a British subject or not) owing either—

(a)   to his duties as a member of any Euratom institution or committee, or as an officer or servant of Euratom; or

(b)   to his dealings in any capacity (official or unofficial) with any Euratom institution or installation or with any Euratom joint enterprise;

has occasion to acquire, or obtain cognisance of, any classified information, he shall be guilty of a misdemeanour if, knowing or having reason to be believe that it is classified information, he communicates it to any unauthorised person or makes any public disclosure of it, whether in the United Kingdom or elsewhere and whether before or after the termination of those duties or dealings; and for this purpose "classified information" means any facts, information, knowledge, documents or objects that are subject to the security rules of a member State or of any Euratom institution.

This subsection shall be construed, and the Official Secrets Acts 1911 to 1939 shall have effect, as if this subsection were contained in the Official Secrets Act 1911, but so that in that Act sections 10 and 11, except section 10(4), shall not apply.

(3)   This section shall not come into force until the entry date.

SECTION 1 – THE TREATY

CONSOLIDATED VERSION OF THE TREATY ON EUROPEAN UNION

TITLE I

COMMON PROVISIONS

Article 1

(ex Article 1 TEU) (1)

By this Treaty, the HIGH CONTRACTING PARTIES establish among themselves a EUROPEAN UNION, hereinafter called 'the Union' on which the Member States confer competences to attain objectives they have in common.

This Treaty marks a new stage in the process of creating an ever closer union among the peoples of Europe, in which decisions are taken as openly as possible and as closely as possible to the citizen. The Union shall be founded on the present Treaty and on the Treaty on the Functioning of the European Union (hereinafter referred to as 'the Treaties'). Those two Treaties shall have the same legal value. The Union shall replace and succeed the European Community.

(1)   These references are merely indicative. For more ample information, please refer to the tables of equivalences between the old and the new numbering of the Treaties.

Article 2

The Union is founded on the values of respect for human dignity, freedom, democracy, equality, the rule of law and respect for human rights, including the rights of persons belonging to minorities. These values are common to the Member States in a society in which pluralism, non-discrimination, tolerance, justice, solidarity and equality between women and men prevail.

Article 3

(ex Article 2 TEU)

1   The Union's aim is to promote peace, its values and the well-being of its peoples.

2   The Union shall offer its citizens an area of freedom, security and justice without internal frontiers, in which the free movement of persons is ensured in conjunction with appropriate measures with respect to external border controls, asylum, immigration and the prevention and combating of crime.

3   The Union shall establish an internal market. It shall work for the sustainable development of Europe based on balanced economic growth and price stability, a highly competitive social market economy, aiming at full employment and social progress, and a high level of protection and improvement of the quality of the environment. It shall promote scientific and technological advance. It shall combat social exclusion and discrimination, and shall promote social justice and protection, equality between women and men, solidarity between generations and protection of the rights of the child. It shall promote economic, social and territorial cohesion, and solidarity among Member States. It shall respect its rich cultural and linguistic diversity, and shall ensure that Europe's cultural heritage is safeguarded and enhanced.

4   The Union shall establish an economic and monetary union whose currency is the euro.

5   In its relations with the wider world, the Union shall uphold and promote its values and interests and contribute to the protection of its citizens. It shall contribute to peace, security, the sustainable development of the Earth, solidarity and mutual respect among peoples, free and fair trade, eradication of poverty and

the protection of human rights, in particular the rights of the child, as well as to the strict observance and the development of international law, including respect for the principles of the United Nations Charter.

6   The Union shall pursue its objectives by appropriate means commensurate with the competences which are conferred upon it in the Treaties.

Article 4

1   In accordance with Article 5, competences not conferred upon the Union in the Treaties remain with the Member States.

2   The Union shall respect the equality of Member States before the Treaties as well as their national identities, inherent in their fundamental structures, political and constitutional, inclusive of regional and local self-government. It shall respect their essential State functions, including ensuring the territorial integrity of the State, maintaining law and order and safeguarding national security. In particular, national security remains the sole responsibility of each Member State.

3   Pursuant to the principle of sincere cooperation, the Union and the Member States shall, in full mutual respect, assist each other in carrying out tasks which flow from the Treaties. The Member States shall take any appropriate measure, general or particular, to ensure fulfilment of the obligations arising out of the Treaties or resulting from the acts of the institutions of the Union. The Member States shall facilitate the achievement of the Union's tasks and refrain from any measure which could jeopardise the attainment of the Union's objectives.

Article 5

(ex Article 5 TEC)

1   The limits of Union competences are governed by the principle of conferral. The use of Union competences is governed by the principles of subsidiarity and proportionality.

2   Under the principle of conferral, the Union shall act only within the limits of the competences conferred upon it by the Member States in the Treaties to attain the objectives set out therein. Competences not conferred upon the Union in the Treaties remain with the Member States.

3   Under the principle of subsidiarity, in areas which do not fall within its exclusive competence, the Union shall act only if and in so far as the objectives of the proposed action cannot be sufficiently achieved by the Member States, either at central level or at regional and local level, but can rather, by reason of the scale or effects of the proposed action, be better achieved at Union level. The institutions of the Union shall apply the principle of subsidiarity as laid down in the Protocol on the application of the principles of subsidiarity and proportionality. National Parliaments ensure compliance with the principle of subsidiarity in accordance with the procedure set out in that Protocol.

4   Under the principle of proportionality, the content and form of Union action shall not exceed what is necessary to achieve the objectives of the Treaties. The institutions of the Union shall apply the principle of proportionality as laid down in the Protocol on the application of the principles of subsidiarity and proportionality.

Article 6

(ex Article 6 TEU)

1   The Union recognises the rights, freedoms and principles set out in the Charter of Fundamental Rights of the European Union of 7 December 2000, as adapted at Strasbourg, on 12 December 2007, which shall have the same legal value as the Treaties. The provisions of the Charter shall not extend in any way the competences of the Union as defined in the Treaties. The rights, freedoms and principles in the Charter shall be interpreted in accordance with the general provisions in Title VII of the Charter governing its

interpretation and application and with due regard to the explanations referred to in the Charter, that set out the sources of those provisions.

2   The Union shall accede to the European Convention for the Protection of Human Rights and Fundamental Freedoms. Such accession shall not affect the Union's competences as defined in the Treaties.

3   Fundamental rights, as guaranteed by the European Convention for the Protection of Human Rights and Fundamental Freedoms and as they result from the constitutional traditions common to the Member States, shall constitute general principles of the Union's law.

Article 7

(ex Article 7 TEU)

1   On a reasoned proposal by one third of the Member States, by the European Parliament or by the European Commission, the Council, acting by a majority of four fifths of its members after obtaining the consent of the European Parliament, may determine that there is a clear risk of a serious breach by a Member State of the values referred to in Article 2. Before making such a determination, the Council shall hear the Member State in question and may address recommendations to it, acting in accordance with the same procedure. The Council shall regularly verify that the grounds on which such a determination was made continue to apply.

2   The European Council, acting by unanimity on a proposal by one third of the Member States or by the Commission and after obtaining the consent of the European Parliament, may determine the existence of a serious and persistent breach by a Member State of the values referred to in Article 2, after inviting the Member State in question to submit its observations.

3   Where a determination under paragraph 2 has been made, the Council, acting by a qualified majority, may decide to suspend certain of the rights deriving from the application of the Treaties to the Member State in question, including the voting rights of the representative of the government of that Member State in the Council. In doing so, the Council shall take into account the possible consequences of such a suspension on the rights and obligations of natural and legal persons.

The obligations of the Member State in question under this Treaty shall in any case continue to be binding on that State.

4   The Council, acting by a qualified majority, may decide subsequently to vary or revoke measures taken under paragraph 3 in response to changes in the situation which led to their being imposed.

5   The voting arrangements applying to the European Parliament, the European Council and the Council for the purposes of this Article are laid down in Article 354 of the Treaty on the Functioning of the European Union.

Article 8

1   The Union shall develop a special relationship with neighbouring countries, aiming to establish an area of prosperity and good neighbourliness, founded on the values of the Union and characterised by close and peaceful relations based on cooperation.

2   For the purposes of paragraph 1, the Union may conclude specific agreements with the countries concerned. These agreements may contain reciprocal rights and obligations as well as the possibility of undertaking activities jointly. Their implementation shall be the subject of periodic consultation.

TITLE II

PROVISIONS ON DEMOCRATIC PRINCIPLES

Article 9

In all its activities, the Union shall observe the principle of the equality of its citizens, who shall receive equal attention from its institutions, bodies, offices and agencies. Every national of a Member State shall be a citizen of the Union. Citizenship of the Union shall be additional to national citizenship and shall not replace it.

Article 10

1   The functioning of the Union shall be founded on representative democracy.

2   Citizens are directly represented at Union level in the European Parliament.

     Member States are represented in the European Council by their Heads of State or Government and in the Council by their governments, themselves democratically accountable either to their national Parliaments, or to their citizens.

3   Every citizen shall have the right to participate in the democratic life of the Union. Decisions shall be taken as openly and as closely as possible to the citizen.

4   Political parties at European level contribute to forming European political awareness and to expressing the will of citizens of the Union.

C 115/20 EN Official Journal of the European Union 9.5.2008

Article 11

1   The institutions shall, by appropriate means, give citizens and representative associations the opportunity to make known and publicly exchange their views in all areas of Union action.

2   The institutions shall maintain an open, transparent and regular dialogue with representative associations and civil society.

3   The European Commission shall carry out broad consultations with parties concerned in order to ensure that the Union's actions are coherent and transparent.

4   Not less than one million citizens who are nationals of a significant number of Member States may take the initiative of inviting the European Commission, within the framework of its powers, to submit any appropriate proposal on matters where citizens consider that a legal act of the Union is required for the purpose of implementing the Treaties. The procedures and conditions required for such a citizens' initiative shall be determined in accordance with the first paragraph of Article 24 of the Treaty on the Functioning of the European Union.

Article 12

National Parliaments contribute actively to the good functioning of the Union:

(a)   through being informed by the institutions of the Union and having draft legislative acts of the Union forwarded to them in accordance with the Protocol on the role of national Parliaments in the European Union;

(b)   by seeing to it that the principle of subsidiarity is respected in accordance with the procedures provided for in the Protocol on the application of the principles of subsidiarity and proportionality;

(c)   by taking part, within the framework of the area of freedom, security and justice, in the evaluation mechanisms for the implementation of the Union policies in that area, in accordance with Article 70 of the Treaty on the Functioning of the European Union, and through being involved in the political monitoring of Europol and the evaluation of Eurojust's activities in accordance with Articles 88 and 85 of that Treaty;

(d)   by taking part in the revision procedures of the Treaties, in accordance with Article 48 of this Treaty;

(e)   by being notified of applications for accession to the Union, in accordance with Article 49 of this Treaty;

(f)   by taking part in the inter-parliamentary cooperation between national Parliaments and with the European Parliament, in accordance with the Protocol on the role of national Parliaments in the European Union.

TITLE III

PROVISIONS ON THE INSTITUTIONS

Article 13

1   The Union shall have an institutional framework which shall aim to promote its values, advance its objectives, serve its interests, those of its citizens and those of the Member States, and ensure the consistency, effectiveness and continuity of its policies and actions. The Union's institutions shall be:

- the European Parliament,
- the European Council,
- the Council,
- the European Commission (hereinafter referred to as 'the Commission'),
- the Court of Justice of the European Union,
- the European Central Bank,
- the Court of Auditors.

2   Each institution shall act within the limits of the powers conferred on it in the Treaties, and in conformity with the procedures, conditions and objectives set out in them. The institutions shall practice mutual sincere cooperation.

3   The provisions relating to the European Central Bank and the Court of Auditors and detailed provisions on the other institutions are set out in the Treaty on the Functioning of the European Union.

4   The European Parliament, the Council and the Commission shall be assisted by an Economic and Social Committee and a Committee of the Regions acting in an advisory capacity.

Article 14

1   The European Parliament shall, jointly with the Council, exercise legislative and budgetary functions. It shall exercise functions of political control and consultation as laid down in the Treaties. It shall elect the President of the Commission.

2   The European Parliament shall be composed of representatives of the Union's citizens. They shall not exceed seven hundred and fifty in number, plus the President. Representation of citizens shall be degressively proportional, with a minimum threshold of six members per Member State. No Member State shall be allocated more than ninety-six seats.

C 115/22 EN Official Journal of the European Union 9.5.2008

The European Council shall adopt by unanimity, on the initiative of the European Parliament and with its consent, a decision establishing the composition of the European Parliament, respecting the principles referred to in the first subparagraph.

3   The members of the European Parliament shall be elected for a term of five years by direct universal suffrage in a free and secret ballot.

4   The European Parliament shall elect its President and its officers from among its members.

Article 15

1   The European Council shall provide the Union with the necessary impetus for its development and shall define the general political directions and priorities thereof. It shall not exercise legislative functions.

2   The European Council shall consist of the Heads of State or Government of the Member States, together with its President and the President of the Commission. The High Representative of the Union for Foreign Affairs and Security Policy shall take part in its work.

3   The European Council shall meet twice every six months, convened by its President. When the agenda so requires, the members of the European Council may decide each to be assisted by a minister and, in the case of the President of the Commission, by a member of the Commission. When the situation so requires, the President shall convene a special meeting of the European Council.

4   Except where the Treaties provide otherwise, decisions of the European Council shall be taken by consensus.

5   The European Council shall elect its President, by a qualified majority, for a term of two and a half years, renewable once. In the event of an impediment or serious misconduct, the European Council can end the President's term of office in accordance with the same procedure.

6   The President of the European Council:

(a)   shall chair it and drive forward its work;

(b)   shall ensure the preparation and continuity of the work of the European Council in cooperation with the President of the Commission, and on the basis of the work of the General Affairs Council;

(c)   shall endeavour to facilitate cohesion and consensus within the European Council;

(d)   shall present a report to the European Parliament after each of the meetings of the European Council.

The President of the European Council shall, at his level and in that capacity, ensure the external representation of the Union on issues concerning its common foreign and security policy, without prejudice to the powers of the High Representative of the Union for Foreign Affairs and Security Policy. The President of the European Council shall not hold a national office.

Article 16

1   The Council shall, jointly with the European Parliament, exercise legislative and budgetary functions. It shall carry out policy-making and coordinating functions as laid down in the Treaties.

2   The Council shall consist of a representative of each Member State at ministerial level, who may commit the government of the Member State in question and cast its vote.

3   The Council shall act by a qualified majority except where the Treaties provide otherwise.

4   As from 1 November 2014, a qualified majority shall be defined as at least 55 % of the members of the Council, comprising at least fifteen of them and representing Member States comprising at least 65 % of

the population of the Union. A blocking minority must include at least four Council members, failing which the qualified majority shall be deemed attained. The other arrangements governing the qualified majority are laid down in Article 238(2) of the Treaty on the Functioning of the European Union.

5   The transitional provisions relating to the definition of the qualified majority which shall be applicable until 31 October 2014 and those which shall be applicable from 1 November 2014 to 31 March 2017 are laid down in the Protocol on transitional provisions.

6   The Council shall meet in different configurations, the list of which shall be adopted in accordance with Article 236 of the Treaty on the Functioning of the European Union. The General Affairs Council shall ensure consistency in the work of the different Council configurations. It shall prepare and ensure the follow-up to meetings of the European Council, in liaison with the President of the European Council and the Commission. The Foreign Affairs Council shall elaborate the Union's external action on the basis of strategic guidelines laid down by the European Council and ensure that the Union's action is consistent.

7   A Committee of Permanent Representatives of the Governments of the Member States shall be responsible for preparing the work of the Council.

8   The Council shall meet in public when it deliberates and votes on a draft legislative act. To this end, each Council meeting shall be divided into two parts, dealing respectively with deliberations on Union legislative acts and non-legislative activities.

9   The Presidency of Council configurations, other than that of Foreign Affairs, shall be held by Member State representatives in the Council on the basis of equal rotation, in accordance with the conditions established in accordance with Article 236 of the Treaty on the Functioning of the European Union.

Article 17

1   The Commission shall promote the general interest of the Union and take appropriate initiatives to that end. It shall ensure the application of the Treaties, and of measures adopted by the institutions pursuant to them. It shall oversee the application of Union law under the control of the Court of Justice of the European Union. It shall execute the budget and manage programmes. It shall exercise coordinating, executive and management functions, as laid down in the Treaties. With the exception of the common foreign and security policy, and other cases provided for in the Treaties, it shall ensure the Union's external representation. It shall initiate the Union's annual and multiannual programming with a view to achieving interinstitutional agreements.

2   Union legislative acts may only be adopted on the basis of a Commission proposal, except where the Treaties provide otherwise. Other acts shall be adopted on the basis of a Commission proposal where the Treaties so provide.

3   The Commission's term of office shall be five years.

The members of the Commission shall be chosen on the ground of their general competence and European commitment from persons whose independence is beyond doubt. In carrying out its responsibilities, the Commission shall be completely independent. Without prejudice to Article 18(2), the members of the Commission shall neither seek nor take instructions from any Government or other institution, body, office or entity. They shall refrain from any action incompatible with their duties or the performance of their tasks.

4   The Commission appointed between the date of entry into force of the Treaty of Lisbon and 31 October 2014, shall consist of one national of each Member State, including its President and the High Representative of the Union for Foreign Affairs and Security Policy who shall be one of its Vice- Presidents.

5   As from 1 November 2014, the Commission shall consist of a number of members, including its President and the High Representative of the Union for Foreign Affairs and Security Policy, corresponding to two thirds of the number of Member States, unless the European Council, acting unanimously, decides to alter this number. The members of the Commission shall be chosen from among the nationals of the Member

States on the basis of a system of strictly equal rotation between the Member States, reflecting the demographic and geographical range of all the Member States. This system shall be established unanimously by the European Council in accordance with Article 244 of the Treaty on the Functioning of the European Union.

6   The President of the Commission shall:

(a)   lay down guidelines within which the Commission is to work;

(b)   decide on the internal organisation of the Commission, ensuring that it acts consistently, efficiently and as a collegiate body;

(c)   appoint Vice-Presidents, other than the High Representative of the Union for Foreign Affairs and Security Policy, from among the members of the Commission. A member of the Commission shall resign if the President so requests. The High Representative of the Union for Foreign Affairs and Security Policy shall resign, in accordance with the procedure set out in Article 18(1), if the President so requests.

7   Taking into account the elections to the European Parliament and after having held the appropriate consultations, the European Council, acting by a qualified majority, shall propose to the European Parliament a candidate for President of the Commission. This candidate shall be elected by the European Parliament by a majority of its component members. If he does not obtain the required majority, the European Council, acting by a qualified majority, shall within one month propose a new candidate who shall be elected by the European Parliament following the same procedure. The Council, by common accord with the President-elect, shall adopt the list of the other persons whom it proposes for appointment as members of the Commission. They shall be selected, on the basis of the suggestions made by Member States, in accordance with the criteria set out in paragraph 3, second subparagraph, and paragraph 5, second subparagraph. The President, the High Representative of the Union for Foreign Affairs and Security Policy and the other members of the Commission shall be subject as a body to a vote of consent by the European Parliament. On the basis of this consent the Commission shall be appointed by the European Council, acting by a qualified majority.

8   The Commission, as a body, shall be responsible to the European Parliament. In accordance with Article 234 of the Treaty on the Functioning of the European Union, the European Parliament may vote on a motion of censure of the Commission. If such a motion is carried, the members of the Commission shall resign as a body and the High Representative of the Union for Foreign Affairs and Security Policy shall resign from the duties that he carries out in the Commission.

Article 18

1   The European Council, acting by a qualified majority, with the agreement of the President of the Commission, shall appoint the High Representative of the Union for Foreign Affairs and Security Policy. The European Council may end his term of office by the same procedure.

2   The High Representative shall conduct the Union's common foreign and security policy. He shall contribute by his proposals to the development of that policy, which he shall carry out as mandated by the Council. The same shall apply to the common security and defence policy.

3   The High Representative shall preside over the Foreign Affairs Council.

4   The High Representative shall be one of the Vice-Presidents of the Commission. He shall ensure the consistency of the Union's external action. He shall be responsible within the Commission for C 115/26 EN Official Journal of the European Union 9.5.2008 responsibilities incumbent on it in external relations and for coordinating other aspects of the Union's external action. In exercising these responsibilities within the Commission, and only for these responsibilities, the High Representative shall be bound by Commission procedures to the extent that this is consistent with paragraphs 2 and 3.

Article 19

1 The Court of Justice of the European Union shall include the Court of Justice, the General Court and specialised courts. It shall ensure that in the interpretation and application of the Treaties the law is observed. Member States shall provide remedies sufficient to ensure effective legal protection in the fields covered by Union law.

2 The Court of Justice shall consist of one judge from each Member State. It shall be assisted by Advocates-General. The General Court shall include at least one judge per Member State.

The Judges and the Advocates-General of the Court of Justice and the Judges of the General Court shall be chosen from persons whose independence is beyond doubt and who satisfy the conditions set out in Articles 253 and 254 of the Treaty on the Functioning of the European Union. They shall be appointed by common accord of the governments of the Member States for six years. Retiring Judges and Advocates-General may be reappointed.

3 The Court of Justice of the European Union shall, in accordance with the Treaties:

(a) rule on actions brought by a Member State, an institution or a natural or legal person;

(b) give preliminary rulings, at the request of courts or tribunals of the Member States, on the interpretation of Union law or the validity of acts adopted by the institutions;

(c) rule in other cases provided for in the Treaties.

TITLE IV

PROVISIONS ON ENHANCED COOPERATION

Article 20

(ex Articles 27a to 27e, 40 to 40b and 43 to 45 TEU and ex Articles 11 and 11a TEC)

1 Member States which wish to establish enhanced cooperation between themselves within the framework of the Union's non-exclusive competences may make use of its institutions and exercise those competences by applying the relevant provisions of the Treaties, subject to the limits and in accordance with the detailed arrangements laid down in this Article and in Articles 326 to 334 of the Treaty on the Functioning of the European Union.

Enhanced cooperation shall aim to further the objectives of the Union, protect its interests and reinforce its integration process. Such cooperation shall be open at any time to all Member States, in accordance with Article 328 of the Treaty on the Functioning of the European Union.

2 The decision authorising enhanced cooperation shall be adopted by the Council as a last resort, when it has established that the objectives of such cooperation cannot be attained within a reasonable period by the Union as a whole, and provided that at least nine Member States participate in it. The Council shall act in accordance with the procedure laid down in Article 329 of the Treaty on the Functioning of the European Union.

3 All members of the Council may participate in its deliberations, but only members of the Council representing the Member States participating in enhanced cooperation shall take part in the vote. The voting rules are set out in Article 330 of the Treaty on the Functioning of the European Union.

4 Acts adopted in the framework of enhanced cooperation shall bind only participating Member States. They shall not be regarded as part of the acquis which has to be accepted by candidate States for accession to the Union.

TITLE V

GENERAL PROVISIONS ON THE UNION'S EXTERNAL ACTION AND SPECIFIC PROVISIONS ON THE COMMON FOREIGN AND SECURITY POLICY

CHAPTER 1

GENERAL PROVISIONS ON THE UNION'S EXTERNAL ACTION

Article 21

1. The Union's action on the international scene shall be guided by the principles which have inspired its own creation, development and enlargement, and which it seeks to advance in the wider world: democracy, the rule of law, the universality and indivisibility of human rights and fundamental freedoms, respect for human dignity, the principles of equality and solidarity, and respect for the principles of the United Nations Charter and international law. The Union shall seek to develop relations and build partnerships with third countries, and international, regional or global organisations which share the principles referred to in the first subparagraph. It shall promote multilateral solutions to common problems, in particular in the framework of the United Nations.

2. The Union shall define and pursue common policies and actions, and shall work for a high degree of cooperation in all fields of international relations, in order to:

    (a) safeguard its values, fundamental interests, security, independence and integrity;

    C 115/28 EN Official Journal of the European Union 9.5.2008

    (b) consolidate and support democracy, the rule of law, human rights and the principles of international law;

    (c) preserve peace, prevent conflicts and strengthen international security, in accordance with the purposes and principles of the United Nations Charter, with the principles of the Helsinki Final Act and with the aims of the Charter of Paris, including those relating to external borders;

    (d) foster the sustainable economic, social and environmental development of developing countries, with the primary aim of eradicating poverty;

    (e) encourage the integration of all countries into the world economy, including through the progressive abolition of restrictions on international trade;

    (f) help develop international measures to preserve and improve the quality of the environment and the sustainable management of global natural resources, in order to ensure sustainable development;

    (g) assist populations, countries and regions confronting natural or man-made disasters; and

    (h) promote an international system based on stronger multilateral cooperation and good global governance.

3. The Union shall respect the principles and pursue the objectives set out in paragraphs 1 and 2 in the development and implementation of the different areas of the Union's external action covered by this Title and by Part Five of the Treaty on the Functioning of the European Union, and of the external aspects of its other policies. The Union shall ensure consistency between the different areas of its external action and between these and its other policies. The Council and the Commission, assisted by the High Representative of the Union for Foreign Affairs and Security Policy, shall ensure that consistency and shall cooperate to that effect.

Article 22

1 On the basis of the principles and objectives set out in Article 21, the European Council shall identify the strategic interests and objectives of the Union. Decisions of the European Council on the strategic interests and objectives of the Union shall relate to the common foreign and security policy and to other areas of the external action of the Union. Such decisions may concern the relations of the Union with a specific country or region or may be thematic in approach. They shall define their duration, and the means to be made available by the Union and the Member States. The European Council shall act unanimously on a recommendation from the Council, adopted by the latter under the arrangements laid down for each area. Decisions of the European Council shall be implemented in accordance with the procedures provided for in the Treaties.

2 The High Representative of the Union for Foreign Affairs and Security Policy, for the area of common foreign and security policy, and the Commission, for other areas of external action, may submit joint proposals to the Council.

CHAPTER 2

SPECIFIC PROVISIONS ON THE COMMON FOREIGN AND SECURITY POLICY

SECTION 1

COMMON PROVISIONS

Article 23

The Union's action on the international scene, pursuant to this Chapter, shall be guided by the principles, shall pursue the objectives of, and be conducted in accordance with, the general provisions laid down in Chapter 1.

Article 24

(ex Article 11 TEU)

1 The Union's competence in matters of common foreign and security policy shall cover all areas of foreign policy and all questions relating to the Union's security, including the progressive framing of a common defence policy that might lead to a common defence. The common foreign and security policy is subject to specific rules and procedures. It shall be defined and implemented by the European Council and the Council acting unanimously, except where the Treaties provide otherwise. The adoption of legislative acts shall be excluded. The common foreign and security policy shall be put into effect by the High Representative of the Union for Foreign Affairs and Security Policy and by Member States, in accordance with the Treaties. The specific role of the European Parliament and of the Commission in this area is defined by the Treaties. The Court of Justice of the European Union shall not have jurisdiction with respect to these provisions, with the exception of its jurisdiction to monitor compliance with Article 40 of this Treaty and to review the legality of certain decisions as provided for by the second paragraph of Article 275 of the Treaty on the Functioning of the European Union.

2 Within the framework of the principles and objectives of its external action, the Union shall conduct, define and implement a common foreign and security policy, based on the development of mutual political solidarity among Member States, the identification of questions of general interest and the achievement of an ever-increasing degree of convergence of Member States' actions.

3 The Member States shall support the Union's external and security policy actively and unreservedly in a spirit of loyalty and mutual solidarity and shall comply with the Union's action in this area.

The Member States shall work together to enhance and develop their mutual political solidarity. They shall refrain from any action which is contrary to the interests of the Union or likely to impair its effectiveness as a cohesive force in international relations. The Council and the High Representative shall ensure compliance with these principles.

Article 25

(ex Article 12 TEU)

The Union shall conduct the common foreign and security policy by:

(a)   defining the general guidelines;

(b)   adopting decisions defining:

     (i)   actions to be undertaken by the Union;

     (ii)   positions to be taken by the Union;

     (iii)   arrangements for the implementation of the decisions referred to in points (i) and (ii); and by

(c)   strengthening systematic cooperation between Member States in the conduct of policy.

Article 26

(ex Article 13 TEU)

1   The European Council shall identify the Union's strategic interests, determine the objectives of and define general guidelines for the common foreign and security policy, including for matters with defence implications. It shall adopt the necessary decisions. If international developments so require, the President of the European Council shall convene an extraordinary meeting of the European Council in order to define the strategic lines of the Union's policy in the face of such developments.

2   The Council shall frame the common foreign and security policy and take the decisions necessary for defining and implementing it on the basis of the general guidelines and strategic lines defined by the European Council. The Council and the High Representative of the Union for Foreign Affairs and Security Policy shall ensure the unity, consistency and effectiveness of action by the Union.

3   The common foreign and security policy shall be put into effect by the High Representative and by the Member States, using national and Union resources.

Article 27

1   The High Representative of the Union for Foreign Affairs and Security Policy, who shall chair the Foreign Affairs Council, shall contribute through his proposals towards the preparation of the common foreign and security policy and shall ensure implementation of the decisions adopted by the European Council and the Council.

2   The High Representative shall represent the Union for matters relating to the common foreign and security policy. He shall conduct political dialogue with third parties on the Union's behalf and shall express the Union's position in international organisations and at international conferences.

3   In fulfilling his mandate, the High Representative shall be assisted by a European External Action Service. This service shall work in cooperation with the diplomatic services of the Member States and shall comprise officials from relevant departments of the General Secretariat of the Council and of the Commission as well as staff seconded from national diplomatic services of the Member States. The organisation and functioning of the European External Action Service shall be established by a decision of the Council. The Council shall act on a proposal from the High Representative after consulting the European Parliament and after obtaining the consent of the Commission.

Article 28

(ex Article 14 TEU)

1   Where the international situation requires operational action by the Union, the Council shall adopt the necessary decisions. They shall lay down their objectives, scope, the means to be made available to the Union, if necessary their duration, and the conditions for their implementation.

If there is a change in circumstances having a substantial effect on a question subject to such a decision, the Council shall review the principles and objectives of that decision and take the necessary decisions.

2   Decisions referred to in paragraph 1 shall commit the Member States in the positions they adopt and in the conduct of their activity.

3   Whenever there is any plan to adopt a national position or take national action pursuant to a decision as referred to in paragraph 1, information shall be provided by the Member State concerned in time to allow, if necessary, for prior consultations within the Council. The obligation to provide prior information shall not apply to measures which are merely a national transposition of Council decisions.

4   In cases of imperative need arising from changes in the situation and failing a review of the Council decision as referred to in paragraph 1, Member States may take the necessary measures as a matter of urgency having regard to the general objectives of that decision. The Member State concerned shall inform the Council immediately of any such measures.

5   Should there be any major difficulties in implementing a decision as referred to in this Article, a Member State shall refer them to the Council which shall discuss them and seek appropriate solutions.

Such solutions shall not run counter to the objectives of the decision referred to in paragraph 1 or impair its effectiveness.

Article 29

(ex Article 15 TEU)

The Council shall adopt decisions which shall define the approach of the Union to a particular matter of a geographical or thematic nature. Member States shall ensure that their national policies conform to the Union positions.

Article 30

(ex Article 22 TEU)

1   Any Member State, the High Representative of the Union for Foreign Affairs and Security Policy, or the High Representative with the Commission's support, may refer any question relating to the common foreign and security policy to the Council and may submit to it initiatives or proposals as appropriate.

2   In cases requiring a rapid decision, the High Representative, of his own motion, or at the request of a Member State, shall convene an extraordinary Council meeting within 48 hours or, in an emergency, within a shorter period.

Article 31

(ex Article 23 TEU)

1   Decisions under this Chapter shall be taken by the European Council and the Council acting unanimously, except where this Chapter provides otherwise. The adoption of legislative acts shall be excluded.

When abstaining in a vote, any member of the Council may qualify its abstention by making a formal declaration under the present subparagraph. In that case, it shall not be obliged to apply the decision, but shall accept that the decision commits the Union. In a spirit of mutual solidarity, the Member State concerned shall refrain from any action likely to conflict with or impede Union action based on that decision and the other Member States shall respect its position. If the members of the Council qualifying their abstention in this way represent at least one third of the Member States comprising at least one third of the population of the Union, the decision shall not be adopted.

2 By derogation from the provisions of paragraph 1, the Council shall act by qualified majority:

- when adopting a decision defining a Union action or position on the basis of a decision of the European Council relating to the Union's strategic interests and objectives, as referred to in Article 22(1),

- when adopting a decision defining a Union action or position, on a proposal which the High Representative of the Union for Foreign Affairs and Security Policy has presented following a specific request from the European Council, made on its own initiative or that of the High Representative,

9.5.2008 EN Official Journal of the European Union C 115/33

- when adopting any decision implementing a decision defining a Union action or position,

- when appointing a special representative in accordance with Article 33.

If a member of the Council declares that, for vital and stated reasons of national policy, it intends to oppose the adoption of a decision to be taken by qualified majority, a vote shall not be taken. The High Representative will, in close consultation with the Member State involved, search for a solution acceptable to it. If he does not succeed, the Council may, acting by a qualified majority, request that the matter be referred to the European Council for a decision by unanimity.

3 The European Council may unanimously adopt a decision stipulating that the Council shall act by a qualified majority in cases other than those referred to in paragraph 2.

4 Paragraphs 2 and 3 shall not apply to decisions having military or defence implications.

5 For procedural questions, the Council shall act by a majority of its members.

Article 32

(ex Article 16 TEU)

Member States shall consult one another within the European Council and the Council on any matter of foreign and security policy of general interest in order to determine a common approach. Before undertaking any action on the international scene or entering into any commitment which could affect the Union's interests, each Member State shall consult the others within the European Council or the Council. Member States shall ensure, through the convergence of their actions, that the Union is able to assert its interests and values on the international scene. Member States shall show mutual solidarity.

When the European Council or the Council has defined a common approach of the Union within the meaning of the first paragraph, the High Representative of the Union for Foreign Affairs and Security Policy and the Ministers for Foreign Affairs of the Member States shall coordinate their activities within the Council.

The diplomatic missions of the Member States and the Union delegations in third countries and at international organisations shall cooperate and shall contribute to formulating and implementing the common approach.

Article 33

(ex Article 18 TEU)

The Council may, on a proposal from the High Representative of the Union for Foreign Affairs and Security Policy, appoint a special representative with a mandate in relation to particular policy issues.

The special representative shall carry out his mandate under the authority of the High Representative.

Article 34

(ex Article 19 TEU)

1   Member States shall coordinate their action in international organisations and at international conferences. They shall uphold the Union's positions in such forums. The High Representative of the Union for Foreign Affairs and Security Policy shall organise this coordination.

In international organisations and at international conferences where not all the Member States participate, those which do take part shall uphold the Union's positions.

2   In accordance with Article 24(3), Member States represented in international organisations or international conferences where not all the Member States participate shall keep the other Member States and the High Representative informed of any matter of common interest. Member States which are also members of the United Nations Security Council will concert and keep the other Member States and the High Representative fully informed. Member States which are members of the Security Council will, in the execution of their functions, defend the positions and the interests of the Union, without prejudice to their responsibilities under the provisions of the United Nations Charter.

When the Union has defined a position on a subject which is on the United Nations Security Council agenda, those Member States which sit on the Security Council shall request that the High Representative be invited to present the Union's position.

Article 35

(ex Article 20 TEU)

The diplomatic and consular missions of the Member States and the Union delegations in third countries and international conferences, and their representations to international organisations, shall cooperate in ensuring that decisions defining Union positions and actions adopted pursuant to this Chapter are complied with and implemented.

They shall step up cooperation by exchanging information and carrying out joint assessments.

They shall contribute to the implementation of the right of citizens of the Union to protection in the territory of third countries as referred to in Article 20(2)(c) of the Treaty on the Functioning of the European Union and of the measures adopted pursuant to Article 23 of that Treaty.

Article 36

(ex Article 21 TEU)

The High Representative of the Union for Foreign Affairs and Security Policy shall regularly consult the European Parliament on the main aspects and the basic choices of the common foreign and security policy and the common security and defence policy and inform it of how those policies evolve. He shall ensure that the views of the European Parliament are duly taken into consideration. Special representatives may be involved in briefing the European Parliament.

The European Parliament may ask questions of the Council or make recommendations to it and to the High Representative. Twice a year it shall hold a debate on progress in implementing the common foreign and security policy, including the common security and defence policy.

Article 37

(ex Article 24 TEU)

The Union may conclude agreements with one or more States or international organisations in areas covered by this Chapter.

Article 38

(ex Article 25 TEU)

Without prejudice to Article 240 of the Treaty on the Functioning of the European Union, a Political and Security Committee shall monitor the international situation in the areas covered by the common foreign and security policy and contribute to the definition of policies by delivering opinions to the Council at the request of the Council or of the High Representative of the Union for Foreign Affairs and Security Policy or on its own initiative. It shall also monitor the implementation of agreed policies, without prejudice to the powers of the High Representative.

Within the scope of this Chapter, the Political and Security Committee shall exercise, under the responsibility of the Council and of the High Representative, the political control and strategic direction of the crisis management operations referred to in Article 43.

The Council may authorise the Committee, for the purpose and for the duration of a crisis management operation, as determined by the Council, to take the relevant decisions concerning the political control and strategic direction of the operation.

Article 39

In accordance with Article 16 of the Treaty on the Functioning of the European Union and by way of derogation from paragraph 2 thereof, the Council shall adopt a decision laying down the rules relating to the protection of individuals with regard to the processing of personal data by the Member States when carrying out activities which fall within the scope of this Chapter, and the rules relating to the free movement of such data. Compliance with these rules shall be subject to the control of independent authorities.

Article 40

(ex Article 47 TEU)

The implementation of the common foreign and security policy shall not affect the application of the procedures and the extent of the powers of the institutions laid down by the Treaties for the exercise of the Union competences referred to in Articles 3 to 6 of the Treaty on the Functioning of the European Union.

Similarly, the implementation of the policies listed in those Articles shall not affect the application of the procedures and the extent of the powers of the institutions laid down by the Treaties for the exercise of the Union competences under this Chapter.

Article 41

(ex Article 28 TEU)

1   Administrative expenditure to which the implementation of this Chapter gives rise for the institutions shall be charged to the Union budget.

2   Operating expenditure to which the implementation of this Chapter gives rise shall also be charged to the Union budget, except for such expenditure arising from operations having military or defence implications and cases where the Council acting unanimously decides otherwise.

In cases where expenditure is not charged to the Union budget, it shall be charged to the Member States in accordance with the gross national product scale, unless the Council acting unanimously decides otherwise. As for expenditure arising from operations having military or defence implications, Member States whose representatives in the Council have made a formal declaration under Article 31(1), second subparagraph, shall not be obliged to contribute to the financing thereof.

3   The Council shall adopt a decision establishing the specific procedures for guaranteeing rapid access to appropriations in the Union budget for urgent financing of initiatives in the framework of the common foreign and security policy, and in particular for preparatory activities for the tasks referred to in Article 42(1) and Article 43. It shall act after consulting the European Parliament.

Preparatory activities for the tasks referred to in Article 42(1) and Article 43 which are not charged to the Union budget shall be financed by a start-up fund made up of Member States' contributions.

The Council shall adopt by a qualified majority, on a proposal from the High Representative of the Union for Foreign Affairs and Security Policy, decisions establishing:

(a)   the procedures for setting up and financing the start-up fund, in particular the amounts allocated to the fund;

(b)   the procedures for administering the start-up fund;

9.5.2008 EN Official Journal of the European Union C 115/37

(c)   the financial control procedures.

When the task planned in accordance with Article 42(1) and Article 43 cannot be charged to the Union budget, the Council shall authorise the High Representative to use the fund. The High Representative shall report to the Council on the implementation of this remit.

SECTION 2

PROVISIONS ON THE COMMON SECURITY AND DEFENCE POLICY

Article 42

(ex Article 17 TEU)

1   The common security and defence policy shall be an integral part of the common foreign and security policy. It shall provide the Union with an operational capacity drawing on civilian and military assets. The Union may use them on missions outside the Union for peace-keeping, conflict prevention and strengthening international security in accordance with the principles of the United Nations Charter. The performance of these tasks shall be undertaken using capabilities provided by the Member States.

2   The common security and defence policy shall include the progressive framing of a common Union defence policy. This will lead to a common defence, when the European Council, acting unanimously, so decides. It shall in that case recommend to the Member States the adoption of such a decision in accordance with their respective constitutional requirements.

The policy of the Union in accordance with this Section shall not prejudice the specific character of the security and defence policy of certain Member States and shall respect the obligations of certain Member States, which see their common defence realised in the North Atlantic Treaty Organisation (NATO), under the North Atlantic Treaty and be compatible with the common security and defence policy established within that framework.

3   Member States shall make civilian and military capabilities available to the Union for the implementation of the common security and defence policy, to contribute to the objectives defined by the Council. Those Member States which together establish multinational forces may also make them available to the common security and defence policy.

     Member States shall undertake progressively to improve their military capabilities. The Agency in the field of defence capabilities development, research, acquisition and armaments (hereinafter referred to as 'the European Defence Agency') shall identify operational requirements, shall promote measures to satisfy those requirements, shall contribute to identifying and, where appropriate, implementing any measure needed to strengthen the industrial and technological base of the defence sector, shall participate in defining a European capabilities and armaments policy, and shall assist the Council in evaluating the improvement of military capabilities.

4   Decisions relating to the common security and defence policy, including those initiating a mission as referred to in this Article, shall be adopted by the Council acting unanimously on a proposal from the High Representative of the Union for Foreign Affairs and Security Policy or an initiative from a Member State. The High Representative may propose the use of both national resources and Union instruments, together with the Commission where appropriate.

5   The Council may entrust the execution of a task, within the Union framework, to a group of Member States in order to protect the Union's values and serve its interests. The execution of such a task shall be governed by Article 44.

6   Those Member States whose military capabilities fulfil higher criteria and which have made more binding commitments to one another in this area with a view to the most demanding missions shall establish permanent structured cooperation within the Union framework. Such cooperation shall be governed by Article 46. It shall not affect the provisions of Article 43.

7   If a Member State is the victim of armed aggression on its territory, the other Member States shall have towards it an obligation of aid and assistance by all the means in their power, in accordance with Article 51 of the United Nations Charter. This shall not prejudice the specific character of the security and defence policy of certain Member States.

     Commitments and cooperation in this area shall be consistent with commitments under the North Atlantic Treaty Organisation, which, for those States which are members of it, remains the foundation of their collective defence and the forum for its implementation.

Article 43

1   The tasks referred to in Article 42(1), in the course of which the Union may use civilian and military means, shall include joint disarmament operations, humanitarian and rescue tasks, military advice and assistance tasks, conflict prevention and peace-keeping tasks, tasks of combat forces in crisis management, including peace-making and post-conflict stabilisation. All these tasks may contribute to the fight against terrorism, including by supporting third countries in combating terrorism in their territories.

2   The Council shall adopt decisions relating to the tasks referred to in paragraph 1, defining their objectives and scope and the general conditions for their implementation. The High Representative of the Union for Foreign Affairs and Security Policy, acting under the authority of the Council and in close and constant contact with the Political and Security Committee, shall ensure coordination of the civilian and military aspects of such tasks.

Article 44

1   Within the framework of the decisions adopted in accordance with Article 43, the Council may entrust the implementation of a task to a group of Member States which are willing and have the necessary capability

for such a task. Those Member States, in association with the High Representative of the Union for Foreign Affairs and Security Policy, shall agree among themselves on the management of the task.

2   Member States participating in the task shall keep the Council regularly informed of its progress on their own initiative or at the request of another Member State. Those States shall inform the Council immediately should the completion of the task entail major consequences or require amendment of the objective, scope and conditions determined for the task in the decisions referred to in paragraph 1. In such cases, the Council shall adopt the necessary decisions.

Article 45

1   The European Defence Agency referred to in Article 42(3), subject to the authority of the Council, shall have as its task to:

(a)   contribute to identifying the Member States' military capability objectives and evaluating observance of the capability commitments given by the Member States;

(b)   promote harmonisation of operational needs and adoption of effective, compatible procurement methods;

(c)   propose multilateral projects to fulfil the objectives in terms of military capabilities, ensure coordination of the programmes implemented by the Member States and management of specific cooperation programmes;

(d)   support defence technology research, and coordinate and plan joint research activities and the study of technical solutions meeting future operational needs;

(e)   contribute to identifying and, if necessary, implementing any useful measure for strengthening the industrial and technological base of the defence sector and for improving the effectiveness of military expenditure.

2   The European Defence Agency shall be open to all Member States wishing to be part of it. The Council, acting by a qualified majority, shall adopt a decision defining the Agency's statute, seat and operational rules. That decision should take account of the level of effective participation in the Agency's activities. Specific groups shall be set up within the Agency bringing together Member States engaged in joint projects. The Agency shall carry out its tasks in liaison with the Commission where necessary.

Article 46

1   Those Member States which wish to participate in the permanent structured cooperation referred to in Article 42(6), which fulfil the criteria and have made the commitments on military capabilities set out in the Protocol on permanent structured cooperation, shall notify their intention to the Council and to the High Representative of the Union for Foreign Affairs and Security Policy.

2   Within three months following the notification referred to in paragraph 1 the Council shall adopt a decision establishing permanent structured cooperation and determining the list of participating Member States. The Council shall act by a qualified majority after consulting the High Representative.

3   Any Member State which, at a later stage, wishes to participate in the permanent structured cooperation shall notify its intention to the Council and to the High Representative.

The Council shall adopt a decision confirming the participation of the Member State concerned which fulfils the criteria and makes the commitments referred to in Articles 1 and 2 of the Protocol on permanent structured cooperation. The Council shall act by a qualified majority after consulting the High Representative. Only members of the Council representing the participating Member States shall take part in the vote.

A qualified majority shall be defined in accordance with Article 238(3)(a) of the Treaty on the Functioning of the European Union.

4   If a participating Member State no longer fulfils the criteria or is no longer able to meet the commitments referred to in Articles 1 and 2 of the Protocol on permanent structured cooperation, the Council may adopt a decision suspending the participation of the Member State concerned.

The Council shall act by a qualified majority. Only members of the Council representing the participating Member States, with the exception of the Member State in question, shall take part in the vote.

A qualified majority shall be defined in accordance with Article 238(3)(a) of the Treaty on the Functioning of the European Union.

5   Any participating Member State which wishes to withdraw from permanent structured cooperation shall notify its intention to the Council, which shall take note that the Member State in question has ceased to participate.

6   The decisions and recommendations of the Council within the framework of permanent structured cooperation, other than those provided for in paragraphs 2 to 5, shall be adopted by unanimity. For the purposes of this paragraph, unanimity shall be constituted by the votes of the representatives of the participating Member States only.

TITLE VI

FINAL PROVISIONS

Article 47

The Union shall have legal personality.

Article 48

(ex Article 48 TEU)

1   The Treaties may be amended in accordance with an ordinary revision procedure. They may also be amended in accordance with simplified revision procedures.

Ordinary revision procedure

2   The Government of any Member State, the European Parliament or the Commission may submit to the Council proposals for the amendment of the Treaties. These proposals may, inter alia, serve either to increase or to reduce the competences conferred on the Union in the Treaties. These proposals shall be submitted to the European Council by the Council and the national Parliaments shall be notified.

3   If the European Council, after consulting the European Parliament and the Commission, adopts by a simple majority a decision in favour of examining the proposed amendments, the President of the European Council shall convene a Convention composed of representatives of the national Parliaments, of the Heads of State or Government of the Member States, of the European Parliament and of the Commission. The European Central Bank shall also be consulted in the case of institutional changes in the monetary area. The Convention shall examine the proposals for amendments and shall adopt by consensus a recommendation to a conference of representatives of the governments of the Member States as provided for in paragraph 4.

The European Council may decide by a simple majority, after obtaining the consent of the European Parliament, not to convene a Convention should this not be justified by the extent of the proposed amendments. In the latter case, the European Council shall define the terms of reference for a conference of representatives of the governments of the Member States.

4   A conference of representatives of the governments of the Member States shall be convened by the President of the Council for the purpose of determining by common accord the amendments to be made to the Treaties.

The amendments shall enter into force after being ratified by all the Member States in accordance with their respective constitutional requirements.

5   If, two years after the signature of a treaty amending the Treaties, four fifths of the Member States have ratified it and one or more Member States have encountered difficulties in proceeding with ratification, the matter shall be referred to the European Council.

Simplified revision procedures

6   The Government of any Member State, the European Parliament or the Commission may submit to the European Council proposals for revising all or part of the provisions of Part Three of the Treaty on the Functioning of the European Union relating to the internal policies and action of the Union.

The European Council may adopt a decision amending all or part of the provisions of Part Three of the Treaty on the Functioning of the European Union. The European Council shall act by unanimity after consulting the European Parliament and the Commission, and the European Central Bank in the case of institutional changes in the monetary area. That decision shall not enter into force until it is approved by the Member States in accordance with their respective constitutional requirements.

The decision referred to in the second subparagraph shall not increase the competences conferred on the Union in the Treaties.

7   Where the Treaty on the Functioning of the European Union or Title V of this Treaty provides for the Council to act by unanimity in a given area or case, the European Council may adopt a decision authorising the Council to act by a qualified majority in that area or in that case. This subparagraph shall not apply to decisions with military implications or those in the area of defence.

Where the Treaty on the Functioning of the European Union provides for legislative acts to be adopted by the Council in accordance with a special legislative procedure, the European Council may adopt a decision allowing for the adoption of such acts in accordance with the ordinary legislative procedure.

Any initiative taken by the European Council on the basis of the first or the second subparagraph shall be notified to the national Parliaments. If a national Parliament makes known its opposition within six months of the date of such notification, the decision referred to in the first or the second subparagraph shall not be adopted. In the absence of opposition, the European Council may adopt the decision.

For the adoption of the decisions referred to in the first and second subparagraphs, the European Council shall act by unanimity after obtaining the consent of the European Parliament, which shall be given by a majority of its component members.

Article 49

(ex Article 49 TEU)

Any European State which respects the values referred to in Article 2 and is committed to promoting them may apply to become a member of the Union. The European Parliament and national Parliaments shall be notified of this application. The applicant State shall address its application to the Council, which shall act unanimously after consulting the Commission and after receiving the consent of the European Parliament, which shall act by a majority of its component members. The conditions of eligibility agreed upon by the European Council shall be taken into account.

The conditions of admission and the adjustments to the Treaties on which the Union is founded, which such admission entails, shall be the subject of an agreement between the Member States and the applicant State. This agreement shall be submitted for ratification by all the contracting States in accordance with their respective constitutional requirements.

Article 50

1   Any Member State may decide to withdraw from the Union in accordance with its own constitutional requirements.

2   A Member State which decides to withdraw shall notify the European Council of its intention.

In the light of the guidelines provided by the European Council, the Union shall negotiate and conclude an agreement with that State, setting out the arrangements for its withdrawal, taking account of the framework for its future relationship with the Union. That agreement shall be negotiated in accordance with Article 218(3) of the Treaty on the Functioning of the European Union. It shall be concluded on behalf of the Union by the Council, acting by a qualified majority, after obtaining the consent of the European Parliament.

3   The Treaties shall cease to apply to the State in question from the date of entry into force of the withdrawal agreement or, failing that, two years after the notification referred to in paragraph 2, unless the European Council, in agreement with the Member State concerned, unanimously decides to extend this period.

4   For the purposes of paragraphs 2 and 3, the member of the European Council or of the Council representing the withdrawing Member State shall not participate in the discussions of the European Council or Council or in decisions concerning it.

A qualified majority shall be defined in accordance with Article 238(3)(b) of the Treaty on the Functioning of the European Union.

5   If a State which has withdrawn from the Union asks to rejoin, its request shall be subject to the procedure referred to in Article 49.

Article 51

The Protocols and Annexes to the Treaties shall form an integral part thereof.

Article 52

1   The Treaties shall apply to the Kingdom of Belgium, the Republic of Bulgaria, the Czech Republic, the Kingdom of Denmark, the Federal Republic of Germany, the Republic of Estonia, Ireland, the Hellenic Republic, the Kingdom of Spain, the French Republic, the Italian Republic, the Republic of Cyprus, the Republic of Latvia, the Republic of Lithuania, the Grand Duchy of Luxembourg, the Republic of Hungary, the Republic of Malta, the Kingdom of the Netherlands, the Republic of Austria, the Republic of Poland, the Portuguese Republic, Romania, the Republic of Slovenia, the Slovak Republic, the Republic of Finland, the Kingdom of Sweden and the United Kingdom of Great Britain and Northern Ireland.

2   The territorial scope of the Treaties is specified in Article 355 of the Treaty on the Functioning of the European Union.

Article 53

(ex Article 51 TEU)

This Treaty is concluded for an unlimited period.

Article 54

(ex Article 52 TEU)

1   This Treaty shall be ratified by the High Contracting Parties in accordance with their respective constitutional requirements. The instruments of ratification shall be deposited with the Government of the Italian Republic.

C 115/44 EN Official Journal of the European Union 9.5.2008

2   This Treaty shall enter into force on 1 January 1993, provided that all the Instruments of ratification have been deposited, or, failing that, on the first day of the month following the deposit of the Instrument of ratification by the last signatory State to take this step.

Article 55

(ex Article 53 TEU)

1   This Treaty, drawn up in a single original in the Bulgarian, Czech, Danish, Dutch, English, Estonian, Finnish, French, German, Greek, Hungarian, Irish, Italian, Latvian, Lithuanian, Maltese, Polish, Portuguese, Romanian, Slovak, Slovenian, Spanish and Swedish languages, the texts in each of these languages being equally authentic, shall be deposited in the archives of the Government of the Italian Republic, which will transmit a certified copy to each of the governments of the other signatory States.

2   This Treaty may also be translated into any other languages as determined by Member States among those which, in accordance with their constitutional order, enjoy official status in all or part of their territory. A certified copy of such translations shall be provided by the Member States concerned to be deposited in the archives of the Council.

CONSOLIDATED VERSION OF THE TREATY ON THE FUNCTIONING OF THE EUROPEAN UNION

PART ONE

PRINCIPLES

Article 1

1   This Treaty organises the functioning of the Union and determines the areas of, delimitation of, and arrangements for exercising its competences.

2   This Treaty and the Treaty on European Union constitute the Treaties on which the Union is founded. These two Treaties, which have the same legal value, shall be referred to as 'the Treaties'.

TITLE I

CATEGORIES AND AREAS OF UNION COMPETENCE

Article 2

1   When the Treaties confer on the Union exclusive competence in a specific area, only the Union may legislate and adopt legally binding acts, the Member States being able to do so themselves only if so empowered by the Union or for the implementation of Union acts.

2   When the Treaties confer on the Union a competence shared with the Member States in a specific area, the Union and the Member States may legislate and adopt legally binding acts in that area. The Member States shall exercise their competence to the extent that the Union has not exercised its competence. The Member States shall again exercise their competence to the extent that the Union has decided to cease exercising its competence.

3   The Member States shall coordinate their economic and employment policies within arrangements as determined by this Treaty, which the Union shall have competence to provide.

4   The Union shall have competence, in accordance with the provisions of the Treaty on European Union, to define and implement a common foreign and security policy, including the progressive framing of a common defence policy.

5   In certain areas and under the conditions laid down in the Treaties, the Union shall have competence to carry out actions to support, coordinate or supplement the actions of the Member States, without thereby superseding their competence in these areas.

Legally binding acts of the Union adopted on the basis of the provisions of the Treaties relating to these areas shall not entail harmonisation of Member States' laws or regulations.

6   The scope of and arrangements for exercising the Union's competences shall be determined by the provisions of the Treaties relating to each area.

Article 3

1   The Union shall have exclusive competence in the following areas:

(a)   customs union;

(b)   the establishing of the competition rules necessary for the functioning of the internal market;

(c)   monetary policy for the Member States whose currency is the euro;

(d)   the conservation of marine biological resources under the common fisheries policy;

(e)   common commercial policy.

2   The Union shall also have exclusive competence for the conclusion of an international agreement when its conclusion is provided for in a legislative act of the Union or is necessary to enable the Union to exercise its internal competence, or in so far as its conclusion may affect common rules or alter their scope.

Article 4

1   The Union shall share competence with the Member States where the Treaties confer on it a competence which does not relate to the areas referred to in Articles 3 and 6.

2   Shared competence between the Union and the Member States applies in the following principal areas:

(a)   internal market;

(b)   social policy, for the aspects defined in this Treaty;

(c)   economic, social and territorial cohesion;

(d)   agriculture and fisheries, excluding the conservation of marine biological resources;

(e)   environment;

(f)   consumer protection;

    (g)   transport;

    (h)   trans-European networks;

    (i)   energy;

    (j)   area of freedom, security and justice;

    (k)   common safety concerns in public health matters, for the aspects defined in this Treaty.

3   In the areas of research, technological development and space, the Union shall have competence to carry out activities, in particular to define and implement programmes; however, the exercise of that competence shall not result in Member States being prevented from exercising theirs.

4   In the areas of development cooperation and humanitarian aid, the Union shall have competence to carry out activities and conduct a common policy; however, the exercise of that competence shall not result in Member States being prevented from exercising theirs.

Article 5

1   The Member States shall coordinate their economic policies within the Union. To this end, the Council shall adopt measures, in particular broad guidelines for these policies.

      Specific provisions shall apply to those Member States whose currency is the euro.

2   The Union shall take measures to ensure coordination of the employment policies of the Member States, in particular by defining guidelines for these policies.

3   The Union may take initiatives to ensure coordination of Member States' social policies.

Article 6

The Union shall have competence to carry out actions to support, coordinate or supplement the actions of the Member States. The areas of such action shall, at European level, be:

(a)   protection and improvement of human health;

(b)   industry;

(c)   culture;

(d)   tourism;

(e)   education, vocational training, youth and sport;

(f)   civil protection;

(g)   administrative cooperation.

TITLE II

PROVISIONS HAVING GENERAL APPLICATION

Article 7

The Union shall ensure consistency between its policies and activities, taking all of its objectives into account and in accordance with the principle of conferral of powers.

Article 8

(ex Article 3(2) TEC) (1)

In all its activities, the Union shall aim to eliminate inequalities, and to promote equality, between men and women.

Article 9

In defining and implementing its policies and activities, the Union shall take into account requirements linked to the promotion of a high level of employment, the guarantee of adequate social protection, the fight against social exclusion, and a high level of education, training and protection of human health.

Article 10

In defining and implementing its policies and activities, the Union shall aim to combat discrimination based on sex, racial or ethnic origin, religion or belief, disability, age or sexual orientation.

Article 11

(ex Article 6 TEC)

Environmental protection requirements must be integrated into the definition and implementation of the Union policies and activities, in particular with a view to promoting sustainable development.

(1) These references are merely indicative. For more ample information, please refer to the tables of equivalences between the old and the new numbering of the Treaties.

Article 12

(ex Article 153(2) TEC)

Consumer protection requirements shall be taken into account in defining and implementing other Union policies and activities.

Article 13

In formulating and implementing the Union's agriculture, fisheries, transport, internal market, research and technological development and space policies, the Union and the Member States shall, since animals are sentient beings, pay full regard to the welfare requirements of animals, while respecting the legislative or administrative provisions and customs of the Member States relating in particular to religious rites, cultural traditions and regional heritage.

Article 14

(ex Article 16 TEC)

Without prejudice to Article 4 of the Treaty on European Union or to Articles 93, 106 and 107 of this Treaty, and given the place occupied by services of general economic interest in the shared values of the Union as well as their role in promoting social and territorial cohesion, the Union and the Member States, each within their respective powers and within the scope of application of the Treaties, shall take care that such services operate on the basis of principles and conditions, particularly economic and financial conditions, which enable them to fulfil their missions. The European Parliament and the Council, acting by means of regulations in accordance with the ordinary legislative procedure, shall establish these principles and set these conditions without prejudice to the competence of Member States, in compliance with the Treaties, to provide, to commission and to fund such services.

Article 15

(ex Article 255 TEC)

1   In order to promote good governance and ensure the participation of civil society, the Union institutions, bodies, offices and agencies shall conduct their work as openly as possible.

2   The European Parliament shall meet in public, as shall the Council when considering and voting on a draft legislative act.

3   Any citizen of the Union, and any natural or legal person residing or having its registered office in a Member State, shall have a right of access to documents of the Union institutions, bodies, offices and agencies, whatever their medium, subject to the principles and the conditions to be defined in accordance with this paragraph.

General principles and limits on grounds of public or private interest governing this right of access to documents shall be determined by the European Parliament and the Council, by means of regulations, acting in accordance with the ordinary legislative procedure.

Each institution, body, office or agency shall ensure that its proceedings are transparent and shall elaborate in its own Rules of Procedure specific provisions regarding access to its documents, in accordance with the regulations referred to in the second subparagraph.

The Court of Justice of the European Union, the European Central Bank and the European Investment Bank shall be subject to this paragraph only when exercising their administrative tasks.

The European Parliament and the Council shall ensure publication of the documents relating to the legislative procedures under the terms laid down by the regulations referred to in the second subparagraph.

Article 16

(ex Article 286 TEC)

1   Everyone has the right to the protection of personal data concerning them.

2   The European Parliament and the Council, acting in accordance with the ordinary legislative procedure, shall lay down the rules relating to the protection of individuals with regard to the processing of personal data by Union institutions, bodies, offices and agencies, and by the Member States when carrying out activities which fall within the scope of Union law, and the rules relating to the free movement of such data. Compliance with these rules shall be subject to the control of independent authorities.

The rules adopted on the basis of this Article shall be without prejudice to the specific rules laid down in Article 39 of the Treaty on European Union.

Article 17

1   The Union respects and does not prejudice the status under national law of churches and religious associations or communities in the Member States.

2   The Union equally respects the status under national law of philosophical and non-confessional organisations.

3   Recognising their identity and their specific contribution, the Union shall maintain an open, transparent and regular dialogue with these churches and organisations.

PART TWO

NON-DISCRIMINATION AND CITIZENSHIP OF THE UNION

Article 18

(ex Article 12 TEC)

Within the scope of application of the Treaties, and without prejudice to any special provisions contained therein, any discrimination on grounds of nationality shall be prohibited.

The European Parliament and the Council, acting in accordance with the ordinary legislative procedure, may adopt rules designed to prohibit such discrimination.

Article 19

(ex Article 13 TEC)

1   Without prejudice to the other provisions of the Treaties and within the limits of the powers conferred by them upon the Union, the Council, acting unanimously in accordance with a special legislative procedure and after obtaining the consent of the European Parliament, may take appropriate action to combat discrimination based on sex, racial or ethnic origin, religion or belief, disability, age or sexual orientation.

2   By way of derogation from paragraph 1, the European Parliament and the Council, acting in accordance with the ordinary legislative procedure, may adopt the basic principles of Union incentive measures, excluding any harmonisation of the laws and regulations of the Member States, to support action taken by the Member States in order to contribute to the achievement of the objectives referred to in paragraph 1.

Article 20

(ex Article 17 TEC)

1   Citizenship of the Union is hereby established. Every person holding the nationality of a Member State shall be a citizen of the Union. Citizenship of the Union shall be additional to and not replace national citizenship.

2   Citizens of the Union shall enjoy the rights and be subject to the duties provided for in the Treaties. They shall have, inter alia:

(a)   the right to move and reside freely within the territory of the Member States;

(b)   the right to vote and to stand as candidates in elections to the European Parliament and in municipal elections in their Member State of residence, under the same conditions as nationals of that State;

(c)   the right to enjoy, in the territory of a third country in which the Member State of which they are nationals is not represented, the protection of the diplomatic and consular authorities of any Member State on the same conditions as the nationals of that State;

(d)   the right to petition the European Parliament, to apply to the European Ombudsman, and to address the institutions and advisory bodies of the Union in any of the Treaty languages and to obtain a reply in the same language.

These rights shall be exercised in accordance with the conditions and limits defined by the Treaties and by the measures adopted thereunder.

Article 21

(ex Article 18 TEC)

1   Every citizen of the Union shall have the right to move and reside freely within the territory of the Member States, subject to the limitations and conditions laid down in the Treaties and by the measures adopted to give them effect.

2   If action by the Union should prove necessary to attain this objective and the Treaties have not provided the necessary powers, the European Parliament and the Council, acting in accordance with the ordinary legislative procedure, may adopt provisions with a view to facilitating the exercise of the rights referred to in paragraph 1.

3   For the same purposes as those referred to in paragraph 1 and if the Treaties have not provided the necessary powers, the Council, acting in accordance with a special legislative procedure, may adopt measures concerning social security or social protection. The Council shall act unanimously after consulting the European Parliament.

Article 22

(ex Article 19 TEC)

1   Every citizen of the Union residing in a Member State of which he is not a national shall have the right to vote and to stand as a candidate at municipal elections in the Member State in which he resides, under the same conditions as nationals of that State. This right shall be exercised subject to detailed arrangements adopted by the Council, acting unanimously in accordance with a special legislative procedure and after consulting the European Parliament; these arrangements may provide for derogations where warranted by problems specific to a Member State.

2   Without prejudice to Article 223(1) and to the provisions adopted for its implementation, every citizen of the Union residing in a Member State of which he is not a national shall have the right to vote and to stand as a candidate in elections to the European Parliament in the Member State in which he resides, under the same conditions as nationals of that State. This right shall be exercised subject to detailed arrangements adopted by the Council, acting unanimously in accordance with a special legislative procedure and after consulting the European Parliament; these arrangements may provide for derogations where warranted by problems specific to a Member State.

Article 23

(ex Article 20 TEC)

Every citizen of the Union shall, in the territory of a third country in which the Member State of which he is a national is not represented, be entitled to protection by the diplomatic or consular authorities of any Member State, on the same conditions as the nationals of that State. Member States shall adopt the necessary provisions and start the international negotiations required to secure this protection.

The Council, acting in accordance with a special legislative procedure and after consulting the European Parliament, may adopt directives establishing the coordination and cooperation measures necessary to facilitate such protection.

Article 24

(ex Article 21 TEC)

The European Parliament and the Council, acting by means of regulations in accordance with the ordinary legislative procedure, shall adopt the provisions for the procedures and conditions required for a citizens' initiative within the meaning of Article 11 of the Treaty on European Union, including the minimum number of Member States from which such citizens must come.

Every citizen of the Union shall have the right to petition the European Parliament in accordance with Article 227.

Every citizen of the Union may apply to the Ombudsman established in accordance with Article 228.

Every citizen of the Union may write to any of the institutions, bodies, offices or agencies referred to in this Article or in Article 13 of the Treaty on European Union in one of the languages mentioned in Article 55(1) of the Treaty on European Union and have an answer in the same language.

Article 25

(ex Article 22 TEC)

The Commission shall report to the European Parliament, to the Council and to the Economic and Social Committee every three years on the application of the provisions of this Part. This report shall take account of the development of the Union.

On this basis, and without prejudice to the other provisions of the Treaties, the Council, acting unanimously in accordance with a special legislative procedure and after obtaining the consent of the European Parliament, may adopt provisions to strengthen or to add to the rights listed in Article 20(2).

These provisions shall enter into force after their approval by the Member States in accordance with their respective constitutional requirements.

PART THREE

UNION POLICIES AND INTERNAL ACTIONS

TITLE I

THE INTERNAL MARKET

Article 26

(ex Article 14 TEC)

1   The Union shall adopt measures with the aim of establishing or ensuring the functioning of the internal market, in accordance with the relevant provisions of the Treaties.

2   The internal market shall comprise an area without internal frontiers in which the free movement of goods, persons, services and capital is ensured in accordance with the provisions of the Treaties.

3   The Council, on a proposal from the Commission, shall determine the guidelines and conditions necessary to ensure balanced progress in all the sectors concerned.

Article 27

(ex Article 15 TEC)

When drawing up its proposals with a view to achieving the objectives set out in Article 26, the Commission shall take into account the extent of the effort that certain economies showing differences in development will have to sustain for the establishment of the internal market and it may propose appropriate provisions.

If these provisions take the form of derogations, they must be of a temporary nature and must cause the least possible disturbance to the functioning of the internal market.

TITLE II

FREE MOVEMENT OF GOODS

Article 28

(ex Article 23 TEC)

1   The Union shall comprise a customs union which shall cover all trade in goods and which shall involve the prohibition between Member States of customs duties on imports and exports and of all charges having equivalent effect, and the adoption of a common customs tariff in their relations with third countries.

2   The provisions of Article 30 and of Chapter 2 of this Title shall apply to products originating in Member States and to products coming from third countries which are in free circulation in Member States.

Article 29

(ex Article 24 TEC)

Products coming from a third country shall be considered to be in free circulation in a Member State if the import formalities have been complied with and any customs duties or charges having equivalent effect which are payable have been levied in that Member State, and if they have not benefited from a total or partial drawback of such duties or charges.

CHAPTER 1

THE CUSTOMS UNION

Article 30

(ex Article 25 TEC)

Customs duties on imports and exports and charges having equivalent effect shall be prohibited between Member States. This prohibition shall also apply to customs duties of a fiscal nature.

Article 31

(ex Article 26 TEC)

Common Customs Tariff duties shall be fixed by the Council on a proposal from the Commission.

Article 32

(ex Article 27 TEC)

In carrying out the tasks entrusted to it under this Chapter the Commission shall be guided by:

(a)   the need to promote trade between Member States and third countries;

(b)   developments in conditions of competition within the Union in so far as they lead to an improvement in the competitive capacity of undertakings;

(c)   the requirements of the Union as regards the supply of raw materials and semi-finished goods; in this connection the Commission shall take care to avoid distorting conditions of competition between Member States in respect of finished goods;

(d)   the need to avoid serious disturbances in the economies of Member States and to ensure rational development of production and an expansion of consumption within the Union.

CHAPTER 2

CUSTOMS COOPERATION

Article 33

(ex Article 135 TEC)

Within the scope of application of the Treaties, the European Parliament and the Council, acting in accordance with the ordinary legislative procedure, shall take measures in order to strengthen customs cooperation between Member States and between the latter and the Commission.

CHAPTER 3

PROHIBITION OF QUANTITATIVE RESTRICTIONS BETWEEN MEMBER STATES

Article 34

(ex Article 28 TEC)

Quantitative restrictions on imports and all measures having equivalent effect shall be prohibited between Member States.

Article 35

(ex Article 29 TEC)

Quantitative restrictions on exports, and all measures having equivalent effect, shall be prohibited between Member States.

Article 36

(ex Article 30 TEC)

The provisions of Articles 34 and 35 shall not preclude prohibitions or restrictions on imports, exports or goods in transit justified on grounds of public morality, public policy or public security; the protection of health and life of humans, animals or plants; the protection of national treasures possessing artistic, historic or archaeological value; or the protection of industrial and commercial property. Such prohibitions or restrictions shall not, however, constitute a means of arbitrary discrimination or a disguised restriction on trade between Member States.

Article 37

(ex Article 31 TEC)

1   Member States shall adjust any State monopolies of a commercial character so as to ensure that no discrimination regarding the conditions under which goods are procured and marketed exists between nationals of Member States.

   The provisions of this Article shall apply to any body through which a Member State, in law or in fact, either directly or indirectly supervises, determines or appreciably influences imports or exports between Member States. These provisions shall likewise apply to monopolies delegated by the State to others.

2   Member States shall refrain from introducing any new measure which is contrary to the principles laid down in paragraph 1 or which restricts the scope of the articles dealing with the prohibition of customs duties and quantitative restrictions between Member States.

3   If a State monopoly of a commercial character has rules which are designed to make it easier to dispose of agricultural products or obtain for them the best return, steps should be taken in applying the rules

contained in this Article to ensure equivalent safeguards for the employment and standard of living of the producers concerned.

TITLE III

AGRICULTURE AND FISHERIES

Article 38

(ex Article 32 TEC)

1   The Union shall define and implement a common agriculture and fisheries policy.

The internal market shall extend to agriculture, fisheries and trade in agricultural products. 'Agricultural products' means the products of the soil, of stockfarming and of fisheries and products of first-stage processing directly related to these products. References to the common agricultural policy or to agriculture, and the use of the term 'agricultural', shall be understood as also referring to fisheries, having regard to the specific characteristics of this sector.

2   Save as otherwise provided in Articles 39 to 44, the rules laid down for the establishment and functioning of the internal market shall apply to agricultural products.

3   The products subject to the provisions of Articles 39 to 44 are listed in Annex I.

4   The operation and development of the internal market for agricultural products must be accompanied by the establishment of a common agricultural policy.

Article 39

(ex Article 33 TEC)

1   The objectives of the common agricultural policy shall be:

(a)   to increase agricultural productivity by promoting technical progress and by ensuring the rational development of agricultural production and the optimum utilisation of the factors of production, in particular labour;

(b)   thus to ensure a fair standard of living for the agricultural community, in particular by increasing the individual earnings of persons engaged in agriculture;

(c)   to stabilise markets;

(d)   to assure the availability of supplies;

(e)   to ensure that supplies reach consumers at reasonable prices.

2   In working out the common agricultural policy and the special methods for its application, account shall be taken of:

(a)   the particular nature of agricultural activity, which results from the social structure of agriculture and from structural and natural disparities between the various agricultural regions;

(b)   the need to effect the appropriate adjustments by degrees;

(c)   the fact that in the Member States agriculture constitutes a sector closely linked with the economy as a whole.

Article 40

(ex Article 34 TEC)

1   In order to attain the objectives set out in Article 39, a common organisation of agricultural markets shall be established.

This organisation shall take one of the following forms, depending on the product concerned:

(a)   common rules on competition;

(b)   compulsory coordination of the various national market organisations;

(c)   a European market organisation.

2   The common organisation established in accordance with paragraph 1 may include all measures required to attain the objectives set out in Article 39, in particular regulation of prices, aids for the production and marketing of the various products, storage and carryover arrangements and common machinery for stabilising imports or exports.

The common organisation shall be limited to pursuit of the objectives set out in Article 39 and shall exclude any discrimination between producers or consumers within the Union.

Any common price policy shall be based on common criteria and uniform methods of calculation.

3   In order to enable the common organisation referred to in paragraph 1 to attain its objectives, one or more agricultural guidance and guarantee funds may be set up.

Article 41

(ex Article 35 TEC)

To enable the objectives set out in Article 39 to be attained, provision may be made within the framework of the common agricultural policy for measures such as:

(a)   an effective coordination of efforts in the spheres of vocational training, of research and of the dissemination of agricultural knowledge; this may include joint financing of projects or institutions;

(b)   joint measures to promote consumption of certain products.

Article 42

(ex Article 36 TEC)

The provisions of the Chapter relating to rules on competition shall apply to production of and trade in agricultural products only to the extent determined by the European Parliament and the Council within the framework of Article 43(2) and in accordance with the procedure laid down therein, account being taken of the objectives set out in Article 39.

The Council, on a proposal from the Commission, may authorise the granting of aid:

(a)   for the protection of enterprises handicapped by structural or natural conditions;

(b)   within the framework of economic development programmes.

Article 43

(ex Article 37 TEC)

1   The Commission shall submit proposals for working out and implementing the common agricultural policy, including the replacement of the national organisations by one of the forms of common organisation provided for in Article 40(1), and for implementing the measures specified in this Title.

These proposals shall take account of the interdependence of the agricultural matters mentioned in this Title.

2   The European Parliament and the Council, acting in accordance with the ordinary legislative procedure and after consulting the Economic and Social Committee, shall establish the common organisation of agricultural markets provided for in Article 40(1) and the other provisions necessary for the pursuit of the objectives of the common agricultural policy and the common fisheries policy.

3   The Council, on a proposal from the Commission, shall adopt measures on fixing prices, levies, aid and quantitative limitations and on the fixing and allocation of fishing opportunities.

4   In accordance with paragraph 1, the national market organisations may be replaced by the common organisation provided for in Article 40(1) if:

(a)   the common organisation offers Member States which are opposed to this measure and which have an organisation of their own for the production in question equivalent safeguards for the employment and standard of living of the producers concerned, account being taken of the adjustments that will be possible and the specialisation that will be needed with the passage of time;

(b)   such an organisation ensures conditions for trade within the Union similar to those existing in a national market.

5   If a common organisation for certain raw materials is established before a common organisation exists for the corresponding processed products, such raw materials as are used for processed products intended for export to third countries may be imported from outside the Union.

Article 44

(ex Article 38 TEC)

Where in a Member State a product is subject to a national market organisation or to internal rules having equivalent effect which affect the competitive position of similar production in another Member State, a countervailing charge shall be applied by Member States to imports of this product coming from the Member State where such organisation or rules exist, unless that State applies a countervailing charge on export.

The Commission shall fix the amount of these charges at the level required to redress the balance; it may also authorise other measures, the conditions and details of which it shall determine.

TITLE IV

FREE MOVEMENT OF PERSONS, SERVICES AND CAPITAL

CHAPTER 1

WORKERS

Article 45

(ex Article 39 TEC)

1   Freedom of movement for workers shall be secured within the Union.

2   Such freedom of movement shall entail the abolition of any discrimination based on nationality between workers of the Member States as regards employment, remuneration and other conditions of work and employment.

3   It shall entail the right, subject to limitations justified on grounds of public policy, public security or public health:

(a)   to accept offers of employment actually made;

(b)   to move freely within the territory of Member States for this purpose;

(c)   to stay in a Member State for the purpose of employment in accordance with the provisions governing the employment of nationals of that State laid down by law, regulation or administrative action;

(d)   to remain in the territory of a Member State after having been employed in that State, subject to conditions which shall be embodied in regulations to be drawn up by the Commission.

4   The provisions of this Article shall not apply to employment in the public service.

Article 46

(ex Article 40 TEC)

The European Parliament and the Council shall, acting in accordance with the ordinary legislative procedure and after consulting the Economic and Social Committee, issue directives or make regulations setting out the measures required to bring about freedom of movement for workers, as defined in Article 45, in particular:

(a)   by ensuring close cooperation between national employment services;

(b)   by abolishing those administrative procedures and practices and those qualifying periods in respect of eligibility for available employment, whether resulting from national legislation or from agreements previously concluded between Member States, the maintenance of which would form an obstacle to liberalisation of the movement of workers;

(c)   by abolishing all such qualifying periods and other restrictions provided for either under national legislation or under agreements previously concluded between Member States as imposed on workers of other Member States conditions regarding the free choice of employment other than those imposed on workers of the State concerned;

(d)   by setting up appropriate machinery to bring offers of employment into touch with applications for employment and to facilitate the achievement of a balance between supply and demand in the employment market in such a way as to avoid serious threats to the standard of living and level of employment in the various regions and industries.

Article 47

(ex Article 41 TEC)

Member States shall, within the framework of a joint programme, encourage the exchange of young workers.

Article 48

(ex Article 42 TEC)

The European Parliament and the Council shall, acting in accordance with the ordinary legislative procedure, adopt such measures in the field of social security as are necessary to provide freedom of movement for workers;

to this end, they shall make arrangements to secure for employed and selfemployed migrant workers and their dependants:

(a) aggregation, for the purpose of acquiring and retaining the right to benefit and of calculating the amount of benefit, of all periods taken into account under the laws of the several countries;

(b) payment of benefits to persons resident in the territories of Member States.

Where a member of the Council declares that a draft legislative act referred to in the first subparagraph would affect important aspects of its social security system, including its scope, cost or financial structure, or would affect the financial balance of that system, it may request that the matter be referred to the European Council. In that case, the ordinary legislative procedure shall be suspended. After discussion, the European Council shall, within four months of this suspension, either:

(a) refer the draft back to the Council, which shall terminate the suspension of the ordinary legislative procedure; or

(b) take no action or request the Commission to submit a new proposal; in that case, the act originally proposed shall be deemed not to have been adopted.

CHAPTER 2

RIGHT OF ESTABLISHMENT

Article 49

(ex Article 43 TEC)

Within the framework of the provisions set out below, restrictions on the freedom of establishment of nationals of a Member State in the territory of another Member State shall be prohibited. Such prohibition shall also apply to restrictions on the setting-up of agencies, branches or subsidiaries by nationals of any Member State established in the territory of any Member State.

Freedom of establishment shall include the right to take up and pursue activities as self-employed persons and to set up and manage undertakings, in particular companies or firms within the meaning of the second paragraph of Article 54, under the conditions laid down for its own nationals by the law of the country where such establishment is effected, subject to the provisions of the Chapter relating to capital.

Article 50

(ex Article 44 TEC)

1 In order to attain freedom of establishment as regards a particular activity, the European Parliament and the Council, acting in accordance with the ordinary legislative procedure and after consulting the Economic and Social Committee, shall act by means of directives.

2 The European Parliament, the Council and the Commission shall carry out the duties devolving upon them under the preceding provisions, in particular:

(a) by according, as a general rule, priority treatment to activities where freedom of establishment makes a particularly valuable contribution to the development of production and trade;

(b) by ensuring close cooperation between the competent authorities in the Member States in order to ascertain the particular situation within the Union of the various activities concerned;

(c)   by abolishing those administrative procedures and practices, whether resulting from national legislation or from agreements previously concluded between Member States, the maintenance of which would form an obstacle to freedom of establishment;

(d)   by ensuring that workers of one Member State employed in the territory of another Member State may remain in that territory for the purpose of taking up activities therein as self-employed persons, where they satisfy the conditions which they would be required to satisfy if they were entering that State at the time when they intended to take up such activities;

(e)   by enabling a national of one Member State to acquire and use land and buildings situated in the territory of another Member State, in so far as this does not conflict with the principles laid down in Article 39(2);

(f)   by effecting the progressive abolition of restrictions on freedom of establishment in every branch of activity under consideration, both as regards the conditions for setting up agencies, branches or subsidiaries in the territory of a Member State and as regards the subsidiaries in the territory of a Member State and as regards the conditions governing the entry of personnel belonging to the main establishment into managerial or supervisory posts in such agencies, branches or subsidiaries;

(g)   by coordinating to the necessary extent the safeguards which, for the protection of the interests of members and others, are required by Member States of companies or firms within the meaning of the second paragraph of Article 54 with a view to making such safeguards equivalent throughout the Union;

(h)   by satisfying themselves that the conditions of establishment are not distorted by aids granted by Member States.

Article 51

(ex Article 45 TEC)

The provisions of this Chapter shall not apply, so far as any given Member State is concerned, to activities which in that State are connected, even occasionally, with the exercise of official authority.

The European Parliament and the Council, acting in accordance with the ordinary legislative procedure, may rule that the provisions of this Chapter shall not apply to certain activities.

Article 52

(ex Article 46 TEC)

1   The provisions of this Chapter and measures taken in pursuance thereof shall not prejudice the applicability of provisions laid down by law, regulation or administrative action providing for special treatment for foreign nationals on grounds of public policy, public security or public health.

2   The European Parliament and the Council shall, acting in accordance with the ordinary legislative procedure, issue directives for the coordination of the abovementioned provisions.

Article 53

(ex Article 47 TEC)

1   In order to make it easier for persons to take up and pursue activities as self-employed persons, the European Parliament and the Council shall, acting in accordance with the ordinary legislative procedure, issue directives for the mutual recognition of diplomas, certificates and other evidence of formal qualifications and for the coordination of the provisions laid down by law, regulation or administrative action in Member States concerning the taking-up and pursuit of activities as selfemployed persons.

2   In the case of the medical and allied and pharmaceutical professions, the progressive abolition of restrictions shall be dependent upon coordination of the conditions for their exercise in the various Member States.

Article 54

(ex Article 48 TEC)

Companies or firms formed in accordance with the law of a Member State and having their registered office, central administration or principal place of business within the Union shall, for the purposes of this Chapter, be treated in the same way as natural persons who are nationals of Member States.

'Companies or firms' means companies or firms constituted under civil or commercial law, including cooperative societies, and other legal persons governed by public or private law, save for those which are non-profit-making.

Article 55

(ex Article 294 TEC)

Member States shall accord nationals of the other Member States the same treatment as their own nationals as regards participation in the capital of companies or firms within the meaning of Article 54, without prejudice to the application of the other provisions of the Treaties.

CHAPTER 3

SERVICES

Article 56

(ex Article 49 TEC)

Within the framework of the provisions set out below, restrictions on freedom to provide services within the Union shall be prohibited in respect of nationals of Member States who are established in a Member State other than that of the person for whom the services are intended.

The European Parliament and the Council, acting in accordance with the ordinary legislative procedure, may extend the provisions of the Chapter to nationals of a third country who provide services and who are established within the Union.

Article 57

(ex Article 50 TEC)

Services shall be considered to be 'services' within the meaning of the Treaties where they are normally provided for remuneration, in so far as they are not governed by the provisions relating to freedom of movement for goods, capital and persons.

'Services' shall in particular include:

(a)   activities of an industrial character;

(b)   activities of a commercial character;

(c)   activities of craftsmen;

(d)   activities of the professions.

Without prejudice to the provisions of the Chapter relating to the right of establishment, the person providing a service may, in order to do so, temporarily pursue his activity in the Member State where the service is provided, under the same conditions as are imposed by that State on its own nationals.

Article 58

(ex Article 51 TEC)

1   Freedom to provide services in the field of transport shall be governed by the provisions of the Title relating to transport.

2   The liberalisation of banking and insurance services connected with movements of capital shall be effected in step with the liberalisation of movement of capital.

Article 59

(ex Article 52 TEC)

1   In order to achieve the liberalisation of a specific service, the European Parliament and the Council, acting in accordance with the ordinary legislative procedure and after consulting the Economic and Social Committee, shall issue directives.

2   As regards the directives referred to in paragraph 1, priority shall as a general rule be given to those services which directly affect production costs or the liberalisation of which helps to promote trade in goods.

Article 60

(ex Article 53 TEC)

The Member States shall endeavour to undertake the liberalisation of services beyond the extent required by the directives issued pursuant to Article 59(1), if their general economic situation and the situation of the economic sector concerned so permit.

To this end, the Commission shall make recommendations to the Member States concerned.

Article 61

(ex Article 54 TEC)

As long as restrictions on freedom to provide services have not been abolished, each Member State shall apply such restrictions without distinction on grounds of nationality or residence to all persons providing services within the meaning of the first paragraph of Article 56.

Article 62

(ex Article 55 TEC)

The provisions of Articles 51 to 54 shall apply to the matters covered by this Chapter.

CHAPTER 4

CAPITAL AND PAYMENTS

Article 63

(ex Article 56 TEC)

1   Within the framework of the provisions set out in this Chapter, all restrictions on the movement of capital between Member States and between Member States and third countries shall be prohibited.

2   Within the framework of the provisions set out in this Chapter, all restrictions on payments between Member States and between Member States and third countries shall be prohibited.

Article 64

(ex Article 57 TEC)

1   The provisions of Article 63 shall be without prejudice to the application to third countries of any restrictions which exist on 31 December 1993 under national or Union law adopted in respect of the movement of capital to or from third countries involving direct investment — including in real estate — establishment, the provision of financial services or the admission of securities to capital markets. In respect of restrictions existing under national law in Bulgaria, Estonia and Hungary, the relevant date shall be 31 December 1999.

2   Whilst endeavouring to achieve the objective of free movement of capital between Member States and third countries to the greatest extent possible and without prejudice to the other Chapters of the Treaties, the European Parliament and the Council, acting in accordance with the ordinary legislative procedure, shall adopt the measures on the movement of capital to or from third countries involving direct investment — including investment in real estate — establishment, the provision of financial services or the admission of securities to capital markets.

3   Notwithstanding paragraph 2, only the Council, acting in accordance with a special legislative procedure, may unanimously, and after consulting the European Parliament, adopt measures which constitute a step backwards in Union law as regards the liberalisation of the movement of capital to or from third countries.

Article 65

(ex Article 58 TEC)

1   The provisions of Article 63 shall be without prejudice to the right of Member States:

(a)   to apply the relevant provisions of their tax law which distinguish between taxpayers who are not in the same situation with regard to their place of residence or with regard to the place where their capital is invested;

(b)   to take all requisite measures to prevent infringements of national law and regulations, in particular in the field of taxation and the prudential supervision of financial institutions, or to lay down procedures for the declaration of capital movements for purposes of administrative or statistical information, or to take measures which are justified on grounds of public policy or public security.

2   The provisions of this Chapter shall be without prejudice to the applicability of restrictions on the right of establishment which are compatible with the Treaties.

3   The measures and procedures referred to in paragraphs 1 and 2 shall not constitute a means of arbitrary discrimination or a disguised restriction on the free movement of capital and payments as defined in Article 63.

4   In the absence of measures pursuant to Article 64(3), the Commission or, in the absence of a Commission decision within three months from the request of the Member State concerned, the Council, may adopt a decision stating that restrictive tax measures adopted by a Member State concerning one or more third countries are to be considered compatible with the Treaties in so far as they are justified by one of the objectives of the Union and compatible with the proper functioning of the internal market. The Council shall act unanimously on application by a Member State.

Article 66

(ex Article 59 TEC)

Where, in exceptional circumstances, movements of capital to or from third countries cause, or threaten to cause, serious difficulties for the operation of economic and monetary union, the Council, on a proposal from the Commission and after consulting the European Central Bank, may take safeguard measures with regard to third countries for a period not exceeding six months if such measures are strictly necessary.

TITLE V

AREA OF FREEDOM, SECURITY AND JUSTICE

CHAPTER 1

GENERAL PROVISIONS

Article 67

(ex Article 61 TEC and ex Article 29 TEU)

1   The Union shall constitute an area of freedom, security and justice with respect for fundamental rights and the different legal systems and traditions of the Member States.

2   It shall ensure the absence of internal border controls for persons and shall frame a common policy on asylum, immigration and external border control, based on solidarity between Member States, which is fair towards third-country nationals. For the purpose of this Title, stateless persons shall be treated as third-country nationals.

3   The Union shall endeavour to ensure a high level of security through measures to prevent and combat crime, racism and xenophobia, and through measures for coordination and cooperation between police and judicial authorities and other competent authorities, as well as through the mutual recognition of judgments in criminal matters and, if necessary, through the approximation of criminal laws.

4   The Union shall facilitate access to justice, in particular through the principle of mutual recognition of judicial and extrajudicial decisions in civil matters.

Article 68

The European Council shall define the strategic guidelines for legislative and operational planning within the area of freedom, security and justice.

Article 69

National Parliaments ensure that the proposals and legislative initiatives submitted under Chapters 4 and 5 comply with the principle of subsidiarity, in accordance with the arrangements laid down by the Protocol on the application of the principles of subsidiarity and proportionality.

Article 70

Without prejudice to Articles 258, 259 and 260, the Council may, on a proposal from the Commission, adopt measures laying down the arrangements whereby Member States, in collaboration with the Commission, conduct objective and impartial evaluation of the implementation of the Union policies referred to in this Title by Member States' authorities, in particular in order to facilitate full application of the principle of mutual recognition. The European Parliament and national Parliaments shall be informed of the content and results of the evaluation.

Article 71

(ex Article 36 TEU)

A standing committee shall be set up within the Council in order to ensure that operational cooperation on internal security is promoted and strengthened within the Union. Without prejudice to Article 240, it shall facilitate coordination of the action of Member States' competent authorities.

Representatives of the Union bodies, offices and agencies concerned may be involved in the proceedings of this committee. The European Parliament and national Parliaments shall be kept informed of the proceedings.

Article 72

(ex Article 64(1) TEC and ex Article 33 TEU)

This Title shall not affect the exercise of the responsibilities incumbent upon Member States with regard to the maintenance of law and order and the safeguarding of internal security.

Article 73

It shall be open to Member States to organise between themselves and under their responsibility such forms of cooperation and coordination as they deem appropriate between the competent departments of their administrations responsible for safeguarding national security.

Article 74

(ex Article 66 TEC)

The Council shall adopt measures to ensure administrative cooperation between the relevant departments of the Member States in the areas covered by this Title, as well as between those departments and the Commission. It shall act on a Commission proposal, subject to Article 76, and after consulting the European Parliament.

Article 75

(ex Article 60 TEC)

Where necessary to achieve the objectives set out in Article 67, as regards preventing and combating terrorism and related activities, the European Parliament and the Council, acting by means of regulations in accordance with the ordinary legislative procedure, shall define a framework for administrative measures with regard to capital movements and payments, such as the freezing of funds, financial assets or economic gains belonging to, or owned or held by, natural or legal persons, groups or non-State entities.

The Council, on a proposal from the Commission, shall adopt measures to implement the framework referred to in the first paragraph.

The acts referred to in this Article shall include necessary provisions on legal safeguards.

Article 76

The acts referred to in Chapters 4 and 5, together with the measures referred to in Article 74 which ensure administrative cooperation in the areas covered by these Chapters, shall be adopted:

(a)   on a proposal from the Commission, or

(b)   on the initiative of a quarter of the Member States.

CHAPTER 2

POLICIES ON BORDER CHECKS, ASYLUM AND IMMIGRATION

Article 77

(ex Article 62 TEC)

1   The Union shall develop a policy with a view to:

 (a)   ensuring the absence of any controls on persons, whatever their nationality, when crossing internal borders;

 (b)   carrying out checks on persons and efficient monitoring of the crossing of external borders;

 (c)   the gradual introduction of an integrated management system for external borders.

2   For the purposes of paragraph 1, the European Parliament and the Council, acting in accordance with the ordinary legislative procedure, shall adopt measures concerning:

 (a)   the common policy on visas and other short-stay residence permits;

 (b)   the checks to which persons crossing external borders are subject;

 (c)   the conditions under which nationals of third countries shall have the freedom to travel within the Union for a short period;

 (d)   any measure necessary for the gradual establishment of an integrated management system for external borders;

 (e)   the absence of any controls on persons, whatever their nationality, when crossing internal borders.

3   If action by the Union should prove necessary to facilitate the exercise of the right referred to in Article 20(2)(a), and if the Treaties have not provided the necessary powers, the Council, acting in accordance with a special legislative procedure, may adopt provisions concerning passports, identity cards, residence permits or any other such document. The Council shall act unanimously after consulting the European Parliament.

4   This Article shall not affect the competence of the Member States concerning the geographical demarcation of their borders, in accordance with international law.

Article 78

(ex Articles 63, points 1 and 2, and 64(2) TEC)

1   The Union shall develop a common policy on asylum, subsidiary protection and temporary protection with a view to offering appropriate status to any third-country national requiring international protection and ensuring compliance with the principle of non-refoulement. This policy must be in accordance with the Geneva Convention of 28 July 1951 and the Protocol of 31 January 1967 relating to the status of refugees, and other relevant treaties.

2   For the purposes of paragraph 1, the European Parliament and the Council, acting in accordance with the ordinary legislative procedure, shall adopt measures for a common European asylum system comprising:

 (a)   a uniform status of asylum for nationals of third countries, valid throughout the Union;

 (b)   a uniform status of subsidiary protection for nationals of third countries who, without obtaining European asylum, are in need of international protection;

(c)   a common system of temporary protection for displaced persons in the event of a massive inflow;

(d)   common procedures for the granting and withdrawing of uniform asylum or subsidiary protection status;

(e)   criteria and mechanisms for determining which Member State is responsible for considering an application for asylum or subsidiary protection;

(f)   standards concerning the conditions for the reception of applicants for asylum or subsidiary protection;

(g)   partnership and cooperation with third countries for the purpose of managing inflows of people applying for asylum or subsidiary or temporary protection.

3   In the event of one or more Member States being confronted by an emergency situation characterised by a sudden inflow of nationals of third countries, the Council, on a proposal from the Commission, may adopt provisional measures for the benefit of the Member State(s) concerned. It shall act after consulting the European Parliament.

Article 79

(ex Article 63, points 3 and 4, TEC)

1   The Union shall develop a common immigration policy aimed at ensuring, at all stages, the efficient management of migration flows, fair treatment of third-country nationals residing legally in Member States, and the prevention of, and enhanced measures to combat, illegal immigration and trafficking in human beings.

2   For the purposes of paragraph 1, the European Parliament and the Council, acting in accordance with the ordinary legislative procedure, shall adopt measures in the following areas:

(a)   the conditions of entry and residence, and standards on the issue by Member States of long-term visas and residence permits, including those for the purpose of family reunification;

(b)   the definition of the rights of third-country nationals residing legally in a Member State, including the conditions governing freedom of movement and of residence in other Member States;

(c)   illegal immigration and unauthorised residence, including removal and repatriation of persons residing without authorisation;

(d)   combating trafficking in persons, in particular women and children.

3   The Union may conclude agreements with third countries for the readmission to their countries of origin or provenance of third-country nationals who do not or who no longer fulfil the conditions for entry, presence or residence in the territory of one of the Member States.

4   The European Parliament and the Council, acting in accordance with the ordinary legislative procedure, may establish measures to provide incentives and support for the action of Member States with a view to promoting the integration of third-country nationals residing legally in their territories, excluding any harmonisation of the laws and regulations of the Member States.

5   This Article shall not affect the right of Member States to determine volumes of admission of third-country nationals coming from third countries to their territory in order to seek work, whether employed or self-employed.

Article 80

The policies of the Union set out in this Chapter and their implementation shall be governed by the principle of solidarity and fair sharing of responsibility, including its financial implications, between the Member States.

Whenever necessary, the Union acts adopted pursuant to this Chapter shall contain appropriate measures to give effect to this principle.

CHAPTER 3

JUDICIAL COOPERATION IN CIVIL MATTERS

Article 81

(ex Article 65 TEC)

1   The Union shall develop judicial cooperation in civil matters having cross-border implications, based on the principle of mutual recognition of judgments and of decisions in extrajudicial cases. Such cooperation may include the adoption of measures for the approximation of the laws and regulations of the Member States.

2   For the purposes of paragraph 1, the European Parliament and the Council, acting in accordance with the ordinary legislative procedure, shall adopt measures, particularly when necessary for the proper functioning of the internal market, aimed at ensuring:

   (a)   the mutual recognition and enforcement between Member States of judgments and of decisions in extrajudicial cases;

   (b)   the cross-border service of judicial and extrajudicial documents;

   (c)   the compatibility of the rules applicable in the Member States concerning conflict of laws and of jurisdiction;

   (d)   cooperation in the taking of evidence;

   (e)   effective access to justice;

   (f)   the elimination of obstacles to the proper functioning of civil proceedings, if necessary by promoting the compatibility of the rules on civil procedure applicable in the Member States;

      (g)   the development of alternative methods of dispute settlement;

   (h)   support for the training of the judiciary and judicial staff.

3   Notwithstanding paragraph 2, measures concerning family law with cross-border implications shall be established by the Council, acting in accordance with a special legislative procedure. The Council shall act unanimously after consulting the European Parliament.

The Council, on a proposal from the Commission, may adopt a decision determining those aspects of family law with cross-border implications which may be the subject of acts adopted by the ordinary legislative procedure. The Council shall act unanimously after consulting the European Parliament.

The proposal referred to in the second subparagraph shall be notified to the national Parliaments. If a national Parliament makes known its opposition within six months of the date of such notification, the decision shall not be adopted. In the absence of opposition, the Council may adopt the decision.

CHAPTER 4

JUDICIAL COOPERATION IN CRIMINAL MATTERS

Article 82

(ex Article 31 TEU)

1   Judicial cooperation in criminal matters in the Union shall be based on the principle of mutual recognition of judgments and judicial decisions and shall include the approximation of the laws and regulations of the Member States in the areas referred to in paragraph 2 and in Article 83.

The European Parliament and the Council, acting in accordance with the ordinary legislative procedure, shall adopt measures to:

(a)   lay down rules and procedures for ensuring recognition throughout the Union of all forms of judgments and judicial decisions;

(b)   prevent and settle conflicts of jurisdiction between Member States;

(c)   support the training of the judiciary and judicial staff;

(d)   facilitate cooperation between judicial or equivalent authorities of the Member States in relation to proceedings in criminal matters and the enforcement of decisions.

2   To the extent necessary to facilitate mutual recognition of judgments and judicial decisions and police and judicial cooperation in criminal matters having a cross-border dimension, the European Parliament and the Council may, by means of directives adopted in accordance with the ordinary legislative procedure, establish minimum rules. Such rules shall take into account the differences between the legal traditions and systems of the Member States.

They shall concern:

(a)   mutual admissibility of evidence between Member States;

(b)   the rights of individuals in criminal procedure;

(c)   the rights of victims of crime;

(d)   any other specific aspects of criminal procedure which the Council has identified in advance by a decision; for the adoption of such a decision, the Council shall act unanimously after obtaining the consent of the European Parliament.

Adoption of the minimum rules referred to in this paragraph shall not prevent Member States from maintaining or introducing a higher level of protection for individuals.

3   Where a member of the Council considers that a draft directive as referred to in paragraph 2 would affect fundamental aspects of its criminal justice system, it may request that the draft directive be referred to the European Council. In that case, the ordinary legislative procedure shall be suspended.

After discussion, and in case of a consensus, the European Council shall, within four months of this suspension, refer the draft back to the Council, which shall terminate the suspension of the ordinary legislative procedure.

Within the same timeframe, in case of disagreement, and if at least nine Member States wish to establish enhanced cooperation on the basis of the draft directive concerned, they shall notify the European Parliament, the Council and the Commission accordingly. In such a case, the authorisation to proceed with enhanced cooperation referred to in Article 20(2) of the Treaty on European Union and Article 329(1) of this Treaty shall be deemed to be granted and the provisions on enhanced cooperation shall apply.

Article 83

(ex Article 31 TEU)

1   The European Parliament and the Council may, by means of directives adopted in accordance with the ordinary legislative procedure, establish minimum rules concerning the definition of criminal offences and sanctions in the areas of particularly serious crime with a cross-border dimension resulting from the nature or impact of such offences or from a special need to combat them on a common basis.

These areas of crime are the following: terrorism, trafficking in human beings and sexual exploitation of women and children, illicit drug trafficking, illicit arms trafficking, money laundering, corruption, counterfeiting of means of payment, computer crime and organised crime.

On the basis of developments in crime, the Council may adopt a decision identifying other areas of crime that meet the criteria specified in this paragraph. It shall act unanimously after obtaining the consent of the European Parliament.

2   If the approximation of criminal laws and regulations of the Member States proves essential to ensure the effective implementation of a Union policy in an area which has been subject to harmonisation measures, directives may establish minimum rules with regard to the definition of criminal offences and sanctions in the area concerned. Such directives shall be adopted by the same ordinary or special legislative procedure as was followed for the adoption of the harmonisation measures in question, without prejudice to Article 76.

3   Where a member of the Council considers that a draft directive as referred to in paragraph 1 or 2 would affect fundamental aspects of its criminal justice system, it may request that the draft directive be referred to the European Council. In that case, the ordinary legislative procedure shall be suspended.

After discussion, and in case of a consensus, the European Council shall, within four months of this suspension, refer the draft back to the Council, which shall terminate the suspension of the ordinary legislative procedure.

Within the same timeframe, in case of disagreement, and if at least nine Member States wish to establish enhanced cooperation on the basis of the draft directive concerned, they shall notify the European Parliament, the Council and the Commission accordingly. In such a case, the authorisation to proceed with enhanced cooperation referred to in Article 20(2) of the Treaty on European Union and Article 329(1) of this Treaty shall be deemed to be granted and the provisions on enhanced cooperation shall apply.

Article 84

The European Parliament and the Council, acting in accordance with the ordinary legislative procedure, may establish measures to promote and support the action of Member States in the field of crime prevention, excluding any harmonisation of the laws and regulations of the Member States.

Article 85

(ex Article 31 TEU)

1   Eurojust's mission shall be to support and strengthen coordination and cooperation between national investigating and prosecuting authorities in relation to serious crime affecting two or more Member States or requiring a prosecution on common bases, on the basis of operations conducted and information supplied by the Member States' authorities and by Europol.

In this context, the European Parliament and the Council, by means of regulations adopted in accordance with the ordinary legislative procedure, shall determine Eurojust's structure, operation, field of action and tasks. These tasks may include:

(a)   the initiation of criminal investigations, as well as proposing the initiation of prosecutions conducted by competent national authorities, particularly those relating to offences against the financial interests of the Union;

(b)   the coordination of investigations and prosecutions referred to in point (a);

(c)   the strengthening of judicial cooperation, including by resolution of conflicts of jurisdiction and by close cooperation with the European Judicial Network.

These regulations shall also determine arrangements for involving the European Parliament and national Parliaments in the evaluation of Eurojust's activities.

2   In the prosecutions referred to in paragraph 1, and without prejudice to Article 86, formal acts of judicial procedure shall be carried out by the competent national officials.

Article 86

1   In order to combat crimes affecting the financial interests of the Union, the Council, by means of regulations adopted in accordance with a special legislative procedure, may establish a European Public Prosecutor's Office from Eurojust. The Council shall act unanimously after obtaining the consent of the European Parliament.

In the absence of unanimity in the Council, a group of at least nine Member States may request that the draft regulation be referred to the European Council. In that case, the procedure in the Council shall be suspended. After discussion, and in case of a consensus, the European Council shall, within four months of this suspension, refer the draft back to the Council for adoption.

Within the same timeframe, in case of disagreement, and if at least nine Member States wish to establish enhanced cooperation on the basis of the draft regulation concerned, they shall notify the European Parliament, the Council and the Commission accordingly. In such a case, the authorisation to proceed with enhanced cooperation referred to in Article 20(2) of the Treaty on European Union and Article 329(1) of this Treaty shall be deemed to be granted and the provisions on enhanced cooperation shall apply.

2   The European Public Prosecutor's Office shall be responsible for investigating, prosecuting and bringing to judgment, where appropriate in liaison with Europol, the perpetrators of, and accomplices in, offences against the Union's financial interests, as determined by the regulation provided for in paragraph 1. It shall exercise the functions of prosecutor in the competent courts of the Member States in relation to such offences.

3   The regulations referred to in paragraph 1 shall determine the general rules applicable to the European Public Prosecutor's Office, the conditions governing the performance of its functions, the rules of procedure applicable to its activities, as well as those governing the admissibility of evidence, and the rules applicable to the judicial review of procedural measures taken by it in the performance of its functions.

4   The European Council may, at the same time or subsequently, adopt a decision amending paragraph 1 in order to extend the powers of the European Public Prosecutor's Office to include serious crime having a cross-border dimension and amending accordingly paragraph 2 as regards the perpetrators of, and accomplices in, serious crimes affecting more than one Member State. The European Council shall act unanimously after obtaining the consent of the European Parliament and after consulting the Commission.

CHAPTER 5

POLICE COOPERATION

Article 87

(ex Article 30 TEU)

1   The Union shall establish police cooperation involving all the Member States' competent authorities, including police, customs and other specialised law enforcement services in relation to the prevention, detection and investigation of criminal offences.

2   For the purposes of paragraph 1, the European Parliament and the Council, acting in accordance with the ordinary legislative procedure, may establish measures concerning:

(a)   the collection, storage, processing, analysis and exchange of relevant information;

(b)   support for the training of staff, and cooperation on the exchange of staff, on equipment and on research into crime-detection;

(c)   common investigative techniques in relation to the detection of serious forms of organised crime.

3   The Council, acting in accordance with a special legislative procedure, may establish measures concerning operational cooperation between the authorities referred to in this Article. The Council shall act unanimously after consulting the European Parliament.

In case of the absence of unanimity in the Council, a group of at least nine Member States may request that the draft measures be referred to the European Council. In that case, the procedure in the Council shall be suspended. After discussion, and in case of a consensus, the European Council shall, within four months of this suspension, refer the draft back to the Council for adoption.

Within the same timeframe, in case of disagreement, and if at least nine Member States wish to establish enhanced cooperation on the basis of the draft measures concerned, they shall notify the European Parliament, the Council and the Commission accordingly. In such a case, the authorisation to proceed with enhanced cooperation referred to in Article 20(2) of the Treaty on European Union and Article 329(1) of this Treaty shall be deemed to be granted and the provisions on enhanced cooperation shall apply.

The specific procedure provided for in the second and third subparagraphs shall not apply to acts which constitute a development of the Schengen acquis.

Article 88

(ex Article 30 TEU)

1   Europol's mission shall be to support and strengthen action by the Member States' police authorities and other law enforcement services and their mutual cooperation in preventing and combating serious crime affecting two or more Member States, terrorism and forms of crime which affect a common interest covered by a Union policy.

2   The European Parliament and the Council, by means of regulations adopted in accordance with the ordinary legislative procedure, shall determine Europol's structure, operation, field of action and tasks. These tasks may include:

(a)   the collection, storage, processing, analysis and exchange of information, in particular that forwarded by the authorities of the Member States or third countries or bodies;

(b)   the coordination, organisation and implementation of investigative and operational action carried out jointly with the Member States' competent authorities or in the context of joint investigative teams, where appropriate in liaison with Eurojust.

These regulations shall also lay down the procedures for scrutiny of Europol's activities by the European Parliament, together with national Parliaments.

3   Any operational action by Europol must be carried out in liaison and in agreement with the authorities of the Member State or States whose territory is concerned. The application of coercive measures shall be the exclusive responsibility of the competent national authorities.

Article 89

(ex Article 32 TEU)

The Council, acting in accordance with a special legislative procedure, shall lay down the conditions and limitations under which the competent authorities of the Member States referred to in Articles 82 and 87 may operate in the territory of another Member State in liaison and in agreement with the authorities of that State. The Council shall act unanimously after consulting the European Parliament.

TITLE VII

COMMON RULES ON COMPETITION, TAXATION AND APPROXIMATION OF LAWS

CHAPTER 1

RULES ON COMPETITION

SECTION 1

RULES APPLYING TO UNDERTAKINGS

Article 101

(ex Article 81 TEC)

1   The following shall be prohibited as incompatible with the internal market: all agreements between undertakings, decisions by associations of undertakings and concerted practices which may affect trade between Member States and which have as their object or effect the prevention, restriction or distortion of competition within the internal market, and in particular those which:

(a)   directly or indirectly fix purchase or selling prices or any other trading conditions;

(b)   limit or control production, markets, technical development, or investment;

(c)   share markets or sources of supply;

(d)   apply dissimilar conditions to equivalent transactions with other trading parties, thereby placing them at a competitive disadvantage;

(e)   make the conclusion of contracts subject to acceptance by the other parties of supplementary obligations which, by their nature or according to commercial usage, have no connection with the subject of such contracts.

2   Any agreements or decisions prohibited pursuant to this Article shall be automatically void.

3   The provisions of paragraph 1 may, however, be declared inapplicable in the case of:

- any agreement or category of agreements between undertakings,

- any decision or category of decisions by associations of undertakings,

- any concerted practice or category of concerted practices, which contributes to improving the production or distribution of goods or to promoting technical or economic progress, while allowing consumers a fair share of the resulting benefit, and which does not:

    (a)   impose on the undertakings concerned restrictions which are not indispensable to the attainment of these objectives;

    (b)   afford such undertakings the possibility of eliminating competition in respect of a substantial part of the products in question.

Article 102

(ex Article 82 TEC)

Any abuse by one or more undertakings of a dominant position within the internal market or in a substantial part of it shall be prohibited as incompatible with the internal market in so far as it may affect trade between Member States.

Such abuse may, in particular, consist in:

(a)   directly or indirectly imposing unfair purchase or selling prices or other unfair trading conditions;

(b)   limiting production, markets or technical development to the prejudice of consumers;

(c)   applying dissimilar conditions to equivalent transactions with other trading parties, thereby placing them at a competitive disadvantage;

(d)   making the conclusion of contracts subject to acceptance by the other parties of supplementary obligations which, by their nature or according to commercial usage, have no connection with the subject of such contracts.

Article 103

(ex Article 83 TEC)

1   The appropriate regulations or directives to give effect to the principles set out in Articles 101 and 102 shall be laid down by the Council, on a proposal from the Commission and after consulting the European Parliament.

2   The regulations or directives referred to in paragraph 1 shall be designed in particular:

(a)   to ensure compliance with the prohibitions laid down in Article 101(1) and in Article 102 by making provision for fines and periodic penalty payments;

9 (b)   to lay down detailed rules for the application of Article 101(3), taking into account the need to ensure effective supervision on the one hand, and to simplify administration to the greatest possible extent on the other;

(c)   to define, if need be, in the various branches of the economy, the scope of the provisions of Articles 101 and 102;

(d)   to define the respective functions of the Commission and of the Court of Justice of the European Union in applying the provisions laid down in this paragraph;

(e)   to determine the relationship between national laws and the provisions contained in this Section or adopted pursuant to this Article.

Article 104

(ex Article 84 TEC)

Until the entry into force of the provisions adopted in pursuance of Article 103, the authorities in Member States shall rule on the admissibility of agreements, decisions and concerted practices and on abuse of a dominant position in the internal market in accordance with the law of their country and with the provisions of Article 101, in particular paragraph 3, and of Article 102.

Article 105

(ex Article 85 TEC)

1   Without prejudice to Article 104, the Commission shall ensure the application of the principles laid down in Articles 101 and 102. On application by a Member State or on its own initiative, and in cooperation with the competent authorities in the Member States, which shall give it their assistance, the Commission shall investigate cases of suspected infringement of these principles. If it finds that there has been an infringement, it shall propose appropriate measures to bring it to an end.

2   If the infringement is not brought to an end, the Commission shall record such infringement of the principles in a reasoned decision. The Commission may publish its decision and authorise Member States to take the measures, the conditions and details of which it shall determine, needed to remedy the situation.

3   The Commission may adopt regulations relating to the categories of agreement in respect of which the Council has adopted a regulation or a directive pursuant to Article 103(2)(b).

Article 106

(ex Article 86 TEC)

1   In the case of public undertakings and undertakings to which Member States grant special or exclusive rights, Member States shall neither enact nor maintain in force any measure contrary to the rules contained in the Treaties, in particular to those rules provided for in Article 18 and Articles 101 to 109.

2   Undertakings entrusted with the operation of services of general economic interest or having the character of a revenue-producing monopoly shall be subject to the rules contained in the Treaties, in particular to the rules on competition, in so far as the application of such rules does not obstruct the performance, in law or in fact, of the particular tasks assigned to them. The development of trade must not be affected to such an extent as would be contrary to the interests of the Union.

3   The Commission shall ensure the application of the provisions of this Article and shall, where necessary, address appropriate directives or decisions to Member States.

SECTION 2

AIDS GRANTED BY STATES

Article 107

(ex Article 87 TEC)

1   Save as otherwise provided in the Treaties, any aid granted by a Member State or through State resources in any form whatsoever which distorts or threatens to distort competition by favouring certain undertakings

or the production of certain goods shall, in so far as it affects trade between Member States, be incompatible with the internal market.

2   The following shall be compatible with the internal market:

(a)   aid having a social character, granted to individual consumers, provided that such aid is granted without discrimination related to the origin of the products concerned;

(b)   aid to make good the damage caused by natural disasters or exceptional occurrences;

(c)   aid granted to the economy of certain areas of the Federal Republic of Germany affected by the division of Germany, in so far as such aid is required in order to compensate for the economic disadvantages caused by that division. Five years after the entry into force of the Treaty of Lisbon, the Council, acting on a proposal from the Commission, may adopt a decision repealing this point.

3   The following may be considered to be compatible with the internal market:

(a)   aid to promote the economic development of areas where the standard of living is abnormally low or where there is serious underemployment, and of the regions referred to in Article 349, in view of their structural, economic and social situation;

(b)   aid to promote the execution of an important project of common European interest or to remedy a serious disturbance in the economy of a Member State;

(c)   aid to facilitate the development of certain economic activities or of certain economic areas, where such aid does not adversely affect trading conditions to an extent contrary to the common interest;

(d)   aid to promote culture and heritage conservation where such aid does not affect trading conditions and competition in the Union to an extent that is contrary to the common interest;

(e)   such other categories of aid as may be specified by decision of the Council on a proposal from the Commission.

Article 108

(ex Article 88 TEC)

1   The Commission shall, in cooperation with Member States, keep under constant review all systems of aid existing in those States. It shall propose to the latter any appropriate measures required by the progressive development or by the functioning of the internal market.

2   If, after giving notice to the parties concerned to submit their comments, the Commission finds that aid granted by a State or through State resources is not compatible with the internal market having regard to Article 107, or that such aid is being misused, it shall decide that the State concerned shall abolish or alter such aid within a period of time to be determined by the Commission.

If the State concerned does not comply with this decision within the prescribed time, the Commission or any other interested State may, in derogation from the provisions of Articles 258 and 259, refer the matter to the Court of Justice of the European Union direct.

On application by a Member State, the Council may, acting unanimously, decide that aid which that State is granting or intends to grant shall be considered to be compatible with the internal market, in derogation from the provisions of Article 107 or from the regulations provided for in Article 109, if such a decision is justified by exceptional circumstances. If, as regards the aid in question, the Commission has already initiated the procedure provided for in the first subparagraph of this paragraph, the fact that the State concerned has made its application to the Council shall have the effect of suspending that procedure until the Council has made its attitude known.

If, however, the Council has not made its attitude known within three months of the said application being made, the Commission shall give its decision on the case.

3   The Commission shall be informed, in sufficient time to enable it to submit its comments, of any plans to grant or alter aid. If it considers that any such plan is not compatible with the internal market having regard to Article 107, it shall without delay initiate the procedure provided for in paragraph 2. The Member State concerned shall not put its proposed measures into effect until this procedure has resulted in a final decision.

4   The Commission may adopt regulations relating to the categories of State aid that the Council has, pursuant to Article 109, determined may be exempted from the procedure provided for by paragraph 3 of this Article.

Article 109

(ex Article 89 TEC)

The Council, on a proposal from the Commission and after consulting the European Parliament, may make any appropriate regulations for the application of Articles 107 and 108 and may in particular determine the conditions in which Article 108(3) shall apply and the categories of aid exempted from this procedure.

CHAPTER 2

TAX PROVISIONS

Article 110

(ex Article 90 TEC)

No Member State shall impose, directly or indirectly, on the products of other Member States any internal taxation of any kind in excess of that imposed directly or indirectly on similar domestic products.

Furthermore, no Member State shall impose on the products of other Member States any internal taxation of such a nature as to afford indirect protection to other products.

Article 111

(ex Article 91 TEC)

Where products are exported to the territory of any Member State, any repayment of internal taxation shall not exceed the internal taxation imposed on them whether directly or indirectly.

Article 112

(ex Article 92 TEC)

In the case of charges other than turnover taxes, excise duties and other forms of indirect taxation, remissions and repayments in respect of exports to other Member States may not be granted and countervailing charges in respect of imports from Member States may not be imposed unless the measures contemplated have been previously approved for a limited period by the Council on a proposal from the Commission.

Article 113

(ex Article 93 TEC)

The Council shall, acting unanimously in accordance with a special legislative procedure and after consulting the European Parliament and the Economic and Social Committee, adopt provisions for the harmonisation of legislation concerning turnover taxes, excise duties and other forms of indirect taxation to the extent that such harmonisation is necessary to ensure the establishment and the functioning of the internal market and to avoid distortion of competition.

CHAPTER 3

APPROXIMATION OF LAWS

Article 114

(ex Article 95 TEC)

1   Save where otherwise provided in the Treaties, the following provisions shall apply for the achievement of the objectives set out in Article 26. The European Parliament and the Council shall, acting in accordance with the ordinary legislative procedure and after consulting the Economic and Social Committee, adopt the measures for the approximation of the provisions laid down by law, regulation or administrative action in Member States which have as their object the establishment and functioning of the internal market.

2   Paragraph 1 shall not apply to fiscal provisions, to those relating to the free movement of persons nor to those relating to the rights and interests of employed persons.

3   The Commission, in its proposals envisaged in paragraph 1 concerning health, safety, environmental protection and consumer protection, will take as a base a high level of protection, taking account in particular of any new development based on scientific facts. Within their respective powers, the European Parliament and the Council will also seek to achieve this objective.

4   If, after the adoption of a harmonisation measure by the European Parliament and the Council, by the Council or by the Commission, a Member State deems it necessary to maintain national provisions on grounds of major needs referred to in Article 36, or relating to the protection of the environment or the working environment, it shall notify the Commission of these provisions as well as the grounds for maintaining them.

5   Moreover, without prejudice to paragraph 4, if, after the adoption of a harmonisation measure by the European Parliament and the Council, by the Council or by the Commission, a Member State deems it necessary to introduce national provisions based on new scientific evidence relating to the protection of the environment or the working environment on grounds of a problem specific to that Member State arising after the adoption of the harmonisation measure, it shall notify the Commission of the envisaged provisions as well as the grounds for introducing them.

6   The Commission shall, within six months of the notifications as referred to in paragraphs 4 and 5, approve or reject the national provisions involved after having verified whether or not they are a means of arbitrary discrimination or a disguised restriction on trade between Member States and whether or not they shall constitute an obstacle to the functioning of the internal market.

   In the absence of a decision by the Commission within this period the national provisions referred to in paragraphs 4 and 5 shall be deemed to have been approved.

   When justified by the complexity of the matter and in the absence of danger for human health, the Commission may notify the Member State concerned that the period referred to in this paragraph may be extended for a further period of up to six months.

7   When, pursuant to paragraph 6, a Member State is authorised to maintain or introduce national provisions derogating from a harmonisation measure, the Commission shall immediately examine whether to propose an adaptation to that measure.

8   When a Member State raises a specific problem on public health in a field which has been the subject of prior harmonisation measures, it shall bring it to the attention of the Commission which shall immediately examine whether to propose appropriate measures to the Council.

9   By way of derogation from the procedure laid down in Articles 258 and 259, the Commission and any Member State may bring the matter directly before the Court of Justice of the European Union if it considers that another Member State is making improper use of the powers provided for in this Article.

10   The harmonisation measures referred to above shall, in appropriate cases, include a safeguard clause authorising the Member States to take, for one or more of the non-economic reasons referred to in Article 36, provisional measures subject to a Union control procedure.

Article 115

(ex Article 94 TEC)

Without prejudice to Article 114, the Council shall, acting unanimously in accordance with a special legislative procedure and after consulting the European Parliament and the Economic and Social Committee, issue directives for the approximation of such laws, regulations or administrative provisions of the Member States as directly affect the establishment or functioning of the internal market.

Article 116

(ex Article 96 TEC)

Where the Commission finds that a difference between the provisions laid down by law, regulation or administrative action in Member States is distorting the conditions of competition in the internal market and that the resultant distortion needs to be eliminated, it shall consult the Member States concerned.

If such consultation does not result in an agreement eliminating the distortion in question, the European, Parliament and the Council, acting in accordance with the ordinary legislative procedure, shall issue the necessary directives. Any other appropriate measures provided for in the Treaties may be adopted.

Article 117

(ex Article 97 TEC)

1   Where there is a reason to fear that the adoption or amendment of a provision laid down by law, regulation or administrative action may cause distortion within the meaning of Article 116, a Member State desiring to proceed therewith shall consult the Commission. After consulting the Member States, the Commission shall recommend to the States concerned such measures as may be appropriate to avoid the distortion in question.

2   If a State desiring to introduce or amend its own provisions does not comply with the recommendation addressed to it by the Commission, other Member States shall not be required, pursuant to Article 116, to amend their own provisions in order to eliminate such distortion. If the Member State which has ignored the recommendation of the Commission causes distortion detrimental only to itself, the provisions of Article 116 shall not apply.

Article 118

In the context of the establishment and functioning of the internal market, the European Parliament and the Council, acting in accordance with the ordinary legislative procedure, shall establish measures for the creation of European intellectual property rights to provide uniform protection of intellectual property rights throughout the Union and for the setting up of centralised Union-wide authorisation, coordination and supervision arrangements.

The Council, acting in accordance with a special legislative procedure, shall by means of regulations establish language arrangements for the European intellectual property rights. The Council shall act unanimously after consulting the European Parliament.

TITLE VIII
ECONOMIC AND MONETARY POLICY
Article 119

(ex Article 4 TEC)

1   For the purposes set out in Article 3 of the Treaty on European Union, the activities of the Member States and the Union shall include, as provided in the Treaties, the adoption of an economic policy which is based on the close coordination of Member States' economic policies, on the internal market and on the definition of common objectives, and conducted in accordance with the principle of an open market economy with free competition.

2   Concurrently with the foregoing, and as provided in the Treaties and in accordance with the procedures set out therein, these activities shall include a single currency, the euro, and the definition and conduct of a single monetary policy and exchange-rate policy the primary objective of both of which shall be to maintain price stability and, without prejudice to this objective, to support the general economic policies in the Union, in accordance with the principle of an open market economy with free competition.

3   These activities of the Member States and the Union shall entail compliance with the following guiding principles: stable prices, sound public finances and monetary conditions and a sustainable balance of payments.

CHAPTER 1
ECONOMIC POLICY
Article 120

(ex Article 98 TEC)

Member States shall conduct their economic policies with a view to contributing to the achievement of the objectives of the Union, as defined in Article 3 of the Treaty on European Union, and in the context of the broad guidelines referred to in Article 121(2). The Member States and the Union shall act in accordance with the principle of an open market economy with free competition, favouring an efficient allocation of resources, and in compliance with the principles set out in Article 119.

Article 121

(ex Article 99 TEC)

1   Member States shall regard their economic policies as a matter of common concern and shall coordinate them within the Council, in accordance with the provisions of Article 120.

2   The Council shall, on a recommendation from the Commission, formulate a draft for the broad guidelines of the economic policies of the Member States and of the Union, and shall report its findings to the European Council.

The European Council shall, acting on the basis of the report from the Council, discuss a conclusion on the broad guidelines of the economic policies of the Member States and of the Union.

On the basis of this conclusion, the Council shall adopt a recommendation setting out these broad guidelines. The Council shall inform the European Parliament of its recommendation.

3   In order to ensure closer coordination of economic policies and sustained convergence of the economic performances of the Member States, the Council shall, on the basis of reports submitted by the Commission, monitor economic developments in each of the Member States and in the Union as well as the consistency of economic policies with the broad guidelines referred to in paragraph 2, and regularly carry out an overall assessment.

For the purpose of this multilateral surveillance, Member States shall forward information to the Commission about important measures taken by them in the field of their economic policy and such other information as they deem necessary.

4   Where it is established, under the procedure referred to in paragraph 3, that the economic policies of a Member State are not consistent with the broad guidelines referred to in paragraph 2 or that they risk jeopardising the proper functioning of economic and monetary union, the Commission may address a warning to the Member State concerned. The Council, on a recommendation from the Commission, may address the necessary recommendations to the Member State concerned. The Council may, on a proposal from the Commission, decide to make its recommendations public.

Within the scope of this paragraph, the Council shall act without taking into account the vote of the member of the Council representing the Member State concerned.

A qualified majority of the other members of the Council shall be defined in accordance with Article 238(3)(a).

5   The President of the Council and the Commission shall report to the European Parliament on the results of multilateral surveillance. The President of the Council may be invited to appear before the competent committee of the European Parliament if the Council has made its recommendations public.

6   The European Parliament and the Council, acting by means of regulations in accordance with the ordinary legislative procedure, may adopt detailed rules for the multilateral surveillance procedure referred to in paragraphs 3 and 4.

Article 122

(ex Article 100 TEC)

1   Without prejudice to any other procedures provided for in the Treaties, the Council, on a proposal from the Commission, may decide, in a spirit of solidarity between Member States, upon the measures appropriate to the economic situation, in particular if severe difficulties arise in the supply of certain products, notably in the area of energy.

2   Where a Member State is in difficulties or is seriously threatened with severe difficulties caused by natural disasters or exceptional occurrences beyond its control, the Council, on a proposal from the Commission, may grant, under certain conditions, Union financial assistance to the Member State concerned. The President of the Council shall inform the European Parliament of the decision taken.

Article 123

(ex Article 101 TEC)

1   Overdraft facilities or any other type of credit facility with the European Central Bank or with the central banks of the Member States (hereinafter referred to as 'national central banks') in favour of Union institutions, bodies, offices or agencies, central governments, regional, local or other public authorities, other bodies governed by public law, or public undertakings of Member States shall be prohibited, as

shall the purchase directly from them by the European Central Bank or national central banks of debt instruments.

2   Paragraph 1 shall not apply to publicly owned credit institutions which, in the context of the supply of reserves by central banks, shall be given the same treatment by national central banks and the European Central Bank as private credit institutions.

Article 124

(ex Article 102 TEC)

Any measure, not based on prudential considerations, establishing privileged access by Union institutions, bodies, offices or agencies, central governments, regional, local or other public authorities, other bodies governed by public law, or public undertakings of Member States to financial institutions, shall be prohibited.

Article 125

(ex Article 103 TEC)

1   The Union shall not be liable for or assume the commitments of central governments, regional, local or other public authorities, other bodies governed by public law, or public undertakings of any Member State, without prejudice to mutual financial guarantees for the joint execution of a specific project. A Member State shall not be liable for or assume the commitments of central governments, regional, local or other public authorities, other bodies governed by public law, or public undertakings of another Member State, without prejudice to mutual financial guarantees for the joint execution of a specific project.

2   The Council, on a proposal from the Commission and after consulting the European Parliament, may, as required, specify definitions for the application of the prohibitions referred to in Articles 123 and 124 and in this Article.

Article 126

(ex Article 104 TEC)

1   Member States shall avoid excessive government deficits.

     9

2   The Commission shall monitor the development of the budgetary situation and of the stock of government debt in the Member States with a view to identifying gross errors. In particular it shall examine compliance with budgetary discipline on the basis of the following two criteria:

(a)   whether the ratio of the planned or actual government deficit to gross domestic product exceeds a reference value, unless:

     ▸   either the ratio has declined substantially and continuously and reached a level that comes close to the reference value,

     ▸   or, alternatively, the excess over the reference value is only exceptional and temporary and the ratio remains close to the reference value;

(b)   whether the ratio of government debt to gross domestic product exceeds a reference value, unless the ratio is sufficiently diminishing and approaching the reference value at a satisfactory pace. The reference values are specified in the Protocol on the excessive deficit procedure annexed to the Treaties.

3   If a Member State does not fulfil the requirements under one or both of these criteria, the Commission shall prepare a report. The report of the Commission shall also take into account whether the government deficit exceeds government investment expenditure and take into account all other relevant factors, including the

medium-term economic and budgetary position of the Member State. The Commission may also prepare a report if, notwithstanding the fulfilment of the requirements under the criteria, it is of the opinion that there is a risk of an excessive deficit in a Member State.

4　The Economic and Financial Committee shall formulate an opinion on the report of the Commission.

5　If the Commission considers that an excessive deficit in a Member State exists or may occur, it shall address an opinion to the Member State concerned and shall inform the Council accordingly.

6　The Council shall, on a proposal from the Commission, and having considered any observations which the Member State concerned may wish to make, decide after an overall assessment whether an excessive deficit exists.

7　Where the Council decides, in accordance with paragraph 6, that an excessive deficit exists, it shall adopt, without undue delay, on a recommendation from the Commission, recommendations addressed to the Member State concerned with a view to bringing that situation to an end within a given period. Subject to the provisions of paragraph 8, these recommendations shall not be made public.

8　Where it establishes that there has been no effective action in response to its recommendations within the period laid down, the Council may make its recommendations public.

9　If a Member State persists in failing to put into practice the recommendations of the Council, the Council may decide to give notice to the Member State to take, within a specified time limit, measures for the deficit reduction which is judged necessary by the Council in order to remedy the situation. In such a case, the Council may request the Member State concerned to submit reports in accordance with a specific timetable in order to examine the adjustment efforts of that Member State.

10　The rights to bring actions provided for in Articles 258 and 259 may not be exercised within the framework of paragraphs 1 to 9 of this Article.

11　As long as a Member State fails to comply with a decision taken in accordance with paragraph 9, the Council may decide to apply or, as the case may be, intensify one or more of the following measures:

- ▸　to require the Member State concerned to publish additional information, to be specified by the Council, before issuing bonds and securities,

- ▸　to invite the European Investment Bank to reconsider its lending policy towards the Member State concerned,

- ▸　to require the Member State concerned to make a non-interest-bearing deposit of an appropriate size with the Union until the excessive deficit has, in the view of the Council, been corrected,

- ▸　to impose fines of an appropriate size.

The President of the Council shall inform the European Parliament of the decisions taken.

12　The Council shall abrogate some or all of its decisions or recommendations referred to in paragraphs 6 to 9 and 11 to the extent that the excessive deficit in the Member State concerned has, in the view of the Council, been corrected. If the Council has previously made public recommendations, it shall, as soon as the decision under paragraph 8 has been abrogated, make a public statement that an excessive deficit in the Member State concerned no longer exists.

13　When taking the decisions or recommendations referred to in paragraphs 8, 9, 11 and 12, the Council shall act on a recommendation from the Commission. When the Council adopts the measures referred to in paragraphs 6 to 9, 11 and 12, it shall act without taking into account the vote of the member of the Council representing the Member State concerned. A qualified majority of the other members of the Council shall be defined in accordance with Article 238(3)(a).

14　Further provisions relating to the implementation of the procedure described in this Article are set out in the Protocol on the excessive deficit procedure annexed to the Treaties.

The Council shall, acting unanimously in accordance with a special legislative procedure and after consulting the European Parliament and the European Central Bank, adopt the appropriate provisions which shall then replace the said Protocol.

Subject to the other provisions of this paragraph, the Council shall, on a proposal from the Commission and after consulting the European Parliament, lay down detailed rules and definitions for the application of the provisions of the said Protocol.

TITLE IX

EMPLOYMENT

Article 145

(ex Article 125 TEC)

Member States and the Union shall, in accordance with this Title, work towards developing a coordinated strategy for employment and particularly for promoting a skilled, trained and adaptable workforce and labour markets responsive to economic change with a view to achieving the objectives defined in Article 3 of the Treaty on European Union.

Article 146

(ex Article 126 TEC)

1　Member States, through their employment policies, shall contribute to the achievement of the objectives referred to in Article 145 in a way consistent with the broad guidelines of the economic policies of the Member States and of the Union adopted pursuant to Article 121(2).

2　Member States, having regard to national practices related to the responsibilities of management and labour, shall regard promoting employment as a matter of common concern and shall coordinate their action in this respect within the Council, in accordance with the provisions of Article 148.

Article 147

(ex Article 127 TEC)

1　The Union shall contribute to a high level of employment by encouraging cooperation between Member States and by supporting and, if necessary, complementing their action. In doing so, the competences of the Member States shall be respected.

2　The objective of a high level of employment shall be taken into consideration in the formulation and implementation of Union policies and activities.

Article 148

(ex Article 128 TEC)

1　The European Council shall each year consider the employment situation in the Union and adopt conclusions thereon, on the basis of a joint annual report by the Council and the Commission.

2　On the basis of the conclusions of the European Council, the Council, on a proposal from the Commission and after consulting the European Parliament, the Economic and Social Committee, the Committee of the

Regions and the Employment Committee referred to in Article 150, shall each year draw up guidelines which the Member States shall take into account in their employment policies.

These guidelines shall be consistent with the broad guidelines adopted pursuant to Article 121(2).

3   Each Member State shall provide the Council and the Commission with an annual report on the principal measures taken to implement its employment policy in the light of the guidelines for employment as referred to in paragraph 2.

4   The Council, on the basis of the reports referred to in paragraph 3 and having received the views of the Employment Committee, shall each year carry out an examination of the implementation of the employment policies of the Member States in the light of the guidelines for employment. The Council, on a recommendation from the Commission, may, if it considers it appropriate in the light of that examination, make recommendations to Member States.

5   On the basis of the results of that examination, the Council and the Commission shall make a joint annual report to the European Council on the employment situation in the Union and on the implementation of the guidelines for employment.

Article 149

(ex Article 129 TEC)

The European Parliament and the Council, acting in accordance with the ordinary legislative procedure and after consulting the Economic and Social Committee and the Committee of the Regions, may adopt incentive measures designed to encourage cooperation between Member States and to support their action in the field of employment through initiatives aimed at developing exchanges of information and best practices, providing comparative analysis and advice as well as promoting innovative approaches and evaluating experiences, in particular by recourse to pilot projects. Those measures shall not include harmonisation of the laws and regulations of the Member States.

Article 150

(ex Article 130 TEC)

The Council, acting by a simple majority after consulting the European Parliament, shall establish an Employment Committee with advisory status to promote coordination between Member States on employment and labour market policies. The tasks of the Committee shall be:

▶   to monitor the employment situation and employment policies in the Member States and the Union,

▶   without prejudice to Article 240, to formulate opinions at the request of either the Council or the Commission or on its own initiative, and to contribute to the preparation of the Council proceedings referred to in Article 148. In fulfilling its mandate, the Committee shall consult management and labour.

Each Member State and the Commission shall appoint two members of the Committee.

TITLE X

SOCIAL POLICY

Article 151

(ex Article 136 TEC)

The Union and the Member States, having in mind fundamental social rights such as those set out in the European Social Charter signed at Turin on 18 October 1961 and in the 1989 Community Charter of the Fundamental

Social Rights of Workers, shall have as their objectives the promotion of employment, improved living and working conditions, so as to make possible their harmonisation while the improvement is being maintained, proper social protection, dialogue between management and labour, the development of human resources with a view to lasting high employment and the combating of exclusion.

To this end the Union and the Member States shall implement measures which take account of the diverse forms of national practices, in particular in the field of contractual relations, and the need to maintain the competitiveness of the Union economy. They believe that such a development will ensue not only from the functioning of the internal market, which will favour the harmonisation of social systems, but also from the procedures provided for in the Treaties and from the approximation of provisions laid down by law, regulation or administrative action.

Article 152

The Union recognises and promotes the role of the social partners at its level, taking into account the diversity of national systems. It shall facilitate dialogue between the social partners, respecting their autonomy.

The Tripartite Social Summit for Growth and Employment shall contribute to social dialogue.

Article 153

(ex Article 137 TEC)

1   With a view to achieving the objectives of Article 151, the Union shall support and complement the activities of the Member States in the following fields:

   (a)   improvement in particular of the working environment to protect workers' health and safety;

   (b)   working conditions;

   (c)   social security and social protection of workers;

   (d)   protection of workers where their employment contract is terminated;

   (e)   the information and consultation of workers;

   (f)   representation and collective defence of the interests of workers and employers, including codetermination, subject to paragraph 5;

   (g)   conditions of employment for third-country nationals legally residing in Union territory;

   (h)   the integration of persons excluded from the labour market, without prejudice to Article 166;

   (i)   equality between men and women with regard to labour market opportunities and treatment at work;

   (j)   the combating of social exclusion;

   (k)   the modernisation of social protection systems without prejudice to point (c).

2   To this end, the European Parliament and the Council:

   (a)   may adopt measures designed to encourage cooperation between Member States through initiatives aimed at improving knowledge, developing exchanges of information and best practices, promoting innovative approaches and evaluating experiences, excluding any harmonisation of the laws and regulations of the Member States;

   (b)   may adopt, in the fields referred to in paragraph 1(a) to (i), by means of directives, minimum requirements for gradual implementation, having regard to the conditions and technical rules obtaining in each of the Member States. Such directives shall avoid imposing administrative, financial and legal constraints in a way which would hold back the creation and development of small and medium-sized undertakings.

The European Parliament and the Council shall act in accordance with the ordinary legislative procedure after consulting the Economic and Social Committee and the Committee of the Regions.

In the fields referred to in paragraph 1(c), (d), (f) and (g), the Council shall act unanimously, in accordance with a special legislative procedure, after consulting the European Parliament and the said Committees.

The Council, acting unanimously on a proposal from the Commission, after consulting the European Parliament, may decide to render the ordinary legislative procedure applicable to paragraph 1(d), (f) and (g).

3   A Member State may entrust management and labour, at their joint request, with the implementation of directives adopted pursuant to paragraph 2, or, where appropriate, with the implementation of a Council decision adopted in accordance with Article 155. In this case, it shall ensure that, no later than the date on which a directive or a decision must be transposed or implemented, management and labour have introduced the necessary measures by agreement, the Member State concerned being required to take any necessary measure enabling it at any time to be in a position to guarantee the results imposed by that directive or that decision.

4   The provisions adopted pursuant to this Article:

▸   shall not affect the right of Member States to define the fundamental principles of their social security systems and must not significantly affect the financial equilibrium thereof,

▸   shall not prevent any Member State from maintaining or introducing more stringent protective measures compatible with the Treaties.

5   The provisions of this Article shall not apply to pay, the right of association, the right to strike or the right to impose lock-outs.

Article 154

(ex Article 138 TEC)

1   The Commission shall have the task of promoting the consultation of management and labour at Union level and shall take any relevant measure to facilitate their dialogue by ensuring balanced support for the parties.

2   To this end, before submitting proposals in the social policy field, the Commission shall consult management and labour on the possible direction of Union action.

3   If, after such consultation, the Commission considers Union action advisable, it shall consult management and labour on the content of the envisaged proposal. Management and labour shall forward to the Commission an opinion or, where appropriate, a recommendation.

4   On the occasion of the consultation referred to in paragraphs 2 and 3, management and labour may inform the Commission of their wish to initiate the process provided for in Article 155.

The duration of this process shall not exceed nine months, unless the management and labour concerned and the Commission decide jointly to extend it.

Article 155

(ex Article 139 TEC)

1   Should management and labour so desire, the dialogue between them at Union level may lead to contractual relations, including agreements.

2   Agreements concluded at Union level shall be implemented either in accordance with the procedures and practices specific to management and labour and the Member States or, in matters covered by Article 153, at the joint request of the signatory parties, by a Council decision on a proposal from the Commission. The European Parliament shall be informed.

     The Council shall act unanimously where the agreement in question contains one or more provisions relating to one of the areas for which unanimity is required pursuant to Article 153(2).

Article 156

(ex Article 140 TEC)

With a view to achieving the objectives of Article 151 and without prejudice to the other provisions of the Treaties, the Commission shall encourage cooperation between the Member States and facilitate the coordination of their action in all social policy fields under this Chapter, particularly in matters relating to:

▶   employment,

▶   labour law and working conditions,

▶   basic and advanced vocational training,

▶   social security,

▶   prevention of occupational accidents and diseases,

▶   occupational hygiene,

▶   the right of association and collective bargaining between employers and workers.

To this end, the Commission shall act in close contact with Member States by making studies, delivering opinions and arranging consultations both on problems arising at national level and on those of concern to international organisations, in particular initiatives aiming at the establishment of guidelines and indicators, the organisation of exchange of best practice, and the preparation of the necessary elements for periodic monitoring and evaluation. The European Parliament shall be kept fully informed.

Before delivering the opinions provided for in this Article, the Commission shall consult the Economic and Social Committee.

Article 157

(ex Article 141 TEC)

1   Each Member State shall ensure that the principle of equal pay for male and female workers for equal work or work of equal value is applied.

2   For the purpose of this Article, 'pay' means the ordinary basic or minimum wage or salary and any other consideration, whether in cash or in kind, which the worker receives directly or indirectly, in respect of his employment, from his employer.

     Equal pay without discrimination based on sex means:

     (a)   that pay for the same work at piece rates shall be calculated on the basis of the same unit of measurement;

          (b)   that pay for work at time rates shall be the same for the same job.

3   The European Parliament and the Council, acting in accordance with the ordinary legislative procedure, and after consulting the Economic and Social Committee, shall adopt measures to ensure the application of the principle of equal opportunities and equal treatment of men and women in matters of employment and occupation, including the principle of equal pay for equal work or work of equal value.

4   With a view to ensuring full equality in practice between men and women in working life, the principle of equal treatment shall not prevent any Member State from maintaining or adopting measures providing for specific advantages in order to make it easier for the underrepresented sex to pursue a vocational activity or to prevent or compensate for disadvantages in professional careers.

Article 158

(ex Article 142 TEC)

Member States shall endeavour to maintain the existing equivalence between paid holiday schemes.

Article 159

(ex Article 143 TEC)

The Commission shall draw up a report each year on progress in achieving the objectives of Article 151, including the demographic situation in the Union. It shall forward the report to the European Parliament, the Council and the Economic and Social Committee.

Article 160

(ex Article 144 TEC)

The Council, acting by a simple majority after consulting the European Parliament, shall establish a Social Protection Committee with advisory status to promote cooperation on social protection policies between Member States and with the Commission. The tasks of the Committee shall be:

▶   to monitor the social situation and the development of social protection policies in the Member States and the Union,

▶   to promote exchanges of information, experience and good practice between Member States and with the Commission,

▶   without prejudice to Article 240, to prepare reports, formulate opinions or undertake other work within its fields of competence, at the request of either the Council or the Commission or on its own initiative.

In fulfilling its mandate, the Committee shall establish appropriate contacts with management and labour.

Each Member State and the Commission shall appoint two members of the Committee.

Article 161

(ex Article 145 TEC)

The Commission shall include a separate chapter on social developments within the Union in its annual report to the European Parliament.

The European Parliament may invite the Commission to draw up reports on any particular problems concerning social conditions.

TITLE XII

EDUCATION, VOCATIONAL TRAINING, YOUTH AND SPORT

Article 165

(ex Article 149 TEC)

1   The Union shall contribute to the development of quality education by encouraging cooperation between Member States and, if necessary, by supporting and supplementing their action, while fully respecting the responsibility of the Member States for the content of teaching and the organisation of education systems and their cultural and linguistic diversity.

The Union shall contribute to the promotion of European sporting issues, while taking account of the specific nature of sport, its structures based on voluntary activity and its social and educational function.

2   Union action shall be aimed at:

▶   developing the European dimension in education, particularly through the teaching and dissemination of the languages of the Member States,

▶   encouraging mobility of students and teachers, by encouraging inter alia, the academic recognition of diplomas and periods of study,

▶   promoting cooperation between educational establishments,

▶   developing exchanges of information and experience on issues common to the education systems of the Member States,

▶   encouraging the development of youth exchanges and of exchanges of socio-educational instructors, and encouraging the participation of young people in democratic life in Europe,

▶   encouraging the development of distance education,

▶   developing the European dimension in sport, by promoting fairness and openness in sporting competitions and cooperation between bodies responsible for sports, and by protecting the physical and moral integrity of sportsmen and sportswomen, especially the youngest sportsmen and sportswomen.

3   The Union and the Member States shall foster cooperation with third countries and the competent international organisations in the field of education and sport, in particular the Council of Europe.

4   In order to contribute to the achievement of the objectives referred to in this Article:

▶   the European Parliament and the Council, acting in accordance with the ordinary legislative procedure, after consulting the Economic and Social Committee and the Committee of the Regions, shall adopt incentive measures, excluding any harmonisation of the laws and regulations of the Member States,

▶   the Council, on a proposal from the Commission, shall adopt recommendations.

Article 166

(ex Article 150 TEC)

1   The Union shall implement a vocational training policy which shall support and supplement the action of the Member States, while fully respecting the responsibility of the Member States for the content and organisation of vocational training.

2   Union action shall aim to:

- ▸ facilitate adaptation to industrial changes, in particular through vocational training and retraining,

- ▸ improve initial and continuing vocational training in order to facilitate vocational integration and reintegration into the labour market,

- ▸ facilitate access to vocational training and encourage mobility of instructors and trainees and particularly young people,

- ▸ stimulate cooperation on training between educational or training establishments and firms,

- ▸ develop exchanges of information and experience on issues common to the training systems of the Member States.

3   The Union and the Member States shall foster cooperation with third countries and the competent international organisations in the sphere of vocational training.

4   The European Parliament and the Council, acting in accordance with the ordinary legislative procedure and after consulting the Economic and Social Committee and the Committee of the Regions, shall adopt measures to contribute to the achievement of the objectives referred to in this Article, excluding any harmonisation of the laws and regulations of the Member States, and the Council, on a proposal from the Commission, shall adopt recommendations.

PART SIX

INSTITUTIONAL AND FINANCIAL PROVISIONS

TITLE I

INSTITUTIONAL PROVISIONS

CHAPTER 1

THE INSTITUTIONS

SECTION 1

THE EUROPEAN PARLIAMENT

Article 223

(ex Article 190(4) and (5) TEC)

1   The European Parliament shall draw up a proposal to lay down the provisions necessary for the election of its Members by direct universal suffrage in accordance with a uniform procedure in all Member States or in accordance with principles common to all Member States.

The Council, acting unanimously in accordance with a special legislative procedure and after obtaining the consent of the European Parliament, which shall act by a majority of its component Members, shall lay down the necessary provisions. These provisions shall enter into force following their approval by the Member States in accordance with their respective constitutional requirements.

2   The European Parliament, acting by means of regulations on its own initiative in accordance with a special legislative procedure after seeking an opinion from the Commission and with the approval of the Council, shall lay down the regulations and general conditions governing the performance of the duties of its Members. All rules or conditions relating to the taxation of Members or former Members shall require unanimity within the Council.

Article 224

(ex Article 191, second subparagraph, TEC)

The European Parliament and the Council, acting in accordance with the ordinary legislative procedure, by means of regulations, shall lay down the regulations governing political parties at European level referred to in Article 10(4) of the Treaty on European Union and in particular the rules regarding their funding.

Article 225

(ex Article 192, second subparagraph, TEC)

The European Parliament may, acting by a majority of its component Members, request the Commission to submit any appropriate proposal on matters on which it considers that a Union act is required for the purpose of implementing the Treaties. If the Commission does not submit a proposal, it shall inform the European Parliament of the reasons.

Article 226

(ex Article 193 TEC)

In the course of its duties, the European Parliament may, at the request of a quarter of its component Members, set up a temporary Committee of Inquiry to investigate, without prejudice to the powers conferred by the Treaties on other institutions or bodies, alleged contraventions or maladministration in the implementation of Union law, except where the alleged facts are being examined before a court and while the case is still subject to legal proceedings. The temporary Committee of Inquiry shall cease to exist on the submission of its report. The detailed provisions governing the exercise of the right of inquiry shall be determined by the European Parliament, acting by means of regulations on its own initiative in accordance with a special legislative procedure, after obtaining the consent of the Council and the Commission.

Article 227

(ex Article 194 TEC)

Any citizen of the Union, and any natural or legal person residing or having its registered office in a Member State, shall have the right to address, individually or in association with other citizens or persons, a petition to the European Parliament on a matter which comes within the Union's fields of activity and which affects him, her or it directly.

Article 228

(ex Article 195 TEC)

1	A European Ombudsman, elected by the European Parliament, shall be empowered to receive complaints from any citizen of the Union or any natural or legal person residing or having its registered office in a Member State concerning instances of maladministration in the activities of the Union institutions, bodies, offices or agencies, with the exception of the Court of Justice of the European Union acting in its judicial role. He or she shall examine such complaints and report on them.

In accordance with his duties, the Ombudsman shall conduct inquiries for which he finds grounds, either on his own initiative or on the basis of complaints submitted to him direct or through a Member of the European Parliament, except where the alleged facts are or have been the subject of legal proceedings. Where the Ombudsman establishes an instance of maladministration, he shall refer the matter to the institution, body, office or agency concerned, which shall have a period of three months in which to inform him of its views. The Ombudsman shall then forward a report to the European Parliament and the institution, body, office or agency concerned. The person lodging the complaint shall be informed of the outcome of such inquiries.

The Ombudsman shall submit an annual report to the European Parliament on the outcome of his inquiries.

2   The Ombudsman shall be elected after each election of the European Parliament for the duration of its term of office. The Ombudsman shall be eligible for reappointment.

The Ombudsman may be dismissed by the Court of Justice at the request of the European Parliament if he no longer fulfils the conditions required for the performance of his duties or if he is guilty of serious misconduct.

3   The Ombudsman shall be completely independent in the performance of his duties. In the performance of those duties he shall neither seek nor take instructions from any Government, institution, body, office or entity. The Ombudsman may not, during his term of office, engage in any other occupation, whether gainful or not.

4   The European Parliament acting by means of regulations on its own initiative in accordance with a special legislative procedure shall, after seeking an opinion from the Commission and with the approval of the Council, lay down the regulations and general conditions governing the performance of the Ombudsman's duties.

Article 229

(ex Article 196 TEC)

The European Parliament shall hold an annual session. It shall meet, without requiring to be convened, on the second Tuesday in March.

The European Parliament may meet in extraordinary part-session at the request of a majority of its component Members or at the request of the Council or of the Commission.

Article 230

(ex Article 197, second, third and fourth paragraph, TEC)

The Commission may attend all the meetings and shall, at its request, be heard.

The Commission shall reply orally or in writing to questions put to it by the European Parliament or by its Members.

The European Council and the Council shall be heard by the European Parliament in accordance with the conditions laid down in the Rules of Procedure of the European Council and those of the Council.

Article 231

(ex Article 198 TEC)

Save as otherwise provided in the Treaties, the European Parliament shall act by a majority of the votes cast.

The Rules of Procedure shall determine the quorum.

Article 232

(ex Article 199 TEC)

The European Parliament shall adopt its Rules of Procedure, acting by a majority of its Members.

The proceedings of the European Parliament shall be published in the manner laid down in the Treaties and in its Rules of Procedure.

Article 233

(ex Article 200 TEC)

The European Parliament shall discuss in open session the annual general report submitted to it by the Commission.

Article 234

(ex Article 201 TEC)

If a motion of censure on the activities of the Commission is tabled before it, the European Parliament shall not vote thereon until at least three days after the motion has been tabled and only by open vote. If the motion of censure is carried by a two-thirds majority of the votes cast, representing a majority of the component Members of the European Parliament, the members of the Commission shall resign as a body and the High Representative of the Union for Foreign Affairs and Security Policy shall resign from duties that he or she carries out in the Commission. They shall remain in office and continue to deal with current business until they are replaced in accordance with Article 17 of the Treaty on European Union. In this case, the term of office of the members of the Commission appointed to replace them shall expire on the date on which the term of office of the members of the Commission obliged to resign as a body would have expired.

SECTION 2

THE EUROPEAN COUNCIL

Article 235

1   Where a vote is taken, any member of the European Council may also act on behalf of not more than one other member.

Article 16(4) of the Treaty on European Union and Article 238(2) of this Treaty shall apply to the

European Council when it is acting by a qualified majority. Where the European Council decides by vote, its President and the President of the Commission shall not take part in the vote.

Abstentions by members present in person or represented shall not prevent the adoption by the European Council of acts which require unanimity.

2   The President of the European Parliament may be invited to be heard by the European Council.

3   The European Council shall act by a simple majority for procedural questions and for the adoption of its Rules of Procedure.

4   The European Council shall be assisted by the General Secretariat of the Council.

Article 236

The European Council shall adopt by a qualified majority:

(a)   a decision establishing the list of Council configurations, other than those of the General Affairs Council and of the Foreign Affairs Council, in accordance with Article 16(6) of the Treaty on European Union;

(b)   a decision on the Presidency of Council configurations, other than that of Foreign Affairs, in accordance with Article 16(9) of the Treaty on European Union.

SECTION 3

THE COUNCIL

Article 237

(ex Article 204 TEC)

The Council shall meet when convened by its President on his own initiative or at the request of one of its Members or of the Commission.

Article 238

(ex Article 205(1) and (2), TEC)

1   Where it is required to act by a simple majority, the Council shall act by a majority of its component members.

2   By way of derogation from Article 16(4) of the Treaty on European Union, as from 1 November 2014 and subject to the provisions laid down in the Protocol on transitional provisions, where the

Council does not act on a proposal from the Commission or from the High Representative of the Union for Foreign Affairs and Security Policy, the qualified majority shall be defined as at least 72 % of the members of the Council, representing Member States comprising at least 65 % of the population of the Union.

3   As from 1 November 2014 and subject to the provisions laid down in the Protocol on transitional provisions, in cases where, under the Treaties, not all the members of the Council participate in voting, a qualified majority shall be defined as follows:

(a)   A qualified majority shall be defined as at least 55 % of the members of the Council representing the participating Member States, comprising at least 65 % of the population of these States.

A blocking minority must include at least the minimum number of Council members representing more than 35 % of the population of the participating Member States, plus one member, failing which the qualified majority shall be deemed attained;

(b)   By way of derogation from point (a), where the Council does not act on a proposal from the Commission or from the High Representative of the Union for Foreign Affairs and Security Policy, the qualified majority shall be defined as at least 72 % of the members of the Council representing the participating Member States, comprising at least 65 % of the population of these States.

4   Abstentions by Members present in person or represented shall not prevent the adoption by the Council of acts which require unanimity.

Article 239

(ex Article 206 TEC)

Where a vote is taken, any Member of the Council may also act on behalf of not more than one other member.

Article 240

(ex Article 207 TEC)

1   A committee consisting of the Permanent Representatives of the Governments of the Member States shall be responsible for preparing the work of the Council and for carrying out the tasks assigned to it by the latter. The Committee may adopt procedural decisions in cases provided for in the Council's Rules of Procedure.

2   The Council shall be assisted by a General Secretariat, under the responsibility of a Secretary- General appointed by the Council.

The Council shall decide on the organisation of the General Secretariat by a simple majority.

3   The Council shall act by a simple majority regarding procedural matters and for the adoption of its Rules of Procedure.

Article 241

(ex Article 208 TEC)

The Council acting by a simple majority may request the Commission to undertake any studies the Council considers desirable for the attainment of the common objectives, and to submit to it any appropriate proposals. If the Commission does not submit a proposal, it shall inform the Council of the reasons.

Article 242

(ex Article 209 TEC)

The Council, acting by a simple majority shall, after consulting the Commission, determine the rules governing the committees provided for in the Treaties.

Article 243

(ex Article 210 TEC)

The Council shall determine the salaries, allowances and pensions of the President of the European Council, the President of the Commission, the High Representative of the Union for Foreign Affairs and Security Policy, the Members of the Commission, the Presidents, Members and Registrars of the Court of Justice of the European Union, and the Secretary-General of the Council. It shall also determine any payment to be made instead of remuneration.

SECTION 4

THE COMMISSION

Article 244

In accordance with Article 17(5) of the Treaty on European Union, the Members of the Commission shall be chosen on the basis of a system of rotation established unanimously by the European Council and on the basis of the following principles:

(a)   Member States shall be treated on a strictly equal footing as regards determination of the sequence of, and the time spent by, their nationals as members of the Commission; consequently, the difference between the total number of terms of office held by nationals of any given pair of Member States may never be more than one;

(b)   subject to point (a), each successive Commission shall be so composed as to reflect satisfactorily the demographic and geographical range of all the Member States.

Article 245

(ex Article 213 TEC)

The Members of the Commission shall refrain from any action incompatible with their duties. Member States shall respect their independence and shall not seek to influence them in the performance of their tasks.

The Members of the Commission may not, during their term of office, engage in any other occupation, whether gainful or not. When entering upon their duties they shall give a solemn undertaking that, both during and after their term of office, they will respect the obligations arising therefrom and in particular their duty to behave with integrity and discretion as regards the acceptance, after they have ceased to hold office, of certain appointments or benefits. In the event of any breach of these obligations, the Court of Justice may, on application by the Council acting by a simple majority or the Commission, rule that the Member concerned be, according to the circumstances, either compulsorily retired in accordance with Article 247 or deprived of his right to a pension or other benefits in its stead.

Article 246

(ex Article 215 TEC)

Apart from normal replacement, or death, the duties of a Member of the Commission shall end when he resigns or is compulsorily retired. A vacancy caused by resignation, compulsory retirement or death shall be filled for the remainder of the Member's term of office by a new Member of the same nationality appointed by the Council, by common accord with the President of the Commission, after consulting the European Parliament and in accordance with the criteria set out in the second subparagraph of Article 17(3) of the Treaty on European Union. The Council may, acting unanimously on a proposal from the President of the Commission, decide that such a vacancy need not be filled, in particular when the remainder of the Member's term of office is short.

In the event of resignation, compulsory retirement or death, the President shall be replaced for the remainder of his term of office. The procedure laid down in the first subparagraph of Article 17(7) of the Treaty on European Union shall be applicable for the replacement of the President.

In the event of resignation, compulsory retirement or death, the High Representative of the Union for Foreign Affairs and Security Policy shall be replaced, for the remainder of his or her term of office, in accordance with Article 18(1) of the Treaty on European Union.

In the case of the resignation of all the Members of the Commission, they shall remain in office and continue to deal with current business until they have been replaced, for the remainder of their term of office, in accordance with Article 17 of the Treaty on European Union.

Article 247

(ex Article 216 TEC)

If any Member of the Commission no longer fulfils the conditions required for the performance of his duties or if he has been guilty of serious misconduct, the Court of Justice may, on application by the Council acting by a simple majority or the Commission, compulsorily retire him.

Article 248

(ex Article 217(2), TEC)

Without prejudice to Article 18(4) of the Treaty on European Union, the responsibilities incumbent upon the Commission shall be structured and allocated among its members by its President, in accordance with Article 17(6) of that Treaty. The President may reshuffle the allocation of those responsibilities during the Commission's term of office. The Members of the Commission shall carry out the duties devolved upon them by the President under his authority.

Article 249

(ex Articles 218(2) and 212 TEC)

1   The Commission shall adopt its Rules of Procedure so as to ensure that both it and its departments operate. It shall ensure that these Rules are published.

2   The Commission shall publish annually, not later than one month before the opening of the session of the European Parliament, a general report on the activities of the Union.

Article 250

(ex Article 219 TEC)

The Commission shall act by a majority of its Members.

Its Rules of Procedure shall determine the quorum.

SECTION 5

THE COURT OF JUSTICE OF THE EUROPEAN UNION

Article 251

(ex Article 221 TEC)

The Court of Justice shall sit in chambers or in a Grand Chamber, in accordance with the rules laid down for that purpose in the Statute of the Court of Justice of the European Union.

When provided for in the Statute, the Court of Justice may also sit as a full Court.

Article 252

(ex Article 222 TEC)

The Court of Justice shall be assisted by eight Advocates-General. Should the Court of Justice so request, the Council, acting unanimously, may increase the number of Advocates-General.

It shall be the duty of the Advocate-General, acting with complete impartiality and independence, to make, in open court, reasoned submissions on cases which, in accordance with the Statute of the Court of Justice of the European Union, require his involvement.

Article 253

(ex Article 223 TEC)

The Judges and Advocates-General of the Court of Justice shall be chosen from persons whose independence is beyond doubt and who possess the qualifications required for appointment to the highest judicial offices in their respective countries or who are jurisconsults of recognised competence; they shall be appointed by common accord of the governments of the Member States for a term of six years, after consultation of the panel provided for in Article 255.

Every three years there shall be a partial replacement of the Judges and Advocates-General, in accordance with the conditions laid down in the Statute of the Court of Justice of the European Union.

The Judges shall elect the President of the Court of Justice from among their number for a term of three years. He may be re-elected. Retiring Judges and Advocates-General may be reappointed.

The Court of Justice shall appoint its Registrar and lay down the rules governing his service.

The Court of Justice shall establish its Rules of Procedure. Those Rules shall require the approval of the Council.

Article 254

(ex Article 224 TEC)

The number of Judges of the General Court shall be determined by the Statute of the Court of Justice of the European Union. The Statute may provide for the General Court to be assisted by Advocates- General.

The members of the General Court shall be chosen from persons whose independence is beyond doubt and who possess the ability required for appointment to high judicial office. They shall be appointed by common accord of the governments of the Member States for a term of six years, after consultation of the panel provided for in Article 255. The membership shall be partially renewed every three years.

Retiring members shall be eligible for reappointment.

The Judges shall elect the President of the General Court from among their number for a term of three years. He may be re-elected.

The General Court shall appoint its Registrar and lay down the rules governing his service.

The General Court shall establish its Rules of Procedure in agreement with the Court of Justice. Those Rules shall require the approval of the Council.

Unless the Statute of the Court of Justice of the European Union provides otherwise, the provisions of the Treaties relating to the Court of Justice shall apply to the General Court.

Article 255

A panel shall be set up in order to give an opinion on candidates' suitability to perform the duties of Judge and Advocate-General of the Court of Justice and the General Court before the governments of the Member States make the appointments referred to in Articles 253 and 254.

The panel shall comprise seven persons chosen from among former members of the Court of Justice and the General Court, members of national supreme courts and lawyers of recognised competence, one of whom shall be proposed by the European Parliament. The Council shall adopt a decision establishing the panel's operating rules and a decision appointing its members. It shall act on the initiative of the President of the Court of Justice.

Article 256

(ex Article 225 TEC)

1   The General Court shall have jurisdiction to hear and determine at first instance actions or proceedings referred to in Articles 263, 265, 268, 270 and 272, with the exception of those assigned to a specialised court set up under Article 257 and those reserved in the Statute for the Court of Justice.

The Statute may provide for the General Court to have jurisdiction for other classes of action or proceeding.

Decisions given by the General Court under this paragraph may be subject to a right of appeal to the Court of Justice on points of law only, under the conditions and within the limits laid down by the Statute.

2   The General Court shall have jurisdiction to hear and determine actions or proceedings brought against decisions of the specialised courts. Decisions given by the General Court under this paragraph may exceptionally be subject to review by the Court of Justice, under the conditions and within the limits laid down by the Statute, where there is a serious risk of the unity or consistency of Union law being affected.

3   The General Court shall have jurisdiction to hear and determine questions referred for a preliminary ruling under Article 267, in specific areas laid down by the Statute.

Where the General Court considers that the case requires a decision of principle likely to affect the unity or consistency of Union law, it may refer the case to the Court of Justice for a ruling. Decisions given by the General Court on questions referred for a preliminary ruling may exceptionally be subject to review by the Court of Justice, under the conditions and within the limits laid down by the Statute, where there is a serious risk of the unity or consistency of Union law being affected.

Article 257

(ex Article 225 A TEC)

The European Parliament and the Council, acting in accordance with the ordinary legislative procedure, may establish specialised courts attached to the General Court to hear and determine at first instance certain classes of action or proceeding brought in specific areas. The European Parliament and the Council shall act by means of regulations either on a proposal from the Commission after consultation of the Court of Justice or at the request of the Court of Justice after consultation of the Commission.

The regulation establishing a specialised court shall lay down the rules on the organisation of the court and the extent of the jurisdiction conferred upon it. Decisions given by specialised courts may be subject to a right of appeal on points of law only or, when provided for in the regulation establishing the specialised court, a right of appeal also on matters of fact, before the General Court.

The members of the specialised courts shall be chosen from persons whose independence is beyond doubt and who possess the ability required for appointment to judicial office. They shall be appointed by the Council, acting unanimously.

The specialised courts shall establish their Rules of Procedure in agreement with the Court of Justice.

Those Rules shall require the approval of the Council.

Unless the regulation establishing the specialised court provides otherwise, the provisions of the Treaties relating to the Court of Justice of the European Union and the provisions of the Statute of the Court of Justice of the European Union shall apply to the specialised courts. Title I of the Statute and Article 64 thereof shall in any case apply to the specialised courts.

Article 258

(ex Article 226 TEC)

If the Commission considers that a Member State has failed to fulfil an obligation under the Treaties, it shall deliver a reasoned opinion on the matter after giving the State concerned the opportunity to submit its observations.

If the State concerned does not comply with the opinion within the period laid down by the Commission, the latter may bring the matter before the Court of Justice of the European Union.

Article 259

(ex Article 227 TEC)

A Member State which considers that another Member State has failed to fulfil an obligation under the Treaties may bring the matter before the Court of Justice of the European Union.

Before a Member State brings an action against another Member State for an alleged infringement of an obligation under the Treaties, it shall bring the matter before the Commission.

The Commission shall deliver a reasoned opinion after each of the States concerned has been given the opportunity to submit its own case and its observations on the other party's case both orally and in writing.

If the Commission has not delivered an opinion within three months of the date on which the matter was brought before it, the absence of such opinion shall not prevent the matter from being brought before the Court.

Article 260

(ex Article 228 TEC)

1   If the Court of Justice of the European Union finds that a Member State has failed to fulfil an obligation under the Treaties, the State shall be required to take the necessary measures to comply with the judgment of the Court.

2   If the Commission considers that the Member State concerned has not taken the necessary measures to comply with the judgment of the Court, it may bring the case before the Court after giving that State the opportunity to submit its observations. It shall specify the amount of the lump sum or penalty payment to be paid by the Member State concerned which it considers appropriate in the circumstances.

If the Court finds that the Member State concerned has not complied with its judgment it may impose a lump sum or penalty payment on it.

This procedure shall be without prejudice to Article 259.

3   When the Commission brings a case before the Court pursuant to Article 258 on the grounds that the Member State concerned has failed to fulfil its obligation to notify measures transposing a directive adopted under a legislative procedure, it may, when it deems appropriate, specify the amount of the lump sum or penalty payment to be paid by the Member State concerned which it considers appropriate in the circumstances. If the Court finds that there is an infringement it may impose a lump sum or penalty payment on the Member State concerned not exceeding the amount specified by the Commission. The payment obligation shall take effect on the date set by the Court in its judgment.

Article 261

(ex Article 229 TEC)

Regulations adopted jointly by the European Parliament and the Council, and by the Council, pursuant to the provisions of the Treaties, may give the Court of Justice of the European Union unlimited jurisdiction with regard to the penalties provided for in such regulations.

Article 262

(ex Article 229 A TEC)

Without prejudice to the other provisions of the Treaties, the Council, acting unanimously in accordance with a special legislative procedure and after consulting the European Parliament, may adopt provisions to confer jurisdiction, to the extent that it shall determine, on the Court of Justice of the European Union in disputes relating to the application of acts adopted on the basis of the Treaties which create European intellectual property rights. These provisions shall enter into force after their approval by the Member States in accordance with their respective constitutional requirements.

Article 263

(ex Article 230 TEC)

The Court of Justice of the European Union shall review the legality of legislative acts, of acts of the Council, of the Commission and of the European Central Bank, other than recommendations and opinions, and of acts of the European Parliament and of the European Council intended to produce legal effects vis-à-vis third parties. It shall also review the legality of acts of bodies, offices or agencies of the Union intended to produce legal effects vis-à-vis third parties.

It shall for this purpose have jurisdiction in actions brought by a Member State, the European Parliament, the Council or the Commission on grounds of lack of competence, infringement of an essential procedural requirement, infringement of the Treaties or of any rule of law relating to their application, or misuse of powers.

The Court shall have jurisdiction under the same conditions in actions brought by the Court of Auditors, by the European Central Bank and by the Committee of the Regions for the purpose of protecting their prerogatives.

Any natural or legal person may, under the conditions laid down in the first and second paragraphs, institute proceedings against an act addressed to that person or which is of direct and individual concern to them, and against a regulatory act which is of direct concern to them and does not entail implementing measures.

Acts setting up bodies, offices and agencies of the Union may lay down specific conditions and arrangements concerning actions brought by natural or legal persons against acts of these bodies, offices or agencies intended to produce legal effects in relation to themThe proceedings provided for in this Article shall be instituted within two months of the publication of the measure, or of its notification to the plaintiff, or, in the absence thereof, of the day on which it came to the knowledge of the latter, as the case may be.

Article 264

(ex Article 231 TEC)

If the action is well founded, the Court of Justice of the European Union shall declare the act concerned to be void.

However, the Court shall, if it considers this necessary, state which of the effects of the act which it has declared void shall be considered as definitive.

Article 265

(ex Article 232 TEC)

Should the European Parliament, the European Council, the Council, the Commission or the European Central Bank, in infringement of the Treaties, fail to act, the Member States and the other institutions of the Union may bring an action before the Court of Justice of the European Union to have the infringement established. This Article shall apply, under the same conditions, to bodies, offices and agencies of the Union which fail to act.

The action shall be admissible only if the institution, body, office or agency concerned has first been called upon to act. If, within two months of being so called upon, the institution, body, office or agency concerned has not defined its position, the action may be brought within a further period of two months.

Any natural or legal person may, under the conditions laid down in the preceding paragraphs, complain to the Court that an institution, body, office or agency of the Union has failed to address to that person any act other than a recommendation or an opinion.

Article 266

(ex Article 233 TEC)

The institution whose act has been declared void or whose failure to act has been declared contrary to the Treaties shall be required to take the necessary measures to comply with the judgment of the Court of Justice of the European Union.

This obligation shall not affect any obligation which may result from the application of the second paragraph of Article 340.

Article 267

(ex Article 234 TEC)

The Court of Justice of the European Union shall have jurisdiction to give preliminary rulings concerning:

(a)   the interpretation of the Treaties;

(b)   the validity and interpretation of acts of the institutions, bodies, offices or agencies of the Union;

Where such a question is raised before any court or tribunal of a Member State, that court or tribunal may, if it considers that a decision on the question is necessary to enable it to give judgment, request the Court to give a ruling thereon.

Where any such question is raised in a case pending before a court or tribunal of a Member State against whose decisions there is no judicial remedy under national law, that court or tribunal shall bring the matter before the Court.

If such a question is raised in a case pending before a court or tribunal of a Member State with regard to a person in custody, the Court of Justice of the European Union shall act with the minimum of delay.

Article 268

(ex Article 235 TEC)

The Court of Justice of the European Union shall have jurisdiction in disputes relating to compensation for damage provided for in the second and third paragraphs of Article 340.

Article 269

The Court of Justice shall have jurisdiction to decide on the legality of an act adopted by the European Council or by the Council pursuant to Article 7 of the Treaty on European Union solely at the request of the Member State concerned by a determination of the European Council or of the Council and in respect solely of the procedural stipulations contained in that Article. Such a request must be made within one month from the date of such determination. The Court shall rule within one month from the date of the request.

Article 270

(ex Article 236 TEC)

The Court of Justice of the European Union shall have jurisdiction in any dispute between the Union and its servants within the limits and under the conditions laid down in the Staff Regulations of Officials and the Conditions of Employment of other servants of the Union.

Article 271

(ex Article 237 TEC)

The Court of Justice of the European Union shall, within the limits hereinafter laid down, have jurisdiction in disputes concerning:

(a)   the fulfilment by Member States of obligations under the Statute of the European Investment Bank. In this connection, the Board of Directors of the Bank shall enjoy the powers conferred upon the Commission by Article 258;

(b)   measures adopted by the Board of Governors of the European Investment Bank. In this connection, any Member State, the Commission or the Board of Directors of the Bank may institute proceedings under the conditions laid down in Article 263;

(c)   measures adopted by the Board of Directors of the European Investment Bank. Proceedings against such measures may be instituted only by Member States or by the Commission, under the conditions laid down in Article 263, and solely on the grounds of non-compliance with the procedure provided for in Article 19(2), (5), (6) and (7) of the Statute of the Bank;

(d)   the fulfilment by national central banks of obligations under the Treaties and the Statute of the ESCB and of the ECB. In this connection the powers of the Governing Council of the European Central Bank in respect of national central banks shall be the same as those conferred upon the Commission in respect of Member States by Article 258. If the Court finds that a national central bank has failed to fulfil an obligation under the Treaties, that bank shall be required to take the necessary measures to comply with the judgment of the Court.

Article 272

(ex Article 238 TEC)

The Court of Justice of the European Union shall have jurisdiction to give judgment pursuant to any arbitration clause contained in a contract concluded by or on behalf of the Union, whether that contract be governed by public or private law.

Article 273

(ex Article 239 TEC)

The Court of Justice shall have jurisdiction in any dispute between Member States which relates to the subject matter of the Treaties if the dispute is submitted to it under a special agreement between the parties.

Article 274

(ex Article 240 TEC)

Save where jurisdiction is conferred on the Court of Justice of the European Union by the Treaties, disputes to which the Union is a party shall not on that ground be excluded from the jurisdiction of the courts or tribunals of the Member States.

Article 275

The Court of Justice of the European Union shall not have jurisdiction with respect to the provisions relating to the common foreign and security policy nor with respect to acts adopted on the basis of those provisions.

However, the Court shall have jurisdiction to monitor compliance with Article 40 of the Treaty on European Union and to rule on proceedings, brought in accordance with the conditions laid down in the fourth paragraph of Article 263 of this Treaty, reviewing the legality of decisions providing for restrictive measures against natural or legal persons adopted by the Council on the basis of Chapter 2 of Title V of the Treaty on European Union.

Article 276

In exercising its powers regarding the provisions of Chapters 4 and 5 of Title V of Part Three relating to the area of freedom, security and justice, the Court of Justice of the European Union shall have no jurisdiction to review the validity or proportionality of operations carried out by the police or other law-enforcement services of a Member State or the exercise of the responsibilities incumbent upon Member States with regard to the maintenance of law and order and the safeguarding of internal security.

Article 277

(ex Article 241 TEC)

Notwithstanding the expiry of the period laid down in Article 263, sixth paragraph, any party may, in proceedings in which an act of general application adopted by an institution, body, office or agency of the Union is at issue, plead the grounds specified in Article 263, second paragraph, in order to invoke before the Court of Justice of the European Union the inapplicability of that act.

Article 278

(ex Article 242 TEC)

Actions brought before the Court of Justice of the European Union shall not have suspensory effect.

The Court may, however, if it considers that circumstances so require, order that application of the contested act be suspended.

Article 279

(ex Article 243 TEC)

The Court of Justice of the European Union may in any cases before it prescribe any necessary interim measures.

Article 280

(ex Article 244 TEC)

The judgments of the Court of Justice of the European Union shall be enforceable under the conditions laid down in Article 299.

Article 281

(ex Article 245 TEC)

The Statute of the Court of Justice of the European Union shall be laid down in a separate Protocol.

The European Parliament and the Council, acting in accordance with the ordinary legislative procedure, may amend the provisions of the Statute, with the exception of Title I and Article 64. The European Parliament and the Council shall act either at the request of the Court of Justice and after consultation of the Commission, or on a proposal from the Commission and after consultation of the Court of Justice.

CHAPTER 2

LEGAL ACTS OF THE UNION, ADOPTION PROCEDURES AND OTHER PROVISIONS

SECTION 1

THE LEGAL ACTS OF THE UNION

Article 288

(ex Article 249 TEC)

To exercise the Union's competences, the institutions shall adopt regulations, directives, decisions, recommendations and opinions.

A regulation shall have general application. It shall be binding in its entirety and directly applicable in all Member States.

A directive shall be binding, as to the result to be achieved, upon each Member State to which it is addressed, but shall leave to the national authorities the choice of form and methods.

A decision shall be binding in its entirety. A decision which specifies those to whom it is addressed shall be binding only on them.

Recommendations and opinions shall have no binding force.

Article 289

1   The ordinary legislative procedure shall consist in the joint adoption by the European Parliament and the Council of a regulation, directive or decision on a proposal from the Commission. This procedure is defined in Article 294.

2   In the specific cases provided for by the Treaties, the adoption of a regulation, directive or decision by the European Parliament with the participation of the Council, or by the latter with the participation of the European Parliament, shall constitute a special legislative procedure.

3   Legal acts adopted by legislative procedure shall constitute legislative acts.

4   In the specific cases provided for by the Treaties, legislative acts may be adopted on the initiative of a group of Member States or of the European Parliament, on a recommendation from the European Central Bank or at the request of the Court of Justice or the European Investment Bank.

Article 290

1   A legislative act may delegate to the Commission the power to adopt non-legislative acts of general application to supplement or amend certain non-essential elements of the legislative act.

The objectives, content, scope and duration of the delegation of power shall be explicitly defined in the legislative acts. The essential elements of an area shall be reserved for the legislative act and accordingly shall not be the subject of a delegation of power.

2   Legislative acts shall explicitly lay down the conditions to which the delegation is subject; these conditions may be as follows:

(a)   the European Parliament or the Council may decide to revoke the delegation;

(b)   the delegated act may enter into force only if no objection has been expressed by the European Parliament or the Council within a period set by the legislative act.

For the purposes of (a) and (b), the European Parliament shall act by a majority of its component members, and the Council by a qualified majority.

3   The adjective 'delegated' shall be inserted in the title of delegated acts.

Article 291

1   Member States shall adopt all measures of national law necessary to implement legally binding Union acts.

2   Where uniform conditions for implementing legally binding Union acts are needed, those acts shall confer implementing powers on the Commission, or, in duly justified specific cases and in the cases provided for in Articles 24 and 26 of the Treaty on European Union, on the Council.

3   For the purposes of paragraph 2, the European Parliament and the Council, acting by means of regulations in accordance with the ordinary legislative procedure, shall lay down in advance the rules and general principles concerning mechanisms for control by Member States of the Commission's exercise of implementing powers.

4   The word 'implementing' shall be inserted in the title of implementing acts.

Article 292

The Council shall adopt recommendations. It shall act on a proposal from the Commission in all cases where the Treaties provide that it shall adopt acts on a proposal from the Commission. It shall act unanimously in those areas in which unanimity is required for the adoption of a Union act. The Commission, and the European Central Bank in the specific cases provided for in the Treaties, shall adopt recommendations.

SECTION 2

PROCEDURES FOR THE ADOPTION OF ACTS AND OTHER PROVISIONS

Article 293

(ex Article 250 TEC)

1   Where, pursuant to the Treaties, the Council acts on a proposal from the Commission, it may amend that proposal only by acting unanimously, except in the cases referred to in paragraphs 10 and 13 of Article 294, in Articles 310, 312 and 314 and in the second paragraph of Article 315.

2   As long as the Council has not acted, the Commission may alter its proposal at any time during the procedures leading to the adoption of a Union act.

Article 294

(ex Article 251 TEC)

1   Where reference is made in the Treaties to the ordinary legislative procedure for the adoption of an act, the following procedure shall apply.

2   The Commission shall submit a proposal to the European Parliament and the Council.

First reading

3   The European Parliament shall adopt its position at first reading and communicate it to the Council.

4   If the Council approves the European Parliament's position, the act concerned shall be adopted in the wording which corresponds to the position of the European Parliament.

5   If the Council does not approve the European Parliament's position, it shall adopt its position at first reading and communicate it to the European Parliament.

6   The Council shall inform the European Parliament fully of the reasons which led it to adopt its position at first reading. The Commission shall inform the European Parliament fully of its position.

Second reading

7   If, within three months of such communication, the European Parliament:

   (a)   approves the Council's position at first reading or has not taken a decision, the act concerned shall be deemed to have been adopted in the wording which corresponds to the position of the Council;

   (b)   rejects, by a majority of its component members, the Council's position at first reading, the proposed act shall be deemed not to have been adopted;

   (c)   proposes, by a majority of its component members, amendments to the Council's position at first reading, the text thus amended shall be forwarded to the Council and to the Commission, which shall deliver an opinion on those amendments.

8   If, within three months of receiving the European Parliament's amendments, the Council, acting by a qualified majority:

   (a)   approves all those amendments, the act in question shall be deemed to have been adopted;

(b)   does not approve all the amendments, the President of the Council, in agreement with the President of the European Parliament, shall within six weeks convene a meeting of the Conciliation Committee.

9   The Council shall act unanimously on the amendments on which the Commission has delivered a negative opinion.

Conciliation

10   The Conciliation Committee, which shall be composed of the members of the Council or their representatives and an equal number of members representing the European Parliament, shall have the task of reaching agreement on a joint text, by a qualified majority of the members of the Council or their representatives and by a majority of the members representing the European Parliament within six weeks of its being convened, on the basis of the positions of the European Parliament and the Council at second reading.

11   The Commission shall take part in the Conciliation Committee's proceedings and shall take all necessary initiatives with a view to reconciling the positions of the European Parliament and the Council.

12   If, within six weeks of its being convened, the Conciliation Committee does not approve the joint text, the proposed act shall be deemed not to have been adopted.

Third reading

13   If, within that period, the Conciliation Committee approves a joint text, the European Parliament, acting by a majority of the votes cast, and the Council, acting by a qualified majority, shall each have a period of six weeks from that approval in which to adopt the act in question in accordance with the joint text. If they fail to do so, the proposed act shall be deemed not to have been adopted.

14   The periods of three months and six weeks referred to in this Article shall be extended by a maximum of one month and two weeks respectively at the initiative of the European Parliament or the Council.

Special provisions

15   Where, in the cases provided for in the Treaties, a legislative act is submitted to the ordinary legislative procedure on the initiative of a group of Member States, on a recommendation by the European Central Bank, or at the request of the Court of Justice, paragraph 2, the second sentence of paragraph 6, and paragraph 9 shall not apply.

In such cases, the European Parliament and the Council shall communicate the proposed act to the Commission with their positions at first and second readings. The European Parliament or the Council may request the opinion of the Commission throughout the procedure, which the Commission may also deliver on its own initiative. It may also, if it deems it necessary, take part in the Conciliation Committee in accordance with paragraph 11.

Article 295

The European Parliament, the Council and the Commission shall consult each other and by common agreement make arrangements for their cooperation. To that end, they may, in compliance with the Treaties, conclude interinstitutional agreements which may be of a binding nature.

Article 296

(ex Article 253 TEC)

Where the Treaties do not specify the type of act to be adopted, the institutions shall select it on a case-by-case basis, in compliance with the applicable procedures and with the principle of proportionality. Legal acts shall state the reasons on which they are based and shall refer to any proposals, initiatives, recommendations, requests or opinions required by the Treaties.

When considering draft legislative acts, the European Parliament and the Council shall refrain from adopting acts not provided for by the relevant legislative procedure in the area in question.

Article 297

(ex Article 254 TEC)

1   Legislative acts adopted under the ordinary legislative procedure shall be signed by the President of the European Parliament and by the President of the Council.

Legislative acts adopted under a special legislative procedure shall be signed by the President of the institution which adopted them.

Legislative acts shall be published in the Official Journal of the European Union. They shall enter into force on the date specified in them or, in the absence thereof, on the twentieth day following that of their publication.

2   Non-legislative acts adopted in the form of regulations, directives or decisions, when the latter do not specify to whom they are addressed, shall be signed by the President of the institution which adopted them. Regulations and directives which are addressed to all Member States, as well as decisions which do not specify to whom they are addressed, shall be published in the Official Journal of the European Union. They shall enter into force on the date specified in them or, in the absence thereof, on the twentieth day following that of their publication.

Other directives, and decisions which specify to whom they are addressed, shall be notified to those to whom they are addressed and shall take effect upon such notification.

Article 298

1   In carrying out their missions, the institutions, bodies, offices and agencies of the Union shall have the support of an open, efficient and independent European administration.

2   In compliance with the Staff Regulations and the Conditions of Employment adopted on the basis of Article 336, the European Parliament and the Council, acting by means of regulations in accordance with the ordinary legislative procedure, shall establish provisions to that end.

Article 299

(ex Article 256 TEC)

Acts of the Council, the Commission or the European Central Bank which impose a pecuniary obligation on persons other than States, shall be enforceable.

Enforcement shall be governed by the rules of civil procedure in force in the State in the territory of which it is carried out. The order for its enforcement shall be appended to the decision, without other formality than verification of the authenticity of the decision, by the national authority which the government of each Member State shall designate for this purpose and shall make known to the Commission and to the Court of Justice of the European Union.

When these formalities have been completed on application by the party concerned, the latter may proceed to enforcement in accordance with the national law, by bringing the matter directly before the competent authority.

Enforcement may be suspended only by a decision of the Court. However, the courts of the country concerned shall have jurisdiction over complaints that enforcement is being carried out in an irregular manner.

SECTION 2 – COMPETITION LAW

COMMISSION NOTICE on the definition of relevant market for the purposes of Community competition law (97/C 372/03)

I. INTRODUCTION

1   The purpose of this notice is to provide guidance as to how the Commission applies the concept of relevant product and geographic market in its ongoing enforcement of Community competition law, in particular the application of Council Regulation No 17 and (EEC) No 4064/89, their equivalents in other sectoral applications such as transport, coal and steel, and agriculture, and the relevant provisions of the EEA Agreement (1). Throughout this notice, references to Articles 85 and 86 of the Treaty and to merger control are to be understood as referring to the equivalent provisions in the EEA Agreement and the ECSC Treaty.

2   Market definition is a tool to identify and define the boundaries of competition between firms. It serves to establish the framework within which competition policy is applied by the Commission. The main purpose of market definition is to identify in a systematic way the competitive constraints that the undertakings involved (2) face. The objective of defining a market in both its product and geographic dimension is to identify those actual competitors of the undertakings involved that are capable of constraining those undertakings' behaviour and of preventing them from behaving independently of effective competitive pressure. It is from this perspective that the market definition makes it possible inter alia to calculate market shares that would convey meaningful information regarding market power for the purposes of assessing dominance or for the purposes of applying Article 85.

3   It follows from point 2 that the concept of 'relevant market` is different from other definitions of market often used in other contexts. For instance, companies often use the term 'market` to refer to the area where it sells its products or to refer broadly to the industry or sector where it belongs.

4   The definition of the relevant market in both its product and its geographic dimensions often has a decisive influence on the assessment of a competition case. By rendering public the procedures which the Commission follows when considering market definition and by indicating the criteria and evidence on which it relies to reach a decision, the Commission expects to increase the transparency of its policy and decision-making in the area of competition policy.

5   Increased transparency will also result in companies and their advisers being able to better anticipate the possibility that the Commission may raise competition concerns in an individual case. Companies could, therefore, take such a possibility into account in their own internal decision-making when contemplating, for instance, acquisitions, the creation of joint ventures, or the establishment of certain agreements. It is also intended that companies should be in a better position to understand what sort of information the Commission considers relevant for the purposes of market definition.

6   The Commission's interpretation of 'relevant market` is without prejudice to the interpretation which may be given by the Court of Justice or the Court of First Instance of the European Communities.

II. DEFINITION OF RELEVANT MARKET

Definition of relevant product market and relevant geographic market

7   The Regulations based on Article 85 and 86 of the Treaty, in particular in section 6 of Form A/B with respect to Regulation No 17, as well as in section 6 of Form CO with respect to Regulation (EEC) No 4064/89 on the control of concentrations having a Community dimension have laid down the following definitions, 'Relevant product markets` are defined as follows:

'A relevant product market comprises all those products and/or services which are regarded as interchangeable or substitutable by the consumer, by reason of the products' characteristics, their prices and their intended use`.

8   'Relevant geographic markets` are defined as follows:

'The relevant geographic market comprises the area in which the undertakings concerned are involved in the supply and demand of products or services, in which the conditions of competition are sufficiently homogeneous and which can be distinguished from neighbouring areas because the conditions of competition are appreciably different in those area`.

9   The relevant market within which to assess a given competition issue is therefore established by the combination of the product and geographic markets. The Commission interprets the definitions in paragraphs 7 an 8 (which reflect the case-law of the Court of Justice and the Court of First Instance as well as its own decision-making practice) according to the orientations defined in this notice.

Concept of relevant market and objectives of Community competition policy

10   The concept of relevant market is closely related to the objectives pursued under Community competition policy. For example, under the Community's merger control, the objective in controlling structural changes in the supply of a product/service is to prevent the creation or reinforcement of a dominant position as a result of which effective competition would be significantly impeded in a substantial part of the common market. Under the Community's competition rules, a dominant position is such that a firm or group of firms would be in a position to behave to an appreciable extent independently of its competitors, customers and ultimately of its consumers (3). Such a position would usually arise when a firm or group of firms accounted for a large share of the supply in any given market, provided that other factors analysed in the assessment (such as entry barriers, customers' capacity to react, etc.) point in the same direction.

11   The same approach is followed by the Commission in its application of Article 86 of the Treaty to firms that enjoy a single or collective dominant position. Within the meaning of Regulation No 17, the Commission has the power to investigate and bring to an end abuses of such a dominant position, which must also be defined by reference to the relevant market. Markets may also need to be defined in the application of Article 85 of the Treaty, in particular, in determining whether an appreciable restriction of competition exists or in establishing if the condition pursuant to Article 85 (3) (b) for an exemption from the application of Article 85 (1) is met.

12   The criteria for defining the relevant market are applied generally for the analysis of certain types of behaviour in the market and for the analysis of structural changes in the supply of products. This methodology, though, might lead to different results depending on the nature of the competition issue being examined. For instance, the scope of the geographic market might be different when analysing a concentration, where the analysis is essentially prospective, from an analysis of past behaviour. The different time horizon considered in each case might lead to the result that different geographic markets are defined for the same products depending on whether the Commission is examining a change in the structure of supply, such as a concentration or a cooperative joint venture, or examining issues relating to certain past behaviour.

Basic principles for market definition

Competitive constraints

13   Firms are subject to three main sources or competitive constraints: demand substitutability, supply substitutability and potential competition. From an economic point of view, for the definition of the relevant market, demand substitution constitutes the most immediate and effective disciplinary force on the suppliers of a given product, in particular in relation to their pricing decisions. A firm or a group of firms cannot have a significant impact on the prevailing conditions of sale, such as prices, if its customers are in a

position to switch easily to available substitute products or to suppliers located elsewhere. Basically, the exercise of market definition consists in identifying the effective alternative sources of supply for the customers of the undertakings involved, in terms both of products/services and of geographic location of suppliers.

14 The competitive constraints arising from supply side substitutability other then those described in paragraphs 20 to 23 and from potential competition are in general less immediate and in any case require an analysis of additional factors. As a result such constraints are taken into account at the assessment stage of competition analysis.

Demand substitution

15 The assessment of demand substitution entails a determination of the range of products which are viewed as substitutes by the consumer. One way of making this determination can be viewed as a speculative experiment, postulating a hypothetical small, lasting change in relative prices and evaluating the likely reactions of customers to that increase. The exercise of market definition focuses on prices for operational and practical purposes, and more precisely on demand substitution arising from small, permanent changes in relative prices. This concept can provide clear indications as to the evidence that is relevant in defining markets.

16 Conceptually, this approach means that, starting from the type of products that the undertakings involved sell and the area in which they sell them, additional products and areas will be included in, or excluded from, the market definition depending on whether competition from these other products and areas affect or restrain sufficiently the pricing of the parties' products in the short term.

17 The question to be answered is whether the parties' customers would switch to readily available substitutes or to suppliers located elsewhere in response to a hypothetical small (in the range 5 % to 10 %) but permanent relative price increase in the products and areas being considered. If substitution were enough to make the price increase unprofitable because of the resulting loss of sales, additional substitutes and areas are included in the relevant market. This would be done until the set of products and geographical areas is such that small, permanent increases in relative prices would be profitable. The equivalent analysis is applicable in cases concerning the concentraiton of buying power, where the starting point would then be the supplier and the price test serves to identify the alternative distribution channels or outlets for the supplier's products. In the application of these principles, careful account should be taken of certain particular situations as described within paragraphs 56 and 58.

18 A practical example of this test can be provided by its application to a merger of, for instance, soft-drink bottlers. An issue to examine in such a case would be to decide whether different flavours of soft drinks belong to the same market. In practice, the question to address would be whether consumers of flavour A would switch to other flavours when confronted with a permanent price increase of 5 % to 10 % for flavour A. If a sufficient number of consumers would switch to, say, flavour B, to such an extent that the price increase for flavour A would not be profitable owing to the resulting loss of sales, then the market would comprise at least flavours A and B. The process would have to be extended in addition to other available flavours until a set of products is identified for which a price rise would not induce a sufficient substitution in demand.

19 Generally, and in particular for the analysis of merger cases, the price to take into account will be the prevailing market price. This may not be the case where the prevailing price has been determined in the absence of sufficient competition. In particular for the investigation of abuses of dominant positions, the fact that the prevailing price might already have been substantially increased will be taken into account.

Supply substitution

20   Supply-side substitutability may also be taken into account when defining markets in those situaitons in which its effects are equivalent to those of demand substitution in terms of effectiveness and immediacy. This means that suppliers are able to switch production to the relevant products and market them in the short term (4) without incurring significant additional costs or risks in response to small and permanent changes in relative prices. When these conditions are met, the additional production that is put on the market will have a disciplinary effect on the competitive behaviour of the companies involved. Such an impact in terms of effectiveness and immediacy is equivalent to the demand substitution effect.

21   These situations typically arise when companies market a wide range of qualities or grades of one product; even if, for a given final customer or group of consumers, the different qualities are not substitutable, the different qualities will be grouped into one product market, provided that most of the suppliers are able to offer and sell the various qualities immediately and without the significant increases in costs described above. In such cases, the relevant product market will encompass all products that are substitutable in demand and supply, and the current sales of those products will be aggregated so as to give the total value or volume of the market. The same reasoning may lead to group different geographic areas.

22   A practical example of the approach to supply-side substitutability when defining product markets is to be found in the case of paper. Paer is usually supplied in a range of different qualities, from standard writing paper to high quality papers to be used, for instance, to publish art books. From a demand point of view, different qualities of paper cannot be used for any given use, i.e. an art book or a high quality publication cannot be based on lower quality papers. However, paper plants are prepared to manufacture the different qualities, and production can be adjusted with negligible costs and in a short time-frame. In the absence of particular difficulties in distribution, paper manufacturers are able therefore, to compete for orders of the various qualities, in particular if orders are placed with sufficient lead time to allow for modification of production plans. Under such circumstances, the Commission would not define a separate market for each quality of paper and its respective use. The various qualities of paper are included in the relevant market, and their sales added up to estimate total market galue and volume.

23   When supply-side substitutability would entail the need to adjust significantly existing tangible and intangible assets, additional investments, strategic decisions or time delays, it will not be considered at the stage of market definition. Examples where supply-side substitution did not induce the Commission to enlarge the market are offered in the area of consumer products, in particular for branded beverages. Although bottling plants may in principle bottle different beverages, there are costs and lead times involved (in terms of advertising, product testing and distribution) before the products can actually be sold. In these cases, the effects of supply-side substitutability and other forms of potential competition would then be examined at a later stage.

Potential competition

24   The third source of competitive constraint, potential competition, is not taken into account when defining markets, since the conditions under which potential competition will actually represent an effective competitive constraint depend on the analysis of specific factors and circumstances related to the conditions of entry. If required, this analysis is only carried out at a subsequent stage, in general once the position of the companies involved in the relevant market has already been ascertained, and when such position gives rise to concerns from a competition point of view.

III. EVIDENCE RELIED ON TO DEFINE RELEVANT MARKETS

The process of defining the relevant market in practice

Product dimension

25   There is a range of evidence permitting an assessment of the extent to which substitution would take place. In individual cases, certain types of evidence will be determinant, depending very much on the characteristics and specificity of the industry and products or services that are being examined. The same type of evidence may be of no importance in other cases. In most cases, a decision will have to be based on the consideration of a number of criteria and different items of evidence. The Commission follows an open approach to empirical evidence, aimed at making an effective use of all available information which may be relevant in individual cases. The Commission does not follow a rigid hierarchy of different sources of information or types of evidence.

26   The process of defining relevant markets may be summarized as follows: on the basis of the preliminary information available or information submitted by the undertakings involved, the Commission will usually be in a position to broadly establish the possible relevant markets within which, for instance, a concentration or a restriction of competition has to be assessed. In general, and for all practical purposes when handling individual cases, the question will usually be to decide on a few alternative possible relevant markets. For instance, with respect to the product market, the issue will often be to establish whether product A and product B belong or do not belong to the same product market. it is often the case that the inclusion of product B would be enough to remove any competition concerns.

27   In such situations it is not necessary to consider whether the market includes additional products, or to reach a definitive conclusion on the precise product market. If under the conceivable alternative market definitions the operation in question does not raise competition concerns, the question of market definition will be left open, reducing thereby the burden on companies to supply information.

Geographic dimension

28   The Commission's approach to geographic market definition might be summarized as follows: it will take a preliminary view of the scope of the geographic market on the basis of broad indications as to the distribution of market shares between the parties and their competitors, as well as a preliminary analysis of pricing and price differences at national and Community or EEA level. This initial view is used basically as a working hypothesis to focus the Commission's enquiries for the purposes of arriving at a precise geographic market definition.

29   The reasons behind any particular configuration of prices and market shares need to be explored. Companies might enjoy high market shares in their domestic markets just because of the weight of the past, and conversely, a homogeneous presence of companies throughout the EEA might be consistent with national or regional geographic markets. The initial working hypothesis will therefore be checked against an analysis of demand characteristics (importance of national or local preferences, current patterns of purchases of customers, product differentiation/brands, other) in order to establish whether companies in different areas do indeed constitute a real alternative source of supply for consumers. The theoretical experiment is again based on substitution arising from changes in relative prices, and the question to answer is again whether the customers of the parties would switch their orders to companies located elsewhere in the short term and at a negligible cost.

30   If necessary, a further check on supply factors will be carried out to ensure that those companies located in differing areas do not face impediments in developing their sales on competitive terms throughout the whole geographic market. This analysis will include an examination of requirements for a local presence in order to sell in that area the conditions of access to distribution channels, costs associated with setting up a distribution network, and the presence or absence of regulatory barriers arising from public

procurement, price regulations, quotas and tariffs limiting trade or production, technical standards, monopolies, freedom of establishment, requirements for administrative authorizations, packaging regulations, etc. In short, the Commission will identify possible obstacles and barriers isolating companies located in a given area from the competitive pressure of companies located outside that area, so as to determine the precise degree of market interpenetration at national, European or global level.

31   The actual pattern and evolution of trade flows offers useful supplementary indications as to the economic importance of each demand or supply factor mentioned above, and the extent to which they may or may not constitute actual barriers creating different geographic markets. The analysis of trade flows will generally address the question of transport costs and the extent to which these may hinder trade between different areas, having regard to plant location, costs of production and relative price levels.

Market integration in the Community

32   Finally, the Commission also takes into account the continuing process of market integration, in particular in the Community, when defining geographic markets, especially in the area of concentrations and structural joint ventures. The measures adopted and implemented in the internal market programme to remove barriers to trade and further integrate the Community markets cannot be ignored when assessing the effects on competition of a concentration or a structural joint venture. A situation where national markets have been artifically isolated from each other because of the existence of legislative barriers that have now been removed will generally lead to a cautious assessment of past evidence regarding prices, market shares or trade patterns. A process of market integration that would, in the short term, lead to wider geographic markets may therefore be taken into consideration when defining the geographic market for the purposes of assessing concentrations and joint ventures.

The process of gathering evidence

33   When a precise market definition is deemed necessary, the Commission will often contact the main customers and the main companies in the industry to enquire into their views about the boudaries of product and geographic markets and to obtain the necessary factual evidence to reach a conclusion. The Commission might also contact the relevant professional associations, and companies active in upstream markets, so as to be able to define, in so far as necessary, separate product and geographic markets, for different levels of production or distribution of the products/services in question. It might also request additional information to the undertakings involved.

34   Where appropriate, the Commission will address written requests for information to the market players mentioned above. These requests will usually include questions relating to the perceptions of companies about reactions to hypothetical price increases and their views of the boundaries of the relevant market. They will also ask for provision of the factual information the Commission deems necessary to reach a conclusion on the extent of the relevant market. The Commission might also discuss with marketing directors or other officers of those companies to gain a better understanding on how negotiations between suppliers and customers take place and better understand issues relating to the definition of the relevant market. Where appropriate, they might also carry out visits or inspections to the premises of the parties, their customers and/or their competitors, in order to better understand how products are manufactured and sold.

35   The type of evidence relevant to reach a conclusion as to the product market can be categorized as follows:

Evidence to define markets - product dimension

36   An analysis of the product characteristics and its intended use allows the Commission, as a first step, to limit the field of investigation of possible substitutes. However, product characteristics and intended use are insufficient to show whether two products are demand substitutes. Functional interchangeability or

similarity in characteristics may not, in themselves, provide sufficient criteria, because the responsiveness of customers to relative price changes may be determinded by other considerations as well. For example, there may be different competitive contraints in the original equipment market for car components and in spare parts, thereby leading to a separate delineation of two relevant markets. Conversely, differences in product characteristics are not in themselves sufficient to exclude demand substitutability, since this will depend to a large extent on how customers value different characteristics.

37   The type of evidence the Commission considers relevant to assess whether two products are demand substitutes can be categorized as follows:

38   Evidence of substitution in the recent past. In certain cases, it is possible to analyse evidence relating to recent past events or shocks in the market that offer actual examples of substituion between two products. When available, this sort of information will normally be fundamental for market definition. If there have been changes in relative prices in the past (all else being equal), the reactions in terms of quantities demanded will be determinant in establishing substitutability. Launches of new products in the past can also offer useful information, when it is possible to precisely analyse which products have lost sales to the new product.

39   There are a number of quantitative tests that have specifically been designed for the purpose of delineating markets. These tests consist of various econometric and statistical approaches estimates of elasticities and cross-price elasticities (5) for the demand of a product, tests based on similarity of price movements over time, the analysis of causality between price series and similarity of price levels and/or their convergence. The Commission takes into account the available quantitative evidence capable of withstanding rigorous scrutiny for the purposes of establishing patterns of substitution in the past.

40   Views of customers and competitors. The Commission often contacts the main customers and competitors of the companies involved in its enquiries, to gather their views on the boundaries of the product market as well as most of the factual information it requires to reach a conclusion on the scope of the market. Reasoned answers of customers and competitors as to what would happen if relative prices for the candidate products were to increase in the candidate geographic area by a small amount (for instance of 5 % to 10 %) are taken into account when they are sufficiently backed by factual evidence.

41   Consumer preferences. In the case of consumer goods, it may be difficult for the Commission to gather the direct views of end consumers about substitute products. Marketing studies that companies have commissioned in the past and that are used by companies in their own decision-making as to pricing of their products and/or marketing actions may provide useful information for the Commission's delineation of the relevant market. Consumer surveys on usage patterns and attitudes, data from consumer's purchasing patterns, the views expressed by retailers and more generally, market research studies submitted by the parties and their competitors are taken into account to establish whether an economically significant proportion of consumers consider two products as substitutable, also taking into account the importance of brands for the products in question. The methodology followed in consumer surveys carried out ad hoc by the undertakings involved or their competitors for the purposes of a merger procedure or a procedure pursuant to Regulation No 17 will usually be scrutinized with utmost care. Unlike pre-existing studies, they have not been prepared in the normal course of business for the adoption of business decisions.

42   Barriers and costs associated with switching demand to potential substitutes. There are a number of barriers and costs that might prevent the Commission from considering two prima facie demand substitutes as belonging to one single product market. It is not possible to provide an exhaustive list of all the possible barriers to substitution and of switching costs. These barriers or obstacles might have a wide range of origins, and in its decisions, the Commission has been confronted with regulatory barriers or other forms of State intervention, constraints arising in downstream markets, need to incur specific capital investment or loss in current output in order to switch to alternative inputs, the location of customers, specific

investment in production process, learning and human capital investment, retooling costs or other investments, uncertainty about quality and reputation of unknown suppliers, and others.

43   Different categories of customers and price discrimination. The extent of the product market might be narrowed in the presence of distinct groups of customers. A distinct group of customers for the relevant product may constitute a narrower, distinct market when such ha group could be subject to price discrimination. This will usually be the case when two conditions are met: (a) it is possible to identify clearly which group an individual customer belongs to at the moment of selling the relevant products to him, and (b) trade among customers or arbitrage by third parties should not be feasible.

Evidence for defining markets - geographic dimension

44   The type of evidence the Commission considers relevant to reach a conclusion as to the geographic market can be categorized as follows:

45   Past evidence of diversion of orders to other areas. In certain cases, evidence on changes in prices between different areas and consequent reactions by customers might be available. Generally, the same quantitative tests used for product market definition might as well be used in geographic market definition, bearing in mind that international comparisons of prices might be more complex due to a number of factors such as exchange rate movements, taxation and product differentiation.

46   Basic demand characteristics. The nature of demand for the relevant product may in itself determine the scope of the geographical market. Factors such as national preferences or preferences for national brands, language, culture and life style, and the need for a local presence have a strong potential to limit the geographic scope of competition.

47   Views of customers and competitors. Where appropriate, the Commission will contact the main customers and competitors of the parties in its enquiries, to gather their views on the boundaries of the geographic market as well as most of the factual information it requires to reach a conclusion on the scope of the market when they are sufficiently backed by factual evidence.

48   Current geographic pattern of purchases. An examination of the customers' current geographic pattern of purchases provides useful evidence as to the possible scope of the geographic market. When customers purchase from companies located anywhere in the Community or the EEA on similar terms, or they procure their supplies through effective tendering procedures in which companies from anywhere in the Community or the EEA submit bids, usually the geographic market will be considered to be Community-wide.

49   Trade flows/pattern of shipments. When the number of customers is so large that it is not possible to obtain through them a clear picture of geographic purchasing patterns, information on trade flows might be used alternatively, provided that the trade statistics are available with a sufficient degree of detail for the relevant products. Trade flows, and above all, the rationale behind trade flows provide useful insights and information for the purpose of establishing the scope of the geographic market but are not in themselves conclusive.

50   Barriers and switching costs associated to divert orders to companies located in other areas. The absence of trans-border purchases or trade flows, for instance, does not necessarily mean that the market is at most national in scope. Still, barriers isolating the national market have to identified before it is concluded that the relevant geographic market in such a case is national. Perhaps the clearest obstacle for a customer to divert its orders to other areas is the impact of transport costs and transport restrictions arising from legislation or from the nature of the relevant products. The impact of transport costs will usually limit the scope of the geographic market for bulky, low-value products, bearing in mind that a transport disadvantage might also be compensated by a comparative advantage in other costs (labour costs or raw materials). Access to distribution in a given area, regulatory barriers still existing in certain sectors, quotas and custom tariffs might also constitute barriers isolating a geographic area from the competitive pressure

of companies located outside that area. Significant switching costs in procuring supplies from companies located in other countries constitute additional sources of such barriers.

51   On the basis of the evidence gathered, the Commission will then define a geographic market that could range from a local dimension to a global one, and there are examples of both local and global markets in past decisions of the Commission.

52   The paragraphs above describe the different factors which might be relevant to define markets. This does not imply that in each individual case it will be necessary to obtain evidence and assess each of these factors. Often in practice the evidence provided by a susbset of these factors will be sufficient to reach a conclusion, as shown in the past decisional practice of the Commission.

IV. CALCULATION OF MARKET SHARE

53   The definition of the relevant market in both its product and geograhic dimensions allows the identification the suppliers and the customers/consumers active on that market. On that basis, a total market size and market shares for each supplier can be calculated on the basis of their sales of the relevant products in the relevant area. In practice, the total market size and market shares are often available from market sources, i.e. companies' estimates, studies commissioned from industry consultants and/or trade associations. When this is not the case, or when available estimates are not reliable, the Commission will usually ask each supplier in the relevant market to provide its own sales in order to calculate total market size and market shares.

54   If sales are usually the reference to calculate market shares, there are nevertheless other indications that, depending on the specific products or industry in question, can offer useful information such as, in particular, capacity, the number of players in bidding markets, units of fleet as in aerospace, or the reserves held in the case of sectors such as mining.

55   As a rule of thumb, both volume sales and value sales provide useful information. In cases of differentiated products, sales in value and their associated market share will usually be considered to better reflect the relative position and strength of each supplier.

V. ADDITIONAL CONSIDERATIONS

56   There are certain areas where the application of the principles above has to be undertaken with care. This is the case when considering primary and secondary markets, in particular, when the behaviour of undertakings at a point in time has to be analysed pursuant to Article 86. The method of defining markets in these cases is the same, i.e. assessing the responses of customers based on their purchasing decisions to relative price changes, but taking into account as well, constraints on substitution imposed by conditions in the connected markets. A narrow definition of market for secondary products, for instance, spare parts, may result when compatibility with the primary product is important. Problems of finding compatible secondary products together with the existence of high prices and a long lifetime of the primary products may render relative price increases of secondary products profitable. A different market definition may result if significant substitution between secondary products is possible or if the characteristics of the primary products make quick and direct consumer responses to relative price increases of the secondary products feasible.

57   In certain cases, the existence of chains of substitution might lead to the definition of a relevant market where products or areas at the extreme of the market are not directly substitutable. An example might be provided by the geographic dimension of a product with significant transport costs. In such cases, deliveries from a given plant are limited to a certain area around each plant by the impact of transport costs. In principle, such an area could constitute the relevant geographic market. However, if the distribution of plants is such that there are considerable overlaps between the areas around different plants, it is possible that the pricing of those products will be constrained by a chain substitution effect, and lead to the definition of a broader geographic market. The same reasoning may apply if product B is

a demand substitute for products A and C. Even if products A and C are not direct demand substitutes, they might be found to be in the same relevant product market since their respective pricing might be constrained by substitution to B.

58   From a practical perspective, the concept of chains of substitution has to be corroborated by actual evidence, for instance related to price interdependence at the extremes of the chains of substitution, in order to lead to an extension of the relevant market in an individual case. Price levels at the extremes of the chains would have to be of the same magnitude as well.

    (1)   The focus of assessment in State aid cases is the aid recipient and the industry/sector concerned rather than identification of competitive constraints faced by the aid recipient. When consideration of market power and therefore of the relevant market are raised in any particular case, elements of the approach outlined here might serve as a basis for the assessment of State aid cases.

    (2)   For the purposes of this notice, the undertakings involved will be, in the case of a concentration, the parties to the concentration; in investigations within the meaning of Article 86 of the Treaty, the undertaking being investigated or the complainants; for investigations within the meaning of Article 85, the parties to the Agreement.

    (3)   Definition given by the Court of Justice in its judgment of 13 February 1979 in Case 85/76, Hoffmann-La Roche [1979] ECR 461, and confirmed in subsequent judgments.

    (4)   That is such a period that does not entail a significant adjustment of existing tangible and intangible assets (see paragraph 23).

    (5)   Own-price elasticity of demand for product X is a measure of the responsiveness of demand for X to percentage change in its own price. Cross-prise elasticity between products X and Y is the responsiveness of demand for product X to percentage change in the price of product Y.

COUNCIL REGULATION (EC) No 2679/98

Article 1

For the purpose of this Regulation:

1   the term 'obstacle' shall mean an obstacle to the free movement of goods among Member States which is attributable to a Member State, whether it involves action or inaction on its part, which may constitute a breach of Articles 30 to 36 of the Treaty and which:

    (a)   leads to serious disruption of the free movement of goods by physically or otherwise preventing, delaying or diverting their import into, export from or transport across a Member State,

    (1) OJ C 10, 15. 1. 1998, p. 14.

    (2) OJ C 359, 23. 11. 1998.

    (3) OJ C 214, 10. 7. 1998, p. 90.

    12. 12. 98 EN Official Journal of the European Communities L 337/9

    (b)   causes serious loss to the individuals affected, and (c) requires immediate action in order to prevent any continuation, increase or intensification of the disruption or loss in question;

2   the term 'inaction' shall cover the case when the competent authorities of a Member State, in the presence of an obstacle caused by actions taken by private individuals, fail to take all necessary and proportionate measures within their powers with a view to removing the obstacle and ensuring the free movement of goods in their territory.

Article 2

This Regulation may not be interpreted as affecting in any way the exercise of fundamental rights as recognised in Member States, including the right or freedom to strike. These rights may also include the right or freedom to take other actions covered by the specific industrial relations systems in Member States.

Article 3

1   When an obstacle occurs or when there is a threat thereof

   (a)   any Member State (whether or not it is the Member State concerned) which has relevant information shall immediately transmit it to the Commission, and

   (b)   the Commission shall immediately transmit to the Member States that information and any information from any other source which it may consider relevant.

2   The Member State concerned shall respond as soon as possible to requests for information from the Commission and from other Member States concerning the nature of the obstacle or threat and the action which it has taken or proposes to take. Information exchange between Member States shall also be transmitted to the Commission.

Article 4

1   When an obstacle occurs, and subject to Article 2, the Member State concerned shall

   (a)   take all necessary and proportionate measures so that the free movement of goods is assured in the territory of the Member State in accordance with the Treaty, and

   (b)   inform the Commission of the actions which its authorities have taken or intend to take.

2   The Commission shall immediately transmit the information received under paragraph 1(b) to the other Member States.

Article 5

1   Where the Commission considers that an obstacle is occurring in a Member State, it shall notify the Member State concerned of the reasons that have led the Commission to such a conclusion and shall request the Member State to take all necessary and proportionate measures to remove the said obstacle within a period which it shall determine with reference to the urgency of the case.

2   In reaching its conclusion, the Commission shall have regard to Article 2.

3   The Commission may publish in the Official Journal of the European Communities the text of the notification which it has sent to the Member State concerned and shall immediately transmit the text to any party which requests it.

4   The Member State shall, within five working days of receipt of the text, either:

   ▸   inform the Commission of the steps which it has taken or intends to take to implement paragraph 1, or

   ▸   communicate a reasoned submission as to why there is no obstacle constituting a breach of Articles 30 to 36 of the Treaty.

5.   In exceptional cases, the Commission may allow an extension of the deadline mentioned in paragraph 4 if the Member State submits a duly substantiated request and the grounds cited are deemed acceptable.

COMMISSION REGULATION (EC) No 2790/1999

Article 1

For the purposes of this Regulation:

(a) "competing undertakings" means actual or potential suppliers in the same product market; the, product market includes goods or services which are regarded by the buyer as interchangeable with or substitutable for the contract goods or services, by reason of the products' characteristics, their prices and their intended use;

(b) "non-compete obligation" means any direct or indirect obligation causing the buyer not to manufacture, purchase, sell or resell goods or services which compete with the contract goods or services, or any direct or indirect obligation on the buyer to purchase from the supplier or from another undertaking designated by the supplier more than 80 % of the buyer's total purchases of the contract goods or services and their substitutes on the relevant market, calculated on the basis of the value of its purchases in the preceding calendar year;

(c) "exclusive supply obligation" means any direct or indirect obligation causing the supplier to sell the goods or services specified in the agreement only to one buyer inside the Community for the purposes of a specific use or for resale;

(d) "Selective distribution system" means a distribution system where the supplier undertakes to sell the contract goods or services, either directly or indirectly, only to distributors selected on the basis of specified criteria and where these distributors undertake not to sell such goods or services to unauthorised distributors;

(e) "intellectual property rights" includes industrial property rights, copyright and neighbouring rights;

(f) "know-how" means a package of non-patented practical information, resulting from experience and testing by the supplier, which is secret, substantial and identified: in this context, "secret" means that the know-how, as a body or in the precise configuration and assembly of its components, is not generally known or easily accessible; "substantial" means that the know-how includes information which is indispensable to the buyer for the use, sale or resale of the contract goods or services; "identified" means that the know-how must be described in a sufficiently comprehensive manner so as to make it possible to verify that it fulfils the criteria of secrecy and substantiality;

(g) "buyer" includes an undertaking which, under an agreement falling within Article 81(1) of the Treaty, sells goods or services on behalf of another undertaking.

Article 2

1   Pursuant to Article 81(3) of the Treaty and subject to the provisions of this Regulation, it is hereby declared that Article 81(1) shall not apply to agreements or concerted practices entered into between two or more undertakings each of which operates, for the purposes of the agreement, at a different level of the production or distribution chain, and relating to the conditions under which the parties may purchase, sell or resell certain goods or services ("vertical agreements").

This exemption shall apply to the extent that such agreements contain restrictions of competition falling within the scope of Article 81(1) ("vertical restraints").

2   The exemption provided for in paragraph 1 shall apply to vertical agreements entered into between an association of undertakings and its members, or between such an association and its suppliers, only if all its members are retailers of goods and if no individual member of the association, together with its connected undertakings, has a total annual turnover exceeding EUR 50 million; vertical agreements entered into by such associations shall be covered by this Regulation without prejudice to the application

of Article 81 to horizontal agreements concluded between the members of the association or decisions adopted by the association.

3   The exemption provided for in paragraph 1 shall apply to vertical agreements containing provisions which relate to the assignment to the buyer or use by the buyer of intellectual property rights, provided that those provisions do not constitute the primary object of such agreements and are directly related to the use, sale or resale of goods or services by the buyer or its customers. The exemption applies on condition that, in relation to the contract goods or services, those provisions do not contain restrictions of competition having the same object or effect as vertical restraints which are not exempted under this Regulation.

4   The exemption provided for in paragraph 1 shall not apply to vertical agreements entered into between competing undertakings; however, it shall apply where competing undertakings enter into a non-reciprocal vertical agreement and:

(a)   the buyer has a total annual turnover not exceeding EUR 100 million, or

(b)   the supplier is a manufacturer and a distributor of goods, while the buyer is a distributor not manufacturing goods competing with the contract goods, or

(c)   the supplier is a provider of services at several levels of trade, while the buyer does not provide competing services at the level of trade where it purchases the contract services.

5   This Regulation shall not apply to vertical agreements the subject matter of which falls within the scope of any other block exemption regulation.

Article 3

1   Subject to paragraph 2 of this Article, the exemption provided for in Article 2 shall apply on condition that the market share held by the supplier does not exceed 30 % of the relevant market on which it sells the contract goods or services.

2   In the case of vertical agreements containing exclusive supply obligations, the exemption provided for in Article 2 shall apply on condition that the market share held by the buyer does not exceed 30 % of the relevant market on which it purchases the contract goods or services.

Article 4

The exemption provided for in Article 2 shall not apply to vertical agreements which, directly or indirectly, in isolation or in combination with other factors under the control of the parties, have as their object:

(a)   the restriction of the buyer's ability to determine its sale price, without prejudice to the possibility of the supplier's imposing a maximum sale price or recommending a sale price, provided that they do not amount to a fixed or minimum sale price as a result of pressure from, or incentives offered by, any of the parties;

(b)   the restriction of the territory into which, or of the customers to whom, the buyer may sell the contract goods or services, except:

▶   the restriction of active sales into the exclusive territory or to an exclusive customer group reserved to the supplier or allocated by the supplier to another buyer, where such a restriction does not limit sales by the customers of the buyer,

▶   the restriction of sales to end users by a buyer operating at the wholesale level of trade,

▶   the restriction of sales to unauthorised distributors by the members of a selective distribution system, and

> the restriction of the buyer's ability to sell components, supplied for the purposes of incorporation, to customers who would use them to manufacture the same type of goods as those produced by the supplier;

(c) the restriction of active or passive sales to end users by members of a selective distribution system operating at the retail level of trade, without prejudice to the possibility of prohibiting a member of the system from operating out of an unauthorised place of establishment;

(d) the restriction of cross-supplies between distributors within a selective distribution system, including between distributors operating at different level of trade;

(e) he restriction agreed between a supplier of components and a buyer who incorporates those components, which limits the supplier to selling the components as spare parts to end-users or to repairers or other service providers not entrusted by the buyer with the repair or servicing of its goods.

Article 5

The exemption provided for in Article 2 shall not apply to any of the following obligations contained in vertical agreements:

(a) any direct or indirect non-compete obligation, the duration of which is indefinite or exceeds five years. A non-compete obligation which is tacitly renewable beyond a period of five years is to be deemed to have been concluded for an indefinite duration. However, the time limitation of five years shall not apply where the contract goods or services are sold by the buyer from premises and land owned by the supplier or leased by the supplier from third parties not connected with the buyer, provided that the duration of the non-compete obligation does not exceed the period of occupancy of the premises and land by the buyer;

(b) any direct or indirect obligation causing the buyer, after termination of the agreement, not to manufacture, purchase, sell or resell goods or services, unless such obligation:

> relates to goods or services which compete with the contract goods or services, and

> is limited to the premises and land from which the buyer has operated during the contract period, and

> is indispensable to protect know-how transferred by the supplier to the buyer,

and provided that the duration of such non-compete obligation is limited to a period of one year after termination of the agreement; this obligation is without prejudice to the possibility of imposing a restriction which is unlimited in time on the use and disclosure of know-how which has not entered the public domain;

(c) any direct or indirect obligation causing the members of a selective distribution system not to sell the brands of particular competing suppliers.

Article 6

The Commission may withdraw the benefit of this Regulation, pursuant to Article 7(1) of Regulation No 19/65/EEC, where it finds in any particular case that vertical agreements to which this Regulation applies nevertheless have effects which are incompatible with the conditions laid down in Article 81(3) of the Treaty, and in particular where access to the relevant market or competition therein is significantly restricted by the cumulative effect of parallel networks of similar vertical restraints implemented by competing suppliers or buyers.

Article 7

Where in any particular case vertical agreements to which the exemption provided for in Article 2 applies have effects incompatible with the conditions laid down in Article 81(3) of the Treaty in the territory of a Member State, or in a part thereof, which has all the characteristics of a distinct geographic market, the competent authority of that Member State may withdraw the benefit of application of this Regulation in respect of that territory, under the same conditions as provided in Article 6.

Article 8

1   Pursuant to Article 1 a of Regulation No 19/65/EEC, the Commission may by regulation declare that, where parallel networks of similar vertical restraints cover more than 50 % of a relevant market, this Regulation shall not apply to vertical agreements containing specific restraints relating to that market.

2   A regulation pursuant to paragraph 1 shall not become applicable earlier than six months following its adoption.

Article 9

1   The market share of 30 % provided for in Article 3(1) shall be calculated on the basis of the market sales value of the contract goods or services and other goods or services sold by the supplier, which are regarded as interchangeable or substitutable by the buyer, by reason of the products' characteristics, their prices and their intended use; if market sales value data are not available, estimates based on other reliable market information, including market sales volumes, may be used to establish the market share of the undertaking concerned. For the purposes of Article 3(2), it is either the market purchase value or estimates thereof which shall be used to calculate the market share.

2   For the purposes of applying the market share, threshold provided for in Article 3 the following rules shall apply:

   (a)   the market share shall be calculated on the basis of data relating to the preceding calendar year;

   (b)   the market share shall include any goods or services supplied to integrated distributors for the purposes of sale;

   (c)   if the market share is initially not more than 30 % but subsequently rises above that level without exceeding 35 %, the exemption provided for in Article 2 shall continue to apply for a period of two consecutive calendar years following the year in which the 30 % market share threshold was first exceeded;

   (d)   if the market share is initially not more than 30 % but subsequently rises above 35 %, the exemption provided for in Article 2 shall continue to apply for one calendar year following the year in which the level of 35 % was first exceeded;

   (e)   the benefit of points (c) and (d) may not be combined so as to exceed a period of two calendar years.

Article 10

1   For the purpose of calculating total annual turnover within the meaning of Article 2(2) and (4), the turnover achieved during the previous financial year by the relevant party to the vertical agreement and the turnover achieved by its connected undertakings in respect of all goods and services, excluding all taxes and other duties, shall be added together. For this purpose, no account shall be taken of dealings between the party to the vertical agreement and its connected undertakings or between its connected undertakings.

2   The exemption provided for in Article 2 shall remain applicable where, for any period of two consecutive financial years, the total annual turnover threshold is exceeded by no more than 10 %.

Article 11

1   For the purposes of this Regulation, the terms "undertaking", "supplier" and "buyer" shall include their respective connected undertakings.

2   "Connected undertakings" are:

(a)   undertakings in which a party to the agreement, directly or indirectly:

▸   has the power to exercise more than half the voting rights, or

▸   has the power to appoint more than half the members of the supervisory board, board of management or bodies legally representing the undertaking, or

▸   has the right to manage the undertaking's affairs;

(b)   undertakings which directly or indirectly have, over a party to the agreement, the rights or powers listed in (a);

(c)   undertakings in which an undertaking referred to in (b) has, directly or indirectly, the rights or powers listed in (a);

(d)   undertakings in which a party to the agreement together with one or more of the undertakings referred to in (a), (b) or (c), or in which two or more of the latter undertakings, jointly have the rights or powers listed in (a);

(e)   undertakings in which the rights or the powers listed in (a) are jointly held by:

▸   parties to the agreement or their respective connected undertakings referred to in (a) to (d), or

▸   one or more of the parties to the agreement or one or more of their connected undertakings referred to in (a) to (d) and one or more third parties.

3   For the purposes of Article 3, the market share held by the undertakings referred to in paragraph 2(e) of this Article shall be apportioned equally to each undertaking having the rights or the powers listed in paragraph 2(a).

Article 12

1   The exemptions provided for in Commission Regulations (EEC) No 1983/83(4), (EEC) No 1984/83(5) and (EEC) No 4087/88(6) shall continue to apply until 31 May 2000.

2   The prohibition laid down in Article 81(1) of the EC Treaty shall not apply during the period from 1 June 2000 to 31 December 2001 in respect of agreements already in force on 31 May 2000 which do not satisfy the conditions for exemption provided for in this Regulation but which satisfy the conditions for exemption provided for in Regulations (EEC) No 1983/83, (EEC) No 1984/83 or (EEC) No 4087/88.

Commission Notice on agreements of minor importance which do not appreciably restrict competition under Article 81(1) of the Treaty establishing the European Community (de minimis) (1) (2001/C 368/07)

I

1   Article 81(1) prohibits agreements between undertakings which may affect trade between Member States and which have as their object or effect the prevention, restriction or distortion of competition within the common market. The Court of Justice of the European Communities has clarified that this provision is not applicable where the impact of the agreement on intra- Community trade or on competition is not appreciable.

2   In this notice the Commission quantifies, with the help of market share thresholds, what is not an appreciable restriction of competition under Article 81 of the EC Treaty. This negative definition of appreciability does not imply that agreements between undertakings which exceed the thresholds set out in

this notice appreciably restrict competition. Such agreements may still have only a negligible effect on competition and may therefore not be prohibited by Article 81(1) (2).

3   Agreements may in addition not fall under Article 81(1) because they are not capable of appreciably affecting trade between Member States. This notice does not deal with this issue. It does not quantify what does not constitute an appreciable effect on trade. It is however acknowledged that agreements between small and medium-sized undertakings, as defined in the Annex to Commission Recommendation 96/280/EC (3), are rarely capable of appreciably affecting trade between Member States. Small and medium-sized undertakings are currently defined in that recommendation as undertakings which have fewer than 250 employees and have either an annual turnover not exceeding EUR 40 million or an annual balance-sheet total not exceeding EUR 27 million.

4   In cases covered by this notice the Commission will not institute proceedings either upon application or on its own initiative. Where undertakings assume in good faith that an agreement is covered by this notice, the Commission will not impose fines. Although not binding on them, this notice also intends to give guidance to the courts and authorities of the Member States in their application of Article 81.

5   This notice also applies to decisions by associations of undertakings and to concerted practices.

6   This notice is without prejudice to any interpretation of Article 81 which may be given by the Court of Justice or the Court of First Instance of the European Communities.

II

7   The Commission holds the view that agreements between undertakings which affect trade between Member States do not appreciably restrict competition within the meaning of Article 81(1):

(a)   if the aggregate market share held by the parties to the agreement does not exceed 10 % on any of the relevant markets affected by the agreement, where the agreement is made between undertakings which are actual or potential competitors on any of these markets (agreements between competitors) (4); or

(b)   if the market share held by each of the parties to the agreement does not exceed 15 % on any of the relevant markets affected by the agreement, where the agreement is made between undertakings which are not actual or potential competitors on any of these markets (agreements between non-competitors).

In cases where it is difficult to classify the agreement as either an agreement between competitors or an agreement between non-competitors the 10 % threshold is applicable. 22.12.2001 EN Official Journal of the European Communities C 368/13

(1)   This notice replaces the notice on agreements of minor importance published in OJ C 372, 9.12.1997.

(2)   See, for instance, the judgment of the Court of Justice in Joined Cases C-215/96 and C-216/96 Bagnasco (Carlos) v Banca Popolare di Novara and Casa di Risparmio di Genova e Imperia (1999) ECR I-135, points 34-35. This notice is also without prejudice to the principles for assessment under Article 81(1) as expressed in the Commission notice .Guidelines on the applicability of Article 81 of the EC Treaty to horizontal cooperation agreements., OJ C 3, 6.1.2001, in particular points 17-31 inclusive, and in the Commission notice .Guidelines on vertical restraints., OJ C 291, 13.10.2000, in particular points 5-20 inclusive.

(3)   OJ L 107, 30.4.1996, p. 4. This recommendation will be revised. It is envisaged to increase the annual turnover threshold from EUR 40 million to EUR 50 million and the annual balance-sheet total threshold from EUR 27 million to EUR 43 million.

(4)   On what are actual or potential competitors, see the Commission notice .Guidelines on the applicability of Article 81 of the EC Treaty to horizontal cooperation agreements., OJ C 3, 6.1.2001, paragraph 9. A firm is treated as an actual competitor if it is either active on the same relevant market or if, in the absence of the agreement, it is able to switch production to the relevant products and market them in the short term without incurring significant additional costs or risks in response to a small and permanent increase in relative prices (immediate supply-side substitutability). A firm is treated as a potential competitor if there is evidence that, absent the agreement, this firm could and would be likely to undertake the necessary additional investments or other necessary switching costs so that it could enter the relevant market in response to a small and permanent increase in relative prices.

8   Where in a relevant market competition is restricted by the cumulative effect of agreements for the sale of goods or services entered into by different suppliers or distributors (cumulative foreclosure effect of parallel networks of agreements having similar effects on the market), the market share thresholds under point 7 are reduced to 5 %, both for agreements between competitors and for agreements between non-competitors. Individual suppliers or distributors with a market share not exceeding 5 % are in general not considered to contribute significantly to a cumulative foreclosure effect (1). A cumulative foreclosure effect is unlikely to exist if less than 30 % of the relevant market is covered by parallel (networks of) agreements having similar effects.

9   The Commission also holds the view that agreements are not restrictive of competition if the market shares do not exceed the thresholds of respectively 10 %, 15 % and 5 % set out in point 7 and 8 during two successive calendar years by more than 2 percentage points.

10   In order to calculate the market share, it is necessary to determine the relevant market. This consists of the relevant product market and the relevant geographic market. When defining the relevant market, reference should be had to the notice on the definition of the relevant market for the purposes of Community competition law (2). The market shares are to be calculated on the basis of sales value data or, where appropriate, purchase value data. If value data are not available, estimates based on other reliable market information, including volume data, may be used.

11   Points 7, 8 and 9 do not apply to agreements containing any of the following hardcore restrictions:

(1)   as regards agreements between competitors as defined in point 7, restrictions which, directly or indirectly, in isolation or in combination with other factors under the control of the parties, have as their object (3):

    (a)   the fixing of prices when selling the products to third parties;

    (b)   the limitation of output or sales;

    (c)   the allocation of markets or customers;

(2)   as regards agreements between non-competitors as defined in point 7, restrictions which, directly or indirectly, in isolation or in combination with other factors under the control of the parties, have as their object:

    (a)   the restriction of the buyer's ability to determine its sale price, without prejudice to the possibility of the supplier imposing a maximum sale price or recommending a sale price, provided that they do not amount to a fixed or minimum sale price as a result of pressure from, or incentives offered by, any of the parties;

    (b)   the restriction of the territory into which, or of the customers to whom, the buyer may sell the contract goods or services, except the following restrictions which are not hardcore:

        ▸   the restriction of active sales into the exclusive territory or to an exclusive customer group reserved to the supplier or allocated by the supplier to another buyer, where such a restriction does not limit sales by the customers of the buyer,

- ▸ the restriction of sales to end users by a buyer operating at the wholesale level of trade,

- ▸ the restriction of sales to unauthorised distributors by the members of a selective distribution system, and

- ▸ the restriction of the buyer's ability to sell components, supplied for the purposes of incorporation, to customers who would use them to manufacture the same type of goods as those produced by the supplier;

(c) the restriction of active or passive sales to end users by members of a selective distribution system operating at the retail level of trade, without prejudice to the possibility of prohibiting a member of the system from operating out of an unauthorised place of establishment;

(d) the restriction of cross-supplies between distributors within a selective distribution system, including between distributors operating at different levels of trade;

C 368/14 EN Official Journal of the European Communities 22.12.2001

(1) See also the Commission notice .Guidelines on vertical restraints., OJ C 291, 13.10.2000, in particular paragraphs 73, 142, 143 and 189. While in the guidelines on vertical restraints in relation to certain restrictions reference is made not only to the total but also to the tied market share of a particular supplier or buyer, in this notice all market share thresholds refer to total market shares.

(2) OJ C 372, 9.12.1997, p. 5.

(3) Without prejudice to situations of joint production with or without joint distribution as defined in Article 5, paragraph 2, of Commission Regulation (EC) No 2658/2000 and Article 5, paragraph 2, of Commission Regulation (EC) No 2659/2000, OJ L 304, 5.12.2000, pp. 3 and 7 respectively.

(e) the restriction agreed between a supplier of components and a buyer who incorporates those components, which limits the supplier's ability to sell the components as spare parts to end users or to repairers or other service providers not entrusted by the buyer with the repair or servicing of its goods;

(3) as regards agreements between competitors as defined in point 7, where the competitors operate, for the purposes of the agreement, at a different level of the production or distribution chain, any of the hardcore restrictions listed in paragraph (1) and (2) above.

12 (1) For the purposes of this notice, the terms .undertaking, .party to the agreement, .distributor, .supplier and buyer shall include their respective connected undertakings.

(2) Connected undertakings are:

(a) undertakings in which a party to the agreement, directly or indirectly:

- ▸ has the power to exercise more than half the voting rights, or

- ▸ has the power to appoint more than half the members of the supervisory board, board of management or bodies legally representing the undertaking, or

- ▸ has the right to manage the undertaking's affairs;

(b) undertakings which directly or indirectly have, over a party to the agreement, the rights or powers listed in (a);

(c) undertakings in which an undertaking referred to in (b) has, directly or indirectly, the rights or powers listed in (a);

(d)   undertakings in which a party to the agreement together with one or more of the undertakings referred to in (a), (b) or (c), or in which two or more of the latter undertakings, jointly have the rights or powers listed in (a);

(e)   undertakings in which the rights or the powers listed in (a) are jointly held by:

▶   parties to the agreement or their respective connected undertakings referred to in (a) to (d), or

▶   one or more of the parties to the agreement or one or more of their connected undertakings referred to in (a) to (d) and one or more third parties.

(3)   For the purposes of paragraph 2(e), the market share held by these jointly held undertakings shall be apportioned equally to each undertaking having the rights or the powers listed in paragraph 2(a).

COUNCIL REGULATION (EC) No 1/2003

CHAPTER I

PRINCIPLES

Article 1

Application of Articles 81 and 82 of the Treaty

1   Agreements, decisions and concerted practices caught by Article 81(1) of the Treaty which do not satisfy the conditions of Article 81(3) of the Treaty shall be prohibited, no prior decision to that effect being required.

2   Agreements, decisions and concerted practices caught by Article 81(1) of the Treaty which satisfy the conditions of Article 81(3) of the Treaty shall not be prohibited, no prior decision to that effect being required.

3   The abuse of a dominant position referred to in Article 82 of the Treaty shall be prohibited, no prior decision to that effect being required.

4.1.2003 EN Official Journal of the European Communities L 1/7

(1)   OJ 124, 28.11.1962, p. 2751/62; Regulation as last amended by Regulation No 1002/67/EEC (OJ 306, 16.12.1967, p. 1).

(2)   Council Regulation (EEC) No 1017/68 of 19 July 1968 applying rules of competition to transport by rail, road and inland waterway (OJ L 175, 23.7.1968, p. 1). Regulation as last amended by the Act of Accession of 1994.

(3)   Council Regulation (EEC) No 4056/86 of 22 December 1986 laying down detailed rules for the application of Articles 81 and 82 (The title of the Regulation has been adjusted to take account of the renumbering of the Articles of the EC Treaty, in accordance with Article 12 of the Treaty of Amsterdam; the original reference was to Articles 85 and 86 of the Treaty) of the Treaty to maritime transport (OJ L 378, 31.12.1986, p. 4). Regulation as last amended by the Act of Accession of 1994.

(4)   Council Regulation (EEC) No 3975/87 of 14 December 1987 laying down the procedure for the application of the rules on competition to undertakings in the air transport sector (OJ L 374, 31.12.1987, p. 1). Regulation as last amended by Regulation (EEC) No 2410/92 (OJ L 240, 24.8.1992, p. 18).

Article 2

Burden of proof

In any national or Community proceedings for the application of Articles 81 and 82 of the Treaty, the burden of proving an infringement of Article 81(1) or of Article 82 of the Treaty shall rest on the party or the authority alleging the infringement. The undertaking or association of undertakings claiming the benefit of Article 81(3) of the Treaty shall bear the burden of proving that the conditions of that paragraph are fulfilled.

Article 3

Relationship between Articles 81 and 82 of the Treaty and national competition laws

1   Where the competition authorities of the Member States or national courts apply national competition law to agreements, decisions by associations of undertakings or concerted practices within the meaning of Article 81(1) of the Treaty which may affect trade between Member States within the meaning of that provision, they shall also apply Article 81 of the Treaty to such agreements, decisions or concerted practices. Where the competition authorities of the Member States or national courts apply national competition law to any abuse prohibited by Article 82 of the Treaty, they shall also apply Article 82 of the Treaty.

2   The application of national competition law may not lead to the prohibition of agreements, decisions by associations of undertakings or concerted practices which may affect trade between Member States but which do not restrict competition within the meaning of Article 81(1) of the Treaty, or which fulfil the conditions of Article 81(3) of the Treaty or which are covered by a Regulation for the application of Article 81(3) of the Treaty. Member States shall not under this Regulation be precluded from adopting and applying on their territory stricter national laws which prohibit or sanction unilateral conduct engaged in by undertakings.

3   Without prejudice to general principles and other provisions of Community law, paragraphs 1 and 2 do not apply when the competition authorities and the courts of the Member States apply national merger control laws nor do they preclude the application of provisions of national law that predominantly pursue an objective different fromthat pursued by Articles 81 and 82 of the Treaty.

CHAPTER II

POWERS

Article 4

Powers of the Commission

For the purpose of applying Articles 81 and 82 of the Treaty, the Commission shall have the powers provided for by this Regulation.

Article 5

Powers of the competition authorities of the Member States

The competition authorities of the Member States shall have the power to apply Articles 81 and 82 of the Treaty in individual cases. For this purpose, acting on their own initiative or on a complaint, they may take the following decisions:

▸   requiring that an infringement be brought to an end,

- ordering interimm easures,

L 1/8 EN Official Journal of the European Communities 4.1.2003

- accepting commitments,

- imposing fines, periodic penalty payments or any other penalty provided for in their national law.

Where on the basis of the information in their possession the conditions for prohibition are not met they may likewise decide that there are no grounds for action on their part.

Article 6

Powers of the national courts

National courts shall have the power to apply Articles 81 and 82 of the Treaty.

CHAPTER III

COMMISSION DECISIONS

Article 7

Finding and termination of infringement

1   Where the Commission, acting on a complaint or on its own initiative, finds that there is an infringement of Article 81 or of Article 82 of the Treaty, it may by decision require the undertakings and associations of undertakings concerned to bring such infringement to an end. For this purpose, it may impose on them any behavioural or structural remedies which are proportionate to the infringement committed and necessary to bring the infringement effectively to an end. Structural remedies can only be imposed either where there is no equally effective behavioural remedy or where any equally effective behavioural remedy would be more burdensome for the undertaking concerned than the structural remedy. If the Commission has a legitimate interest in doing so, it may also find that an infringement has been committed in the past.

2   Those entitled to lodge a complaint for the purposes of paragraph 1 are natural or legal persons who can show a legitimate interest and Member States.

Article 8

Interim measures

1   In cases of urgency due to the risk of serious and irreparable damage to competition, the Commission, acting on its own initiative may by decision, on the basis of a prima facie finding of infringement, order interim measures.

2   A decision under paragraph 1 shall apply for a specified period of time and may be renewed in so far this is necessary and appropriate.

Article 9

Commitments

1   Where the Commission intends to adopt a decision requiring that an infringement be brought to an end and the undertakings concerned offer commitments to meet the concerns expressed to them by the Commission in its preliminary assessment, the Commission may by decision make those commitments

binding on the undertakings. Such a decision may be adopted for a specified period and shall conclude that there are no longer grounds for action by the Commission.

4.1.2003 EN Official Journal of the European Communities L 1/9

2.   The Commission may, upon request or on its own initiative, reopen the proceedings:

(a)   where there has been a material change in any of the facts on which the decision was based;

(b)   where the undertakings concerned act contrary to their commitments; or

(c)   where the decision was based on incomplete, incorrect or misleading information provided by the parties.

Article 10

Finding of inapplicability

Where the Community public interest relating to the application of Articles 81 and 82 of the Treaty so requires, the Commission, acting on its own initiative, may by decision find that Article 81 of the Treaty is not applicable to an agreement, a decision by an association of undertakings or a concerted practice, either because the conditions of Article 81(1) of the Treaty are not fulfilled, or because the conditions of Article 81(3) of the Treaty are satisfied.

The Commission may likewise make such a finding with reference to Article 82 of the Treaty.

CHAPTER IV

COOPERATION

Article 11

Cooperation between the Commission and the competition authorities of the Member States

1   The Commission and the competition authorities of the Member States shall apply the Community competition rules in close cooperation.

2   The Commission shall transmit to the competition authorities of the Member States copies of the most important documents it has collected with a view to applying Articles 7, 8, 9, 10 and Article 29(1).

At the request of the competition authority of a Member State, the Commission shall provide it with a copy of other existing documents necessary for the assessment of the case.

3   The competition authorities of the Member States shall, when acting under Article 81 or Article 82 of the Treaty, inform the Commission in writing before or without delay after commencing the first formal investigative measure. This information may also be made available to the competition authorities of the other Member States.

4   No later than 30 days before the adoption of a decision requiring that an infringement be brought to an end, accepting commitments or withdrawing the benefit of a block exemption Regulation, the competition authorities of the Member States shall inform the Commission. To that effect, they shall provide the Commission with a summary of the case, the envisaged decision or, in the absence thereof, any other document indicating the proposed course of action. This information may also be made available to the competition authorities of the other Member States. At the request of the Commission, the acting competition authority shall make available to the Commission other documents it holds which are

necessary for the assessment of the case. The information supplied to the Commission may be made available to the competition authorities of the other Member States. National competition authorities may also exchange between themselves information necessary for the assessment of a case that they are dealing with under Article 81 or Article 82 of the Treaty.

5   The competition authorities of the Member States may consult the Commission on any case involving the application of Community law.

L 1/10 EN Official Journal of the European Communities 4.1.2003

6   The initiation by the Commission of proceedings for the adoption of a decision under Chapter III shall relieve the competition authorities of the Member States of their competence to apply Articles 81 and 82 of the Treaty. If a competition authority of a Member State is already acting on a case, the Commission shall only initiate proceedings after consulting with that national competition authority.

Article 12

Exchange of information

1   For the purpose of applying Articles 81 and 82 of the Treaty the Commission and the competition authorities of the Member States shall have the power to provide one another with and use in evidence any matter of fact or of law, including confidential information.

2   Information exchanged shall only be used in evidence for the purpose of applying Article 81 or Article 82 of the Treaty and in respect of the subject-matter for which it was collected by the transmitting authority. However, where national competition law is applied in the same case and in parallel to Community competition law and does not lead to a different outcome, information exchanged under this Article may also be used for the application of national competition law.

3   Information exchanged pursuant to paragraph 1 can only be used in evidence to impose sanctions on natural persons where:

  ▶   the law of the transmitting authority foresees sanctions of a similar kind in relation to an infringement of Article 81 or Article 82 of the Treaty or, in the absence thereof,

  ▶   the information has been collected in a way which respects the same level of protection of the rights of defence of natural persons as provided for under the national rules of the receiving authority. However, in this case, the information exchanged cannot be used by the receiving authority to impose custodial sanctions.

Article 13

Suspension or termination of proceedings

1   Where competition authorities of two or more Member States have received a complaint or are acting on their own initiative under Article 81 or Article 82 of the Treaty against the same agreement, decision of an association or practice, the fact that one authority is dealing with the case shall be sufficient grounds for the others to suspend the proceedings before them or to reject the complaint. The Commission may likewise reject a complaint on the ground that a competition authority of a Member State is dealing with the case.

2   Where a competition authority of a Member State or the Commission has received a complaint against an agreement, decision of an association or practice which has already been dealt with by another competition authority, it may reject it.

Article 14

Advisory Committee

1   The Commission shall consult an Advisory Committee on Restrictive Practices and Dominant Positions prior to the taking of any decision under Articles 7, 8, 9, 10, 23, Article 24(2) and Article 29(1).

2   For the discussion of individual cases, the Advisory Committee shall be composed of representatives of the competition authorities of the Member States. For meetings in which issues other than individual cases are being discussed, an additional Member State representative competent in competition matters may be appointed. Representatives may, if unable to attend, be replaced by other representatives.

4.1.2003 EN Official Journal of the European Communities L 1/11

3   The consultation may take place at a meeting convened and chaired by the Commission, held not earlier than 14 days after dispatch of the notice convening it, together with a summary of the case, an indication of the most important documents and a preliminary draft decision. In respect of decisions pursuant to Article 8, the meeting may be held seven days after the dispatch of the operative part of a draft decision.

Where the Commission dispatches a notice convening the meeting which gives a shorter period of notice than those specified above, the meeting may take place on the proposed date in the absence of an objection by any Member State. The Advisory Committee shall deliver a written opinion on the Commission's preliminary draft decision. It may deliver an opinion even if some members are absent and are not represented.

At the request of one or several members, the positions stated in the opinion shall be reasoned.

4   Consultation may also take place by written procedure. However, if any Member State so requests, the Commission shall convene a meeting. In case of written procedure, the Commission shall determine a time-limit of not less than 14 days within which the Member States are to put forward their observations for circulation to all other Member States. In case of decisions to be taken pursuant to Article 8, the timelimit of 14 days is replaced by seven days. Where the Commission determines a time-limit for the written procedure which is shorter than those specified above, the proposed time-limit shall be applicable in the absence of an objection by any Member State.

5   The Commission shall take the utmost account of the opinion delivered by the Advisory Committee.

It shall inform the Committee of the manner in which its opinion has been taken into account.

6   Where the Advisory Committee delivers a written opinion, this opinion shall be appended to the draft decision. If the Advisory Committee recommends publication of the opinion, the Commission shall carry out such publication taking into account the legitimate interest of undertakings in the protection of their business secrets.

7   At the request of a competition authority of a Member State, the Commission shall include on the agenda of the Advisory Committee cases that are being dealt with by a competition authority of a Member State under Article 81 or Article 82 of the Treaty. The Commission may also do so on its own initiative.

In either case, the Commission shall inform the competition authority concerned.

A request may in particular be made by a competition authority of a Member State in respect of a case where the Commission intends to initiate proceedings with the effect of Article 11(6).

The Advisory Committee shall not issue opinions on cases dealt with by competition authorities of the Member States. The Advisory Committee may also discuss general issues of Community competition law.

Article 15

Cooperation with national courts

1   In proceedings for the application of Article 81 or Article 82 of the Treaty, courts of the Member States may ask the Commission to transmit to them information in its possession or its opinion on questions concerning the application of the Community competition rules.

2   Member States shall forward to the Commission a copy of any written judgment of national courts deciding on the application of Article 81 or Article 82 of the Treaty. Such copy shall be forwarded without delay after the full written judgment is notified to the parties.

3   Competition authorities of the Member States, acting on their own initiative, may submit written observations to the national courts of their Member State on issues relating to the application of Article 81 or Article 82 of the Treaty. With the permission of the court in question, they may also submit oral observations to the national courts of their Member State. Where the coherent application of Article 81 or Article 82 of the Treaty so requires, the Commission, acting on its own initiative, may submit written observations to courts of the Member States. With the permission of the court in question, it may also make oral observations.

For the purpose of the preparation of their observations only, the competition authorities of the Member States and the Commission may request the relevant court of the Member State to transmit or ensure the transmission to them of any documents necessary for the assessment of the case.

L 1/12 EN Official Journal of the European Communities 4.1.2003

4   This Article is without prejudice to wider powers to make observations before courts conferred on competition authorities of the Member States under the law of their Member State.

Article 16

Uniform application of Community competition law

1   When national courts rule on agreements, decisions or practices under Article 81 or Article 82 of the Treaty which are already the subject of a Commission decision, they cannot take decisions running counter to the decision adopted by the Commission. They must also avoid giving decisions which would conflict with a decision contemplated by the Commission in proceedings it has initiated. To that effect, the national court may assess whether it is necessary to stay its proceedings. This obligation is without prejudice to the rights and obligations under Article 234 of the Treaty.

2   When competition authorities of the Member States rule on agreements, decisions or practices under Article 81 or Article 82 of the Treaty which are already the subject of a Commission decision, they cannot take decisions which would run counter to the decision adopted by the Commission.

CHAPTER V

POWERS OF INVESTIGATION

Article 17

Investigations into sectors of the economy and into types of agreements

1   Where the trend of trade between Member States, the rigidity of prices or other circumstances suggest that competition may be restricted or distorted within the common market, the Commission may conduct its inquiry into a particular sector of the economy or into a particular type of agreements across various

sectors. In the course of that inquiry, the Commission may request the undertakings or associations of undertakings concerned to supply the information necessary for giving effect to Articles 81 and 82 of the Treaty and may carry out any inspections necessary for that purpose.

The Commission may in particular request the undertakings or associations of undertakings concerned to communicate to it all agreements, decisions and concerted practices.

The Commission may publish a report on the results of its inquiry into particular sectors of the economy or particular types of agreements across various sectors and invite comments from interested parties.

2   Articles 14, 18, 19, 20, 22, 23 and 24 shall apply mutatis mutandis.

Article 18

Requests for information

1   In order to carry out the duties assigned to it by this Regulation, the Commission may, by simple request or by decision, require undertakings and associations of undertakings to provide all necessary information.

2   When sending a simple request for information to an undertaking or association of undertakings, the Commission shall state the legal basis and the purpose of the request, specify what information is required and fix the time-limit within which the information is to be provided, and the penalties provided for in Article 23 for supplying incorrect or misleading information.

4.1.2003 EN Official Journal of the European Communities L 1/13

3   Where the Commission requires undertakings and associations of undertakings to supply information by decision, it shall state the legal basis and the purpose of the request, specify what information is required and fix the time-limit within which it is to be provided. It shall also indicate the penalties provided for in Article 23 and indicate or impose the penalties provided for in Article 24. It shall further indicate the right to have the decision reviewed by the Court of Justice.

4   The owners of the undertakings or their representatives and, in the case of legal persons, companies or firms, or associations having no legal personality, the persons authorised to represent them by law or by their constitution shall supply the information requested on behalf of the undertaking or the association of undertakings concerned. Lawyers duly authorised to act may supply the information on behalf of their clients. The latter shall remain fully responsible if the information supplied is incomplete, incorrect or misleading.

5   The Commission shall without delay forward a copy of the simple request or of the decision to the competition authority of the Member State in whose territory the seat of the undertaking or association of undertakings is situated and the competition authority of the Member State whose territory is affected.

6   At the request of the Commission the governments and competition authorities of the Member States shall provide the Commission with all necessary information to carry out the duties assigned to it by this Regulation.

Article 19

Power to take statements

1   In order to carry out the duties assigned to it by this Regulation, the Commission may interview any natural or legal person who consents to be interviewed for the purpose of collecting information relating to the subject-matter of an investigation.

2   Where an interview pursuant to paragraph 1 is conducted in the premises of an undertaking, the Commission shall inform the competition authority of the Member State in whose territory the interview

takes place. If so requested by the competition authority of that Member State, its officials may assist the officials and other accompanying persons authorised by the Commission to conduct the interview.

Article 20

The Commission's powers of inspection

1   In order to carry out the duties assigned to it by this Regulation, the Commission may conduct all necessary inspections of undertakings and associations of undertakings.

2   The officials and other accompanying persons authorised by the Commission to conduct an inspection are empowered:

(a)   to enter any premises, land and means of transport of undertakings and associations of undertakings;

(b)   to examine the books and other records related to the business, irrespective of the medium on which they are stored;

(c)   to take or obtain in any formcopies of or extracts fromsuch books or records;

(d)   to seal any business premises and books or records for the period and to the extent necessary for the inspection;

(e)   to ask any representative or member of staff of the undertaking or association of undertakings for explanations on facts or documents relating to the subject-matter and purpose of the inspection and to record the answers.

L 1/14 EN Official Journal of the European Communities 4.1.2003

3   The officials and other accompanying persons authorised by the Commission to conduct an inspection shall exercise their powers upon production of a written authorisation specifying the subject matter and purpose of the inspection and the penalties provided for in Article 23 in case the production of the required books or other records related to the business is incomplete or where the answers to questions asked under paragraph 2 of the present Article are incorrect or misleading. In good time before the inspection, the Commission shall give notice of the inspection to the competition authority of the Member State in whose territory it is to be conducted.

4   Undertakings and associations of undertakings are required to submit to inspections ordered by decision of the Commission. The decision shall specify the subject matter and purpose of the inspection, appoint the date on which it is to begin and indicate the penalties provided for in Articles 23 and 24 and the right to have the decision reviewed by the Court of Justice. The Commission shall take such decisions after consulting the competition authority of the Member State in whose territory the inspection is to be conducted.

5   Officials of as well as those authorised or appointed by the competition authority of the Member State in whose territory the inspection is to be conducted · shall, at the request of that authority or of the Commission, actively assist the officials and other accompanying persons authorised by the Commission.

To this end, they shall enjoy the powers specified in paragraph 2.

6   Where the officials and other accompanying persons authorised by the Commission find that an undertaking opposes an inspection ordered pursuant to this Article, the Member State concerned shall afford them the necessary assistance, requesting where appropriate the assistance of the police or of an equivalent enforcement authority, so as to enable them to conduct their inspection.

7   If the assistance provided for in paragraph 6 requires authorisation froma judicial authority according to national rules, such authorisation shall be applied for. Such authorisation may also be applied for as a precautionary measure.

8   Where authorisation as referred to in paragraph 7 is applied for, the national judicial authority shall control that the Commission decision is authentic and that the coercive measures envisaged are neither arbitrary nor excessive having regard to the subject matter of the inspection. In its control of the proportionality of the coercive measures, the national judicial authority may ask the Commission, directly or through the Member State competition authority, for detailed explanations in particular on the grounds the Commission has for suspecting infringement of Articles 81 and 82 of the Treaty, as well as on the seriousness of the suspected infringement and on the nature of the involvement of the undertaking concerned. However, the national judicial authority may not call into question the necessity for the inspection nor demand that it be provided with the information in the Commission's file. The lawfulness of the Commission decision shall be subject to review only by the Court of Justice.

Article 21

Inspection of other premises

1   If a reasonable suspicion exists that books or other records related to the business and to the subjectmatter of the inspection, which may be relevant to prove a serious violation of Article 81 or Article 82 of the Treaty, are being kept in any other premises, land and means of transport, including the homes of directors, managers and other members of staff of the undertakings and associations of undertakings concerned, the Commission can by decision order an inspection to be conducted in such other premises, land and means of transport.

2   The decision shall specify the subject matter and purpose of the inspection, appoint the date on which it is to begin and indicate the right to have the decision reviewed by the Court of Justice. It shall in particular state the reasons that have led the Commission to conclude that a suspicion in the sense of paragraph 1 exists. The Commission shall take such decisions after consulting the competition authority of the Member State in whose territory the inspection is to be conducted.

4.1.2003 EN Official Journal of the European Communities L 1/15

3   A decision adopted pursuant to paragraph 1 cannot be executed without prior authorisation from the national judicial authority of the Member State concerned. The national judicial authority shall control that the Commission decision is authentic and that the coercive measures envisaged are neither arbitrary nor excessive having regard in particular to the seriousness of the suspected infringement, to the importance of the evidence sought, to the involvement of the undertaking concerned and to the reasonable likelihood that business books and records relating to the subject matter of the inspection are kept in the premises for which the authorisation is requested. The national judicial authority may ask the Commission, directly or through the Member State competition authority, for detailed explanations on those elements which are necessary to allow its control of the proportionality of the coercive measures envisaged.

However, the national judicial authority may not call into question the necessity for the inspection nor demand that it be provided with information in the Commission's file. The lawfulness of the Commission decision shall be subject to review only by the Court of Justice.

4   The officials and other accompanying persons authorised by the Commission to conduct an inspection ordered in accordance with paragraph 1 of this Article shall have the powers set out in Article 20(2)(a), (b) and (c). Article 20(5) and (6) shall apply mutatis mutandis.

Article 22

Investigations by competition authorities of Member States

1   The competition authority of a Member State may in its own territory carry out any inspection or other fact-finding measure under its national law on behalf and for the account of the competition authority of another Member State in order to establish whether there has been an infringement of Article 81 or Article 82 of the Treaty. Any exchange and use of the information collected shall be carried out in accordance with Article 12.

2   At the request of the Commission, the competition authorities of the Member States shall undertake the inspections which the Commission considers to be necessary under Article 20(1) or which it has ordered by decision pursuant to Article 20(4). The officials of the competition authorities of the Member States who are responsible for conducting these inspections as well as those authorised or appointed by themshall exercise their powers in accordance with their national law. If so requested by the Commission or by the competition authority of the Member State in whose territory the inspection is to be conducted, officials and other accompanying persons authorised by the Commission may assist the officials of the authority concerned.

CHAPTER VI

PENALTIES

Article 23

Fines

1   The Commission may by decision impose on undertakings and associations of undertakings fines not exceeding 1 % of the total turnover in the preceding business year where, intentionally or negligently:

    (a)   they supply incorrect or misleading information in response to a request made pursuant to Article 17 or Article 18(2);

    (b)   in response to a request made by decision adopted pursuant to Article 17 or Article 18(3), they supply incorrect, incomplete or misleading information or do not supply information within the required time-limit;

    (c)   they produce the required books or other records related to the business in incomplete form during inspections under Article 20 or refuse to submit to inspections ordered by a decision adopted pursuant to Article 20(4);

L 1/16 EN Official Journal of the European Communities 4.1.2003

    (d)   in response to a question asked in accordance with Article 20(2)(e),

        ▸   they give an incorrect or misleading answer,

        ▸   they fail to rectify within a time-limit set by the Commission an incorrect, incomplete or misleading answer given by a member of staff, or

        ▸   they fail or refuse to provide a complete answer on facts relating to the subject-matter and purpose of an inspection ordered by a decision adopted pursuant to Article 20(4);

    (e)   seals affixed in accordance with Article 20(2)(d) by officials or other accompanying persons authorised by the Commission have been broken.

2   The Commission may by decision impose fines on undertakings and associations of undertakings where, either intentionally or negligently:

(a)   they infringe Article 81 or Article 82 of the Treaty; or

(b)   they contravene a decision ordering interim measures under Article 8; or

(c)   they fail to comply with a commitment made binding by a decision pursuant to Article 9.

For each undertaking and association of undertakings participating in the infringement, the fine shall not exceed 10 % of its total turnover in the preceding business year.

Where the infringement of an association relates to the activities of its members, the fine shall not exceed 10 % of the sum of the total turnover of each member active on the market affected by the infringement of the association.

3   In fixing the amount of the fine, regard shall be had both to the gravity and to the duration of the infringement.

4   When a fine is imposed on an association of undertakings taking account of the turnover of its members and the association is not solvent, the association is obliged to call for contributions from its members to cover the amount of the fine.

Where such contributions have not been made to the association within a time-limit fixed by the Commission, the Commission may require payment of the fine directly by any of the undertakings whose representatives were members of the decision-making bodies concerned of the association.

After the Commission has required payment under the second subparagraph, where necessary to ensure full payment of the fine, the Commission may require payment of the balance by any of the members of the association which were active on the market on which the infringement occurred.

However, the Commission shall not require payment under the second or the third subparagraph from undertakings which show that they have not implemented the infringing decision of the association and either were not aware of its existence or have actively distanced themselves from it before the Commission started investigating the case.

The financial liability of each undertaking in respect of the payment of the fine shall not exceed 10 % of its total turnover in the preceding business year.

5   Decisions taken pursuant to paragraphs 1 and 2 shall not be of a criminal law nature.

Article 24

Periodic penalty payments

1   The Commission may, by decision, impose on undertakings or associations of undertakings periodic penalty payments not exceeding 5 % of the average daily turnover in the preceding business year per day and calculated from the date appointed by the decision, in order to compel them:

(a)   to put an end to an infringement of Article 81 or Article 82 of the Treaty, in accordance with a decision taken pursuant to Article 7; 4.1.2003 EN Official Journal of the European Communities L 1/17

(b)   to comply with a decision ordering interim measures taken pursuant to Article 8;

(c)   to comply with a commitment made binding by a decision pursuant to Article 9;

(d)   to supply complete and correct information which it has requested by decision taken pursuant to Article 17 or Article 18(3);

(e)   to submit to an inspection which it has ordered by decision taken pursuant to Article 20(4).

2   Where the undertakings or associations of undertakings have satisfied the obligation which the periodic penalty payment was intended to enforce, the Commission may fix the definitive amount of the periodic penalty payment at a figure lower than that which would arise under the original decision. Article 23(4) shall apply correspondingly.

CHAPTER VII

LIMITATION PERIODS

Article 25

Limitation periods for the imposition of penalties

1   The powers conferred on the Commission by Articles 23 and 24 shall be subject to the following limitation periods:

(a)   three years in the case of infringements of provisions concerning requests for information or the conduct of inspections;

(b)   five years in the case of all other infringements.

2   Time shall begin to run on the day on which the infringement is committed. However, in the case of continuing or repeated infringements, time shall begin to run on the day on which the infringement ceases.

3   Any action taken by the Commission or by the competition authority of a Member State for the purpose of the investigation or proceedings in respect of an infringement shall interrupt the limitation period for the imposition of fines or periodic penalty payments. The limitation period shall be interrupted with effect from the date on which the action is notified to at least one undertaking or association of undertakings which has participated in the infringement. Actions which interrupt the running of the period shall include in particular the following:

(a)   written requests for information by the Commission or by the competition authority of a Member State;

(b)   written authorisations to conduct inspections issued to its officials by the Commission or by the competition authority of a Member State;

(c)   the initiation of proceedings by the Commission or by the competition authority of a Member State;

(d)   notification of the statement of objections of the Commission or of the competition authority of a Member State.

4   The interruption of the limitation period shall apply for all the undertakings or associations of undertakings which have participated in the infringement.

5   Each interruption shall start time running afresh. However, the limitation period shall expire at the latest on the day on which a period equal to twice the limitation period has elapsed without the Commission having imposed a fine or a periodic penalty payment. That period shall be extended by the time during which limitation is suspended pursuant to paragraph 6.

6   The limitation period for the imposition of fines or periodic penalty payments shall be suspended for as long as the decision of the Commission is the subject of proceedings pending before the Court of Justice.

Article 26

Limitation period for the enforcement of penalties

1   The power of the Commission to enforce decisions taken pursuant to Articles 23 and 24 shall be subject to a limitation period of five years.

2   Time shall begin to run on the day on which the decision becomes final.

3   The limitation period for the enforcement of penalties shall be interrupted:

    (a)   by notification of a decision varying the original amount of the fine or periodic penalty payment or refusing an application for variation;

    (b)   by any action of the Commission or of a Member State, acting at the request of the Commission, designed to enforce payment of the fine or periodic penalty payment.

4   Each interruption shall start time running afresh.

5   The limitation period for the enforcement of penalties shall be suspended for so long as:

    (a)   time to pay is allowed;

    (b)   enforcement of payment is suspended pursuant to a decision of the Court of Justice.

CHAPTER VIII

HEARINGS AND PROFESSIONAL SECRECY

Article 27

Hearing of the parties, complainants and others

1   Before taking decisions as provided for in Articles 7, 8, 23 and Article 24(2), the Commission shall give the undertakings or associations of undertakings which are the subject of the proceedings conducted by the Commission the opportunity of being heard on the matters to which the Commission has taken objection. The Commission shall base its decisions only on objections on which the parties concerned have been able to comment. Complainants shall be associated closely with the proceedings.

2   The rights of defence of the parties concerned shall be fully respected in the proceedings. They shall be entitled to have access to the Commission's file, subject to the legitimate interest of undertakings in the protection of their business secrets. The right of access to the file shall not extend to confidential information and internal documents of the Commission or the competition authorities of the Member States. In particular, the right of access shall not extend to correspondence between the Commission and the competition authorities of the Member States, or between the latter, including documents drawn up pursuant to Articles 11 and 14. Nothing in this paragraph shall prevent the Commission from disclosing and using information necessary to prove an infringement.

3   If the Commission considers it necessary, it may also hear other natural or legal persons. Applications to be heard on the part of such persons shall, where they show a sufficient interest, be granted. The competition authorities of the Member States may also ask the Commission to hear other natural or legal persons.

4   Where the Commission intends to adopt a decision pursuant to Article 9 or Article 10, it shall publish a concise summary of the case and the main content of the commitments or of the proposed course of action. Interested third parties may submit their observations within a time limit which is fixed by the Commission

in its publication and which may not be less than one month. Publication shall have regard to the legitimate interest of undertakings in the protection of their business secrets.

4.1.2003 EN Official Journal of the European Communities L 1/19

Article 28

Professional secrecy

1   Without prejudice to Articles 12 and 15, information collected pursuant to Articles 17 to 22 shall be used only for the purpose for which it was acquired.

2   Without prejudice to the exchange and to the use of information foreseen in Articles 11, 12, 14, 15 and 27, the Commission and the competition authorities of the Member States, their officials, servants and other persons working under the supervision of these authorities as well as officials and civil servants of other authorities of the Member States shall not disclose information acquired or exchanged by them pursuant to this Regulation and of the kind covered by the obligation of professional secrecy. This obligation also applies to all representatives and experts of Member States attending meetings of the Advisory Committee pursuant to Article 14.

CHAPTER IX

EXEMPTION REGULATIONS

Article 29

Withdrawal in individual cases

1   Where the Commission, empowered by a Council Regulation, such as Regulations 19/65/EEC, (EEC) No 2821/71, (EEC) No 3976/87, (EEC) No 1534/91 or (EEC) No 479/92, to apply Article 81(3) of the Treaty by regulation, has declared Article 81(1) of the Treaty inapplicable to certain categories of agreements, decisions by associations of undertakings or concerted practices, it may, acting on its own initiative or on a complaint, withdraw the benefit of such an exemption Regulation when it finds that in any particular case an agreement, decision or concerted practice to which the exemption Regulation applies has certain effects which are incompatible with Article 81(3) of the Treaty.

2   Where, in any particular case, agreements, decisions by associations of undertakings or concerted practices to which a Commission Regulation referred to in paragraph 1 applies have effects which are incompatible with Article 81(3) of the Treaty in the territory of a Member State, or in a part thereof, which has all the characteristics of a distinct geographic market, the competition authority of that Member State may withdraw the benefit of the Regulation in question in respect of that territory.

CHAPTER X

GENERAL PROVISIONS

Article 30

Publication of decisions

1   The Commission shall publish the decisions, which it takes pursuant to Articles 7 to 10, 23 and 24.

2   The publication shall state the names of the parties and the main content of the decision, including any penalties imposed. It shall have regard to the legitimate interest of undertakings in the protection of their business secrets.

Article 31

Review by the Court of Justice

The Court of Justice shall have unlimited jurisdiction to review decisions whereby the Commission has fixed a fine or periodic penalty payment. It may cancel, reduce or increase the fine or periodic penalty payment imposed.

L 1/20 EN Official Journal of the European Communities 4.1.2003

Article 32

Exclusions

This Regulation shall not apply to:

(a)   international tramp vessel services as defined in Article 1(3)(a) of Regulation (EEC) No 4056/86;

(b)   a maritime transport service that takes place exclusively between ports in one and the same Member State as foreseen in Article 1(2) of Regulation (EEC) No 4056/86;

(c)   air transport between Community airports and third countries.

Article 33

Implementing provisions

1   The Commission shall be authorised to take such measures as may be appropriate in order to apply this Regulation. The measures may concern, inter alia:

     (a)   the form, content and other details of complaints lodged pursuant to Article 7 and the procedure for rejecting complaints;

     (b)   the practical arrangements for the exchange of information and consultations provided for in Article 11;

     (c)   the practical arrangements for the hearings provided for in Article 27.

2   Before the adoption of any measures pursuant to paragraph 1, the Commission shall publish a draft thereof and invite all interested parties to submit their comments within the time-limit it lays down, which may not be less than one month. Before publishing a draft measure and before adopting it, the Commission shall consult the Advisory Committee on Restrictive Practices and Dominant Positions.

CHAPTER XI

TRANSITIONAL, AMENDING AND FINAL PROVISIONS

Article 34

Transitional provisions

1   Applications made to the Commission under Article 2 of Regulation No 17, notifications made under Articles 4 and 5 of that Regulation and the corresponding applications and notifications made under Regulations (EEC) No 1017/68, (EEC) No 4056/86 and (EEC) No 3975/87 shall lapse as from the date of application of this Regulation.

2   Procedural steps taken under Regulation No 17 and Regulations (EEC) No 1017/68, (EEC) No 4056/86 and (EEC) No 3975/87 shall continue to have effect for the purposes of applying this Regulation.

Article 35

Designation of competition authorities of Member States

1   The Member States shall designate the competition authority or authorities responsible for the application of Articles 81 and 82 of the Treaty in such a way that the provisions of this regulation are effectively complied with. The measures necessary to empower those authorities to apply those Articles shall be taken before 1 May 2004. The authorities designated may include courts.

4.1.2003 EN Official Journal of the European Communities L 1/21

2   When enforcement of Community competition law is entrusted to national administrative and judicial authorities, the Member States may allocate different powers and functions to those different national authorities, whether administrative or judicial.

3   The effects of Article 11(6) apply to the authorities designated by the Member States including courts that exercise functions regarding the preparation and the adoption of the types of decisions foreseen in Article 5. The effects of Article 11(6) do not extend to courts insofar as they act as review courts in respect of the types of decisions foreseen in Article 5.

4   Notwithstanding paragraph 3, in the Member States where, for the adoption of certain types of decisions foreseen in Article 5, an authority brings an action before a judicial authority that is separate and different from the prosecuting authority and provided that the terms of this paragraph are complied with, the effects of Article 11(6) shall be limited to the authority prosecuting the case which shall withdraw its claim before the judicial authority when the Commission opens proceedings and this withdrawal shall bring the national proceedings effectively to an end.

Article 36

Amendment of Regulation (EEC) No 1017/68

Regulation (EEC) No 1017/68 is amended as follows:

1   Article 2 is repealed;

2   in Article 3(1), the words 'The prohibition laid down in Article 2' are replaced by the words 'The prohibition in Article 81(1) of the Treaty';

3   Article 4 is amended as follows:

(a)   In paragraph 1, the words 'The agreements, decisions and concerted practices referred to in Article 2' are replaced by the words 'Agreements, decisions and concerted practices pursuant to Article 81(1) of the Treaty';

(b)   Paragraph 2 is replaced by the following:

'2. If the implementation of any agreement, decision or concerted practice covered by paragraph 1 has, in a given case, effects which are incompatible with the requirements of Article 81(3) of the Treaty, undertakings or associations of undertakings may be required to make such effects cease.'

4   Articles 5 to 29 are repealed with the exception of Article 13(3) which continues to apply to decisions adopted pursuant to Article 5 of Regulation (EEC) No 1017/68 prior to the date of application of this Regulation until the date of expiration of those decisions;

5   in Article 30, paragraphs 2, 3 and 4 are deleted.

Council Regulation (EC) No 139/2004

Article 1

Scope

1   Without prejudice to Article 4(5) and Article 22, this Regulation shall apply to all concentrations with a Community dimension as defined in this Article.

2   A concentration has a Community dimension where:

(a)   the combined aggregate worldwide turnover of all the undertakings concerned is more than EUR 5000 million; and

(b)   the aggregate Community-wide turnover of each of at least two of the undertakings concerned is more than EUR 250 million, unless each of the undertakings concerned achieves more than two-thirds of its aggregate Community-wide turnover within one and the same Member State.

3   A concentration that does not meet the thresholds laid down in paragraph 2 has a Community dimension where:

(a)   the combined aggregate worldwide turnover of all the undertakings concerned is more than EUR 2500 million;

(b)   in each of at least three Member States, the combined aggregate turnover of all the undertakings concerned is more than EUR 100 million;

(c)   in each of at least three Member States included for the purpose of point (b), the aggregate turnover of each of at least two of the undertakings concerned is more than EUR 25 million; and

(d)   the aggregate Community-wide turnover of each of at least two of the undertakings concerned is more than EUR 100 million, unless each of the undertakings concerned achieves more than two-thirds of its aggregate Community-wide turnover within one and the same Member State.

4   On the basis of statistical data that may be regularly provided by the Member States, the Commission shall report to the Council on the operation of the thresholds and criteria set out in paragraphs 2 and 3 by 1 July 2009 and may present proposals pursuant to paragraph 5.

5   Following the report referred to in paragraph 4 and on a proposal from the Commission, the Council, acting by a qualified majority, may revise the thresholds and criteria mentioned in paragraph 3.

Article 2

Appraisal of concentrations

1   Concentrations within the scope of this Regulation shall be appraised in accordance with the objectives of this Regulation and the following provisions with a view to establishing whether or not they are compatible with the common market.

In making this appraisal, the Commission shall take into account:

(a)   the need to maintain and develop effective competition within the common market in view of, among other things, the structure of all the markets concerned and the actual or potential competition from undertakings located either within or outwith the Community;

(b)   the market position of the undertakings concerned and their economic and financial power, the alternatives available to suppliers and users, their access to supplies or markets, any legal or other barriers to entry, supply and demand trends for the relevant goods and services, the interests of the intermediate and ultimate consumers, and the development of technical and economic progress provided that it is to consumers' advantage and does not form an obstacle to competition.

2   A concentration which would not significantly impede effective competition in the common market or in a substantial part of it, in particular as a result of the creation or strengthening of a dominant position, shall be declared compatible with the common market.

3   A concentration which would significantly impede effective competition, in the common market or in a substantial part of it, in particular as a result of the creation or strengthening of a dominant position, shall be declared incompatible with the common market.

4   To the extent that the creation of a joint venture constituting a concentration pursuant to Article 3 has as its object or effect the coordination of the competitive behaviour of undertakings that remain independent, such coordination shall be appraised in accordance with the criteria of Article 81(1) and (3) of the Treaty, with a view to establishing whether or not the operation is compatible with the common market.

5   In making this appraisal, the Commission shall take into account in particular:

   ▶   whether two or more parent companies retain, to a significant extent, activities in the same market as the joint venture or in a market which is downstream or upstream from that of the joint venture or in a neighbouring market closely related to this market,

   ▶   whether the coordination which is the direct consequence of the creation of the joint venture affords the undertakings concerned the possibility of eliminating competition in respect of a substantial part of the products or services in question.

Article 3

Definition of concentration

1   A concentration shall be deemed to arise where a change of control on a lasting basis results from:

   (a)   the merger of two or more previously independent undertakings or parts of undertakings, or

   (b)   the acquisition, by one or more persons already controlling at least one undertaking, or by one or more undertakings, whether by purchase of securities or assets, by contract or by any other means, of direct or indirect control of the whole or parts of one or more other undertakings.

2   Control shall be constituted by rights, contracts or any other means which, either separately or in combination and having regard to the considerations of fact or law involved, confer the possibility of exercising decisive influence on an undertaking, in particular by:

   (a)   ownership or the right to use all or part of the assets of an undertaking;

   (b)   rights or contracts which confer decisive influence on the composition, voting or decisions of the organs of an undertaking.

3   Control is acquired by persons or undertakings which:

   (a)   are holders of the rights or entitled to rights under the contracts concerned; or

   (b)   while not being holders of such rights or entitled to rights under such contracts, have the power to exercise the rights deriving therefrom.

4   The creation of a joint venture performing on a lasting basis all the functions of an autonomous economic entity shall constitute a concentration within the meaning of paragraph 1(b).

5   A concentration shall not be deemed to arise where:

(a)   credit institutions or other financial institutions or insurance companies, the normal activities of which include transactions and dealing in securities for their own account or for the account of others, hold on a temporary basis securities which they have acquired in an undertaking with a view to reselling them, provided that they do not exercise voting rights in respect of those securities with a view to determining the competitive behaviour of that undertaking or provided that they exercise such voting rights only with a view to preparing the disposal of all or part of that undertaking or of its assets or the disposal of those securities and that any such disposal takes place within one year of the date of acquisition; that period may be extended by the Commission on request where such institutions or companies can show that the disposal was not reasonably possible within the period set;

(b)   control is acquired by an office-holder according to the law of a Member State relating to liquidation, winding up, insolvency, cessation of payments, compositions or analogous proceedings;

(c)   the operations referred to in paragraph 1(b) are carried out by the financial holding companies referred to in Article 5(3) of Fourth Council Directive 78/660/EEC of 25 July 1978 based on Article 54(3)(g) of the Treaty on the annual accounts of certain types of companies(6) provided however that the voting rights in respect of the holding are exercised, in particular in relation to the appointment of members of the management and supervisory bodies of the undertakings in which they have holdings, only to maintain the full value of those investments and not to determine directly or indirectly the competitive conduct of those undertakings.

Article 4

Prior notification of concentrations and pre-notification referral at the request of the notifying parties

1   Concentrations with a Community dimension defined in this Regulation shall be notified to the Commission prior to their implementation and following the conclusion of the agreement, the announcement of the public bid, or the acquisition of a controlling interest.

Notification may also be made where the undertakings concerned demonstrate to the Commission a good faith intention to conclude an agreement or, in the case of a public bid, where they have publicly announced an intention to make such a bid, provided that the intended agreement or bid would result in a concentration with a Community dimension.

For the purposes of this Regulation, the term "notified concentration" shall also cover intended concentrations notified pursuant to the second subparagraph. For the purposes of paragraphs 4 and 5 of this Article, the term "concentration" includes intended concentrations within the meaning of the second subparagraph.

2   A concentration which consists of a merger within the meaning of Article 3(1)(a) or in the acquisition of joint control within the meaning of Article 3(1)(b) shall be notified jointly by the parties to the merger or by those acquiring joint control as the case may be. In all other cases, the notification shall be effected by the person or undertaking acquiring control of the whole or parts of one or more undertakings.

3   Where the Commission finds that a notified concentration falls within the scope of this Regulation, it shall publish the fact of the notification, at the same time indicating the names of the undertakings concerned, their country of origin, the nature of the concentration and the economic sectors involved. The Commission shall take account of the legitimate interest of undertakings in the protection of their business secrets.

4   Prior to the notification of a concentration within the meaning of paragraph 1, the persons or undertakings referred to in paragraph 2 may inform the Commission, by means of a reasoned submission, that the concentration may significantly affect competition in a market within a Member State which presents all

the characteristics of a distinct market and should therefore be examined, in whole or in part, by that Member State.

The Commission shall transmit this submission to all Member States without delay. The Member State referred to in the reasoned submission shall, within 15 working days of receiving the submission, express its agreement or disagreement as regards the request to refer the case. Where that Member State takes no such decision within this period, it shall be deemed to have agreed.

Unless that Member State disagrees, the Commission, where it considers that such a distinct market exists, and that competition in that market may be significantly affected by the concentration, may decide to refer the whole or part of the case to the competent authorities of that Member State with a view to the application of that State's national competition law.

The decision whether or not to refer the case in accordance with the third subparagraph shall be taken within 25 working days starting from the receipt of the reasoned submission by the Commission. The Commission shall inform the other Member States and the persons or undertakings concerned of its decision. If the Commission does not take a decision within this period, it shall be deemed to have adopted a decision to refer the case in accordance with the submission made by the persons or undertakings concerned.

If the Commission decides, or is deemed to have decided, pursuant to the third and fourth subparagraphs, to refer the whole of the case, no notification shall be made pursuant to paragraph 1 and national competition law shall apply. Article 9(6) to (9) shall apply mutatis mutandis.

5   With regard to a concentration as defined in Article 3 which does not have a Community dimension within the meaning of Article 1 and which is capable of being reviewed under the national competition laws of at least three Member States, the persons or undertakings referred to in paragraph 2 may, before any notification to the competent authorities, inform the Commission by means of a reasoned submission that the concentration should be examined by the Commission.

The Commission shall transmit this submission to all Member States without delay.

Any Member State competent to examine the concentration under its national competition law may, within 15 working days of receiving the reasoned submission, express its disagreement as regards the request to refer the case.

Where at least one such Member State has expressed its disagreement in accordance with the third subparagraph within the period of 15 working days, the case shall not be referred. The Commission shall, without delay, inform all Member States and the persons or undertakings concerned of any such expression of disagreement.

Where no Member State has expressed its disagreement in accordance with the third subparagraph within the period of 15 working days, the concentration shall be deemed to have a Community dimension and shall be notified to the Commission in accordance with paragraphs 1 and 2. In such situations, no Member State shall apply its national competition law to the concentration.

6   The Commission shall report to the Council on the operation of paragraphs 4 and 5 by 1 July 2009. Following this report and on a proposal from the Commission, the Council, acting by a qualified majority, may revise paragraphs 4 and 5.

Article 5

Calculation of turnover

1   Aggregate turnover within the meaning of this Regulation shall comprise the amounts derived by the undertakings concerned in the preceding financial year from the sale of products and the provision of

services falling within the undertakings' ordinary activities after deduction of sales rebates and of value added tax and other taxes directly related to turnover. The aggregate turnover of an undertaking concerned shall not include the sale of products or the provision of services between any of the undertakings referred to in paragraph 4.

Turnover, in the Community or in a Member State, shall comprise products sold and services provided to undertakings or consumers, in the Community or in that Member State as the case may be.

2   By way of derogation from paragraph 1, where the concentration consists of the acquisition of parts, whether or not constituted as legal entities, of one or more undertakings, only the turnover relating to the parts which are the subject of the concentration shall be taken into account with regard to the seller or sellers.

However, two or more transactions within the meaning of the first subparagraph which take place within a two-year period between the same persons or undertakings shall be treated as one and the same concentration arising on the date of the last transaction.

3   In place of turnover the following shall be used:

   (a)   for credit institutions and other financial institutions, the sum of the following income items as defined in Council Directive 86/635/EEC(7), after deduction of value added tax and other taxes directly related to those items, where appropriate:

      (i)   interest income and similar income;

      (ii)   income from securities:

         ▶   income from shares and other variable yield securities,

         ▶   income from participating interests,

         ▶   income from shares in affiliated undertakings;

      (iii)   commissions receivable;

      (iv)   net profit on financial operations;

      (v)   other operating income.

      The turnover of a credit or financial institution in the Community or in a Member State shall comprise the income items, as defined above, which are received by the branch or division of that institution established in the Community or in the Member State in question, as the case may be;

   (b)   for insurance undertakings, the value of gross premiums written which shall comprise all amounts received and receivable in respect of insurance contracts issued by or on behalf of the insurance undertakings, including also outgoing reinsurance premiums, and after deduction of taxes and parafiscal contributions or levies charged by reference to the amounts of individual premiums or the total volume of premiums; as regards Article 1(2)(b) and (3)(b), (c) and (d) and the final part of Article 1(2) and (3), gross premiums received from Community residents and from residents of one Member State respectively shall be taken into account.

4   Without prejudice to paragraph 2, the aggregate turnover of an undertaking concerned within the meaning of this Regulation shall be calculated by adding together the respective turnovers of the following:

   (a)   the undertaking concerned;

   (b)   those undertakings in which the undertaking concerned, directly or indirectly:

      (i)   owns more than half the capital or business assets, or

(ii)   has the power to exercise more than half the voting rights, or

(iii)   has the power to appoint more than half the members of the supervisory board, the administrative board or bodies legally representing the undertakings, or

(iv)   has the right to manage the undertakings' affairs;

(c)   those undertakings which have in the undertaking concerned the rights or powers listed in (b);

(d)   those undertakings in which an undertaking as referred to in (c) has the rights or powers listed in (b);

(e)   those undertakings in which two or more undertakings as referred to in (a) to (d) jointly have the rights or powers listed in (b).

5   Where undertakings concerned by the concentration jointly have the rights or powers listed in paragraph 4(b), in calculating the aggregate turnover of the undertakings concerned for the purposes of this Regulation:

(a)   no account shall be taken of the turnover resulting from the sale of products or the provision of services between the joint undertaking and each of the undertakings concerned or any other undertaking connected with any one of them, as set out in paragraph 4(b) to (e);

(b)   account shall be taken of the turnover resulting from the sale of products and the provision of services between the joint undertaking and any third undertakings. This turnover shall be apportioned equally amongst the undertakings concerned.

Article 6

Examination of the notification and initiation of proceedings

1   The Commission shall examine the notification as soon as it is received.

(a)   Where it concludes that the concentration notified does not fall within the scope of this Regulation, it shall record that finding by means of a decision.

(b)   Where it finds that the concentration notified, although falling within the scope of this Regulation, does not raise serious doubts as to its compatibility with the common market, it shall decide not to oppose it and shall declare that it is compatible with the common market.

A decision declaring a concentration compatible shall be deemed to cover restrictions directly related and necessary to the implementation of the concentration.

(c)   Without prejudice to paragraph 2, where the Commission finds that the concentration notified falls within the scope of this Regulation and raises serious doubts as to its compatibility with the common market, it shall decide to initiate proceedings. Without prejudice to Article 9, such proceedings shall be closed by means of a decision as provided for in Article 8(1) to (4), unless the undertakings concerned have demonstrated to the satisfaction of the Commission that they have abandoned the concentration.

2   Where the Commission finds that, following modification by the undertakings concerned, a notified concentration no longer raises serious doubts within the meaning of paragraph 1(c), it shall declare the concentration compatible with the common market pursuant to paragraph 1(b).

The Commission may attach to its decision under paragraph 1(b) conditions and obligations intended to ensure that the undertakings concerned comply with the commitments they have entered into vis-à-vis the Commission with a view to rendering the concentration compatible with the common market.

3   The Commission may revoke the decision it took pursuant to paragraph 1(a) or (b) where:

(a)   the decision is based on incorrect information for which one of the undertakings is responsible or where it has been obtained by deceit, or

(b)   the undertakings concerned commit a breach of an obligation attached to the decision.

4   In the cases referred to in paragraph 3, the Commission may take a decision under paragraph 1, without being bound by the time limits referred to in Article 10(1).

5   The Commission shall notify its decision to the undertakings concerned and the competent authorities of the Member States without delay.

Article 7

Suspension of concentrations

1   A concentration with a Community dimension as defined in Article 1, or which is to be examined by the Commission pursuant to Article 4(5), shall not be implemented either before its notification or until it has been declared compatible with the common market pursuant to a decision under Articles 6(1)(b), 8(1) or 8(2), or on the basis of a presumption according to Article 10(6).

2   Paragraph 1 shall not prevent the implementation of a public bid or of a series of transactions in securities including those convertible into other securities admitted to trading on a market such as a stock exchange, by which control within the meaning of Article 3 is acquired from various sellers, provided that:

(a)   the concentration is notified to the Commission pursuant to Article 4 without delay; and

(b)   the acquirer does not exercise the voting rights attached to the securities in question or does so only to maintain the full value of its investments based on a derogation granted by the Commission under paragraph 3.

3   The Commission may, on request, grant a derogation from the obligations imposed in paragraphs 1 or 2. The request to grant a derogation must be reasoned. In deciding on the request, the Commission shall take into account inter alia the effects of the suspension on one or more undertakings concerned by the concentration or on a third party and the threat to competition posed by the concentration. Such a derogation may be made subject to conditions and obligations in order to ensure conditions of effective competition. A derogation may be applied for and granted at any time, be it before notification or after the transaction.

4   The validity of any transaction carried out in contravention of paragraph 1 shall be dependent on a decision pursuant to Article 6(1)(b) or Article 8(1), (2) or (3) or on a presumption pursuant to Article 10(6).

This Article shall, however, have no effect on the validity of transactions in securities including those convertible into other securities admitted to trading on a market such as a stock exchange, unless the buyer and seller knew or ought to have known that the transaction was carried out in contravention of paragraph 1.

Article 8

Powers of decision of the Commission

1   Where the Commission finds that a notified concentration fulfils the criterion laid down in Article 2(2) and, in the cases referred to in Article 2(4), the criteria laid down in Article 81(3) of the Treaty, it shall issue a decision declaring the concentration compatible with the common market.

A decision declaring a concentration compatible shall be deemed to cover restrictions directly related and necessary to the implementation of the concentration.

2   Where the Commission finds that, following modification by the undertakings concerned, a notified concentration fulfils the criterion laid down in Article 2(2) and, in the cases referred to in Article 2(4), the criteria laid down in Article 81(3) of the Treaty, it shall issue a decision declaring the concentration compatible with the common market.

The Commission may attach to its decision conditions and obligations intended to ensure that the undertakings concerned comply with the commitments they have entered into vis-à-vis the Commission with a view to rendering the concentration compatible with the common market.

A decision declaring a concentration compatible shall be deemed to cover restrictions directly related and necessary to the implementation of the concentration.

3   Where the Commission finds that a concentration fulfils the criterion defined in Article 2(3) or, in the cases referred to in Article 2(4), does not fulfil the criteria laid down in Article 81(3) of the Treaty, it shall issue a decision declaring that the concentration is incompatible with the common market.

4   Where the Commission finds that a concentration:

(a)   has already been implemented and that concentration has been declared incompatible with the common market, or

(b)   has been implemented in contravention of a condition attached to a decision taken under paragraph 2, which has found that, in the absence of the condition, the concentration would fulfil the criterion laid down in Article 2(3) or, in the cases referred to in Article 2(4), would not fulfil the criteria laid down in Article 81(3) of the Treaty, the Commission may:

     ▸   require the undertakings concerned to dissolve the concentration, in particular through the dissolution of the merger or the disposal of all the shares or assets acquired, so as to restore the situation prevailing prior to the implementation of the concentration; in circumstances where restoration of the situation prevailing before the implementation of the concentration is not possible through dissolution of the concentration, the Commission may take any other measure appropriate to achieve such restoration as far as possible,

     ▸   order any other appropriate measure to ensure that the undertakings concerned dissolve the concentration or take other restorative measures as required in its decision.

In cases falling within point (a) of the first subparagraph, the measures referred to in that subparagraph may be imposed either in a decision pursuant to paragraph 3 or by separate decision.

5   The Commission may take interim measures appropriate to restore or maintain conditions of effective competition where a concentration:

(a)   has been implemented in contravention of Article 7, and a decision as to the compatibility of the concentration with the common market has not yet been taken;

(b)   has been implemented in contravention of a condition attached to a decision under Article 6(1)(b) or paragraph 2 of this Article;

(c)   has already been implemented and is declared incompatible with the common market.

6   The Commission may revoke the decision it has taken pursuant to paragraphs 1 or 2 where:

(a)   the declaration of compatibility is based on incorrect information for which one of the undertakings is responsible or where it has been obtained by deceit; or

(b)   the undertakings concerned commit a breach of an obligation attached to the decision.

7   The Commission may take a decision pursuant to paragraphs 1 to 3 without being bound by the time limits referred to in Article 10(3), in cases where:

(a) it finds that a concentration has been implemented

    (i) in contravention of a condition attached to a decision under Article 6(1)(b), or

    (ii) in contravention of a condition attached to a decision taken under paragraph 2 and in accordance with Article 10(2), which has found that, in the absence of the condition, the concentration would raise serious doubts as to its compatibility with the common market; or

(b) a decision has been revoked pursuant to paragraph 6.

8   The Commission shall notify its decision to the undertakings concerned and the competent authorities of the Member States without delay.

Article 9

Referral to the competent authorities of the Member States

1   The Commission may, by means of a decision notified without delay to the undertakings concerned and the competent authorities of the other Member States, refer a notified concentration to the competent authorities of the Member State concerned in the following circumstances.

2   Within 15 working days of the date of receipt of the copy of the notification, a Member State, on its own initiative or upon the invitation of the Commission, may inform the Commission, which shall inform the undertakings concerned, that:

(a) a concentration threatens to affect significantly competition in a market within that Member State, which presents all the characteristics of a distinct market, or

(b) a concentration affects competition in a market within that Member State, which presents all the characteristics of a distinct market and which does not constitute a substantial part of the common market.

3   If the Commission considers that, having regard to the market for the products or services in question and the geographical reference market within the meaning of paragraph 7, there is such a distinct market and that such a threat exists, either:

(a) it shall itself deal with the case in accordance with this Regulation; or

(b) it shall refer the whole or part of the case to the competent authorities of the Member State concerned with a view to the application of that State's national competition law.

If, however, the Commission considers that such a distinct market or threat does not exist, it shall adopt a decision to that effect which it shall address to the Member State concerned, and shall itself deal with the case in accordance with this Regulation.

In cases where a Member State informs the Commission pursuant to paragraph 2(b) that a concentration affects competition in a distinct market within its territory that does not form a substantial part of the common market, the Commission shall refer the whole or part of the case relating to the distinct market concerned, if it considers that such a distinct market is affected.

4   A decision to refer or not to refer pursuant to paragraph 3 shall be taken:

(a) as a general rule within the period provided for in Article 10(1), second subparagraph, where the Commission, pursuant to Article 6(1)(b), has not initiated proceedings; or

(b) within 65 working days at most of the notification of the concentration concerned where the Commission has initiated proceedings under Article 6(1)(c), without taking the preparatory steps in order to adopt the necessary measures under Article 8(2), (3) or (4) to maintain or restore effective competition on the market concerned.

5   If within the 65 working days referred to in paragraph 4(b) the Commission, despite a reminder from the Member State concerned, has not taken a decision on referral in accordance with paragraph 3 nor has taken the preparatory steps referred to in paragraph 4(b), it shall be deemed to have taken a decision to refer the case to the Member State concerned in accordance with paragraph 3(b).

6   The competent authority of the Member State concerned shall decide upon the case without undue delay.

Within 45 working days after the Commission's referral, the competent authority of the Member State concerned shall inform the undertakings concerned of the result of the preliminary competition assessment and what further action, if any, it proposes to take. The Member State concerned may exceptionally suspend this time limit where necessary information has not been provided to it by the undertakings concerned as provided for by its national competition law.

Where a notification is requested under national law, the period of 45 working days shall begin on the working day following that of the receipt of a complete notification by the competent authority of that Member State.

7   The geographical reference market shall consist of the area in which the undertakings concerned are involved in the supply and demand of products or services, in which the conditions of competition are sufficiently homogeneous and which can be distinguished from neighbouring areas because, in particular, conditions of competition are appreciably different in those areas. This assessment should take account in particular of the nature and characteristics of the products or services concerned, of the existence of entry barriers or of consumer preferences, of appreciable differences of the undertakings' market shares between the area concerned and neighbouring areas or of substantial price differences.

8   In applying the provisions of this Article, the Member State concerned may take only the measures strictly necessary to safeguard or restore effective competition on the market concerned.

9   In accordance with the relevant provisions of the Treaty, any Member State may appeal to the Court of Justice, and in particular request the application of Article 243 of the Treaty, for the purpose of applying its national competition law.

Article 10

Time limits for initiating proceedings and for decisions

1   Without prejudice to Article 6(4), the decisions referred to in Article 6(1) shall be taken within 25 working days at most. That period shall begin on the working day following that of the receipt of a notification or, if the information to be supplied with the notification is incomplete, on the working day following that of the receipt of the complete information.

That period shall be increased to 35 working days where the Commission receives a request from a Member State in accordance with Article 9(2)or where, the undertakings concerned offer commitments pursuant to Article 6(2) with a view to rendering the concentration compatible with the common market.

2   Decisions pursuant to Article 8(1) or (2) concerning notified concentrations shall be taken as soon as it appears that the serious doubts referred to in Article 6(1)(c) have been removed, particularly as a result of modifications made by the undertakings concerned, and at the latest by the time limit laid down in paragraph 3.

3   Without prejudice to Article 8(7), decisions pursuant to Article 8(1) to (3) concerning notified concentrations shall be taken within not more than 90 working days of the date on which the proceedings are initiated. That period shall be increased to 105 working days where the undertakings concerned offer commitments pursuant to Article 8(2), second subparagraph, with a view to rendering the concentration compatible with the common market, unless these commitments have been offered less than 55 working days after the initiation of proceedings.

The periods set by the first subparagraph shall likewise be extended if the notifying parties make a request to that effect not later than 15 working days after the initiation of proceedings pursuant to Article 6(1)(c). The notifying parties may make only one such request. Likewise, at any time following the initiation of proceedings, the periods set by the first subparagraph may be extended by the Commission with the agreement of the notifying parties. The total duration of any extension or extensions effected pursuant to this subparagraph shall not exceed 20 working days.

4   The periods set by paragraphs 1 and 3 shall exceptionally be suspended where, owing to circumstances for which one of the undertakings involved in the concentration is responsible, the Commission has had to request information by decision pursuant to Article 11 or to order an inspection by decision pursuant to Article 13.

The first subparagraph shall also apply to the period referred to in Article 9(4)(b).

5   Where the Court of Justice gives a judgment which annuls the whole or part of a Commission decision which is subject to a time limit set by this Article, the concentration shall be re-examined by the Commission with a view to adopting a decision pursuant to Article 6(1).

The concentration shall be re-examined in the light of current market conditions.

The notifying parties shall submit a new notification or supplement the original notification, without delay, where the original notification becomes incomplete by reason of intervening changes in market conditions or in the information provided. Where there are no such changes, the parties shall certify this fact without delay.

The periods laid down in paragraph 1 shall start on the working day following that of the receipt of complete information in a new notification, a supplemented notification, or a certification within the meaning of the third subparagraph.

The second and third subparagraphs shall also apply in the cases referred to in Article 6(4) and Article 8(7).

6   Where the Commission has not taken a decision in accordance with Article 6(1)(b), (c), 8(1), (2) or (3) within the time limits set in paragraphs 1 and 3 respectively, the concentration shall be deemed to have been declared compatible with the common market, without prejudice to Article 9.

Article 11

Requests for information

1   In order to carry out the duties assigned to it by this Regulation, the Commission may, by simple request or by decision, require the persons referred to in Article 3(1)(b), as well as undertakings and associations of undertakings, to provide all necessary information.

2   When sending a simple request for information to a person, an undertaking or an association of undertakings, the Commission shall state the legal basis and the purpose of the request, specify what information is required and fix the time limit within which the information is to be provided, as well as the penalties provided for in Article 14 for supplying incorrect or misleading information.

3   Where the Commission requires a person, an undertaking or an association of undertakings to supply information by decision, it shall state the legal basis and the purpose of the request, specify what information is required and fix the time limit within which it is to be provided. It shall also indicate the penalties provided for in Article 14 and indicate or impose the penalties provided for in Article 15. It shall further indicate the right to have the decision reviewed by the Court of Justice.

4   The owners of the undertakings or their representatives and, in the case of legal persons, companies or firms, or associations having no legal personality, the persons authorised to represent them by law or by

their constitution, shall supply the information requested on behalf of the undertaking concerned. Persons duly authorised to act may supply the information on behalf of their clients. The latter shall remain fully responsible if the information supplied is incomplete, incorrect or misleading.

5   The Commission shall without delay forward a copy of any decision taken pursuant to paragraph 3 to the competent authorities of the Member State in whose territory the residence of the person or the seat of the undertaking or association of undertakings is situated, and to the competent authority of the Member State whose territory is affected. At the specific request of the competent authority of a Member State, the Commission shall also forward to that authority copies of simple requests for information relating to a notified concentration.

6   At the request of the Commission, the governments and competent authorities of the Member States shall provide the Commission with all necessary information to carry out the duties assigned to it by this Regulation.

7   In order to carry out the duties assigned to it by this Regulation, the Commission may interview any natural or legal person who consents to be interviewed for the purpose of collecting information relating to the subject matter of an investigation. At the beginning of the interview, which may be conducted by telephone or other electronic means, the Commission shall state the legal basis and the purpose of the interview.

Where an interview is not conducted on the premises of the Commission or by telephone or other electronic means, the Commission shall inform in advance the competent authority of the Member State in whose territory the interview takes place. If the competent authority of that Member State so requests, officials of that authority may assist the officials and other persons authorised by the Commission to conduct the interview.

Article 12

Inspections by the authorities of the Member States

1   At the request of the Commission, the competent authorities of the Member States shall undertake the inspections which the Commission considers to be necessary under Article 13(1), or which it has ordered by decision pursuant to Article 13(4). The officials of the competent authorities of the Member States who are responsible for conducting these inspections as well as those authorised or appointed by them shall exercise their powers in accordance with their national law.

2   If so requested by the Commission or by the competent authority of the Member State within whose territory the inspection is to be conducted, officials and other accompanying persons authorised by the Commission may assist the officials of the authority concerned.

Article 13

The Commission's powers of inspection

1   In order to carry out the duties assigned to it by this Regulation, the Commission may conduct all necessary inspections of undertakings and associations of undertakings.

2   The officials and other accompanying persons authorised by the Commission to conduct an inspection shall have the power:

   (a)   to enter any premises, land and means of transport of undertakings and associations of undertakings;

   (b)   to examine the books and other records related to the business, irrespective of the medium on which they are stored;

(c)   to take or obtain in any form copies of or extracts from such books or records;

(d)   to seal any business premises and books or records for the period and to the extent necessary for the inspection;

(e)   to ask any representative or member of staff of the undertaking or association of undertakings for explanations on facts or documents relating to the subject matter and purpose of the inspection and to record the answers.

3   Officials and other accompanying persons authorised by the Commission to conduct an inspection shall exercise their powers upon production of a written authorisation specifying the subject matter and purpose of the inspection and the penalties provided for in Article 14, in the production of the required books or other records related to the business which is incomplete or where answers to questions asked under paragraph 2 of this Article are incorrect or misleading. In good time before the inspection, the Commission shall give notice of the inspection to the competent authority of the Member State in whose territory the inspection is to be conducted.

4   Undertakings and associations of undertakings are required to submit to inspections ordered by decision of the Commission. The decision shall specify the subject matter and purpose of the inspection, appoint the date on which it is to begin and indicate the penalties provided for in Articles 14 and 15 and the right to have the decision reviewed by the Court of Justice. The Commission shall take such decisions after consulting the competent authority of the Member State in whose territory the inspection is to be conducted.

5   Officials of, and those authorised or appointed by, the competent authority of the Member State in whose territory the inspection is to be conducted shall, at the request of that authority or of the Commission, actively assist the officials and other accompanying persons authorised by the Commission. To this end, they shall enjoy the powers specified in paragraph 2.

6   Where the officials and other accompanying persons authorised by the Commission find that an undertaking opposes an inspection, including the sealing of business premises, books or records, ordered pursuant to this Article, the Member State concerned shall afford them the necessary assistance, requesting where appropriate the assistance of the police or of an equivalent enforcement authority, so as to enable them to conduct their inspection.

7   If the assistance provided for in paragraph 6 requires authorisation from a judicial authority according to national rules, such authorisation shall be applied for. Such authorisation may also be applied for as a precautionary measure.

8   Where authorisation as referred to in paragraph 7 is applied for, the national judicial authority shall ensure that the Commission decision is authentic and that the coercive measures envisaged are neither arbitrary nor excessive having regard to the subject matter of the inspection. In its control of proportionality of the coercive measures, the national judicial authority may ask the Commission, directly or through the competent authority of that Member State, for detailed explanations relating to the subject matter of the inspection. However, the national judicial authority may not call into question the necessity for the inspection nor demand that it be provided with the information in the Commission's file. The lawfulness of the Commission's decision shall be subject to review only by the Court of Justice.

Article 14

Fines

1   The Commission may by decision impose on the persons referred to in Article 3(1)b, undertakings or associations of undertakings, fines not exceeding 1 % of the aggregate turnover of the undertaking or association of undertakings concerned within the meaning of Article 5 where, intentionally or negligently:

(a)   they supply incorrect or misleading information in a submission, certification, notification or supplement thereto, pursuant to Article 4, Article 10(5) or Article 22(3);

(b)   they supply incorrect or misleading information in response to a request made pursuant to Article 11(2);

(c)   in response to a request made by decision adopted pursuant to Article 11(3), they supply incorrect, incomplete or misleading information or do not supply information within the required time limit;

(d)   they produce the required books or other records related to the business in incomplete form during inspections under Article 13, or refuse to submit to an inspection ordered by decision taken pursuant to Article 13(4);

(e)   in response to a question asked in accordance with Article 13(2)(e),

  ▸   they give an incorrect or misleading answer,

  ▸   they fail to rectify within a time limit set by the Commission an incorrect, incomplete or misleading answer given by a member of staff, or

  ▸   they fail or refuse to provide a complete answer on facts relating to the subject matter and purpose of an inspection ordered by a decision adopted pursuant to Article 13(4);

(f)   seals affixed by officials or other accompanying persons authorised by the Commission in accordance with Article 13(2)(d) have been broken.

2   The Commission may by decision impose fines not exceeding 10 % of the aggregate turnover of the undertaking concerned within the meaning of Article 5 on the persons referred to in Article 3(1)b or the undertakings concerned where, either intentionally or negligently, they:

(a)   fail to notify a concentration in accordance with Articles 4 or 22(3) prior to its implementation, unless they are expressly authorised to do so by Article 7(2) or by a decision taken pursuant to Article 7(3);

(b)   implement a concentration in breach of Article 7;

(c)   implement a concentration declared incompatible with the common market by decision pursuant to Article 8(3) or do not comply with any measure ordered by decision pursuant to Article 8(4) or (5);

(d)   fail to comply with a condition or an obligation imposed by decision pursuant to Articles 6(1)(b), Article 7(3) or Article 8(2), second subparagraph.

3   In fixing the amount of the fine, regard shall be had to the nature, gravity and duration of the infringement.

4   Decisions taken pursuant to paragraphs 1, 2 and 3 shall not be of a criminal law nature.

Article 15

Periodic penalty payments

1   The Commission may by decision impose on the persons referred to in Article 3(1)b, undertakings or associations of undertakings, periodic penalty payments not exceeding 5 % of the average daily aggregate turnover of the undertaking or association of undertakings concerned within the meaning of Article 5 for each working day of delay, calculated from the date set in the decision, in order to compel them:

(a)   to supply complete and correct information which it has requested by decision taken pursuant to Article 11(3);

(b)   to submit to an inspection which it has ordered by decision taken pursuant to Article 13(4);

(c)   to comply with an obligation imposed by decision pursuant to Article 6(1)(b), Article 7(3) or Article 8(2), second subparagraph; or;

(d)   to comply with any measures ordered by decision pursuant to Article 8(4) or (5).

2   Where the persons referred to in Article 3(1)(b), undertakings or associations of undertakings have satisfied the obligation which the periodic penalty payment was intended to enforce, the Commission may fix the definitive amount of the periodic penalty payments at a figure lower than that which would arise under the original decision.

Article 16

Review by the Court of Justice

The Court of Justice shall have unlimited jurisdiction within the meaning of Article 229 of the Treaty to review decisions whereby the Commission has fixed a fine or periodic penalty payments; it may cancel, reduce or increase the fine or periodic penalty payment imposed.

Article 17

Professional secrecy

1   Information acquired as a result of the application of this Regulation shall be used only for the purposes of the relevant request, investigation or hearing.

2   Without prejudice to Article 4(3), Articles 18 and 20, the Commission and the competent authorities of the Member States, their officials and other servants and other persons working under the supervision of these authorities as well as officials and civil servants of other authorities of the Member States shall not disclose information they have acquired through the application of this Regulation of the kind covered by the obligation of professional secrecy.

3   Paragraphs 1 and 2 shall not prevent publication of general information or of surveys which do not contain information relating to particular undertakings or associations of undertakings.

Article 18

Hearing of the parties and of third persons

1   Before taking any decision provided for in Article 6(3), Article 7(3), Article 8(2) to (6), and Articles 14 and 15, the Commission shall give the persons, undertakings and associations of undertakings concerned the opportunity, at every stage of the procedure up to the consultation of the Advisory Committee, of making known their views on the objections against them.

2   By way of derogation from paragraph 1, a decision pursuant to Articles 7(3) and 8(5) may be taken provisionally, without the persons, undertakings or associations of undertakings concerned being given the opportunity to make known their views beforehand, provided that the Commission gives them that opportunity as soon as possible after having taken its decision.

3   The Commission shall base its decision only on objections on which the parties have been able to submit their observations. The rights of the defence shall be fully respected in the proceedings. Access to the file shall be open at least to the parties directly involved, subject to the legitimate interest of undertakings in the protection of their business secrets.

4   In so far as the Commission or the competent authorities of the Member States deem it necessary, they may also hear other natural or legal persons. Natural or legal persons showing a sufficient interest and especially members of the administrative or management bodies of the undertakings concerned or the recognised representatives of their employees shall be entitled, upon application, to be heard.

Article 19

Liaison with the authorities of the Member States

1 The Commission shall transmit to the competent authorities of the Member States copies of notifications within three working days and, as soon as possible, copies of the most important documents lodged with or issued by the Commission pursuant to this Regulation. Such documents shall include commitments offered by the undertakings concerned vis-à-vis the Commission with a view to rendering the concentration compatible with the common market pursuant to Article 6(2) or Article 8(2), second subparagraph.

2 The Commission shall carry out the procedures set out in this Regulation in close and constant liaison with the competent authorities of the Member States, which may express their views upon those procedures. For the purposes of Article 9 it shall obtain information from the competent authority of the Member State as referred to in paragraph 2 of that Article and give it the opportunity to make known its views at every stage of the procedure up to the adoption of a decision pursuant to paragraph 3 of that Article; to that end it shall give it access to the file.

3 An Advisory Committee on concentrations shall be consulted before any decision is taken pursuant to Article 8(1) to (6), Articles 14 or 15 with the exception of provisional decisions taken in accordance with Article 18(2).

4 The Advisory Committee shall consist of representatives of the competent authorities of the Member States. Each Member State shall appoint one or two representatives; if unable to attend, they may be replaced by other representatives. At least one of the representatives of a Member State shall be competent in matters of restrictive practices and dominant positions.

5 Consultation shall take place at a joint meeting convened at the invitation of and chaired by the Commission. A summary of the case, together with an indication of the most important documents and a preliminary draft of the decision to be taken for each case considered, shall be sent with the invitation. The meeting shall take place not less than 10 working days after the invitation has been sent. The Commission may in exceptional cases shorten that period as appropriate in order to avoid serious harm to one or more of the undertakings concerned by a concentration.

6 The Advisory Committee shall deliver an opinion on the Commission's draft decision, if necessary by taking a vote. The Advisory Committee may deliver an opinion even if some members are absent and unrepresented. The opinion shall be delivered in writing and appended to the draft decision. The Commission shall take the utmost account of the opinion delivered by the Committee. It shall inform the Committee of the manner in which its opinion has been taken into account.

7 The Commission shall communicate the opinion of the Advisory Committee, together with the decision, to the addressees of the decision. It shall make the opinion public together with the decision, having regard to the legitimate interest of undertakings in the protection of their business secrets.

Article 20

Publication of decisions

1 The Commission shall publish the decisions which it takes pursuant to Article 8(1) to (6), Articles 14 and 15 with the exception of provisional decisions taken in accordance with Article 18(2) together with the opinion of the Advisory Committee in the Official Journal of the European Union.

2 The publication shall state the names of the parties and the main content of the decision; it shall have regard to the legitimate interest of undertakings in the protection of their business secrets.

Article 21

Application of the Regulation and jurisdiction

1. This Regulation alone shall apply to concentrations as defined in Article 3, and Council Regulations (EC) No 1/2003(8), (EEC) No 1017/68(9), (EEC) No 4056/86(10) and (EEC) No 3975/87(11) shall not apply, except in relation to joint ventures that do not have a Community dimension and which have as their object or effect the coordination of the competitive behaviour of undertakings that remain independent.

2. Subject to review by the Court of Justice, the Commission shall have sole jurisdiction to take the decisions provided for in this Regulation.

3. No Member State shall apply its national legislation on competition to any concentration that has a Community dimension.

   The first subparagraph shall be without prejudice to any Member State's power to carry out any enquiries necessary for the application of Articles 4(4), 9(2) or after referral, pursuant to Article 9(3), first subparagraph, indent (b), or Article 9(5), to take the measures strictly necessary for the application of Article 9(8).

4. Notwithstanding paragraphs 2 and 3, Member States may take appropriate measures to protect legitimate interests other than those taken into consideration by this Regulation and compatible with the general principles and other provisions of Community law.

   Public security, plurality of the media and prudential rules shall be regarded as legitimate interests within the meaning of the first subparagraph.

   Any other public interest must be communicated to the Commission by the Member State concerned and shall be recognised by the Commission after an assessment of its compatibility with the general principles and other provisions of Community law before the measures referred to above may be taken. The Commission shall inform the Member State concerned of its decision within 25 working days of that communication.

Article 22

Referral to the Commission

1. One or more Member States may request the Commission to examine any concentration as defined in Article 3 that does not have a Community dimension within the meaning of Article 1 but affects trade between Member States and threatens to significantly affect competition within the territory of the Member State or States making the request.

   Such a request shall be made at most within 15 working days of the date on which the concentration was notified, or if no notification is required, otherwise made known to the Member State concerned.

2. The Commission shall inform the competent authorities of the Member States and the undertakings concerned of any request received pursuant to paragraph 1 without delay.

   Any other Member State shall have the right to join the initial request within a period of 15 working days of being informed by the Commission of the initial request.

   All national time limits relating to the concentration shall be suspended until, in accordance with the procedure set out in this Article, it has been decided where the concentration shall be examined. As soon as a Member State has informed the Commission and the undertakings concerned that it does not wish to join the request, the suspension of its national time limits shall end.

3   The Commission may, at the latest 10 working days after the expiry of the period set in paragraph 2, decide to examine, the concentration where it considers that it affects trade between Member States and threatens to significantly affect competition within the territory of the Member State or States making the request. If the Commission does not take a decision within this period, it shall be deemed to have adopted a decision to examine the concentration in accordance with the request.

The Commission shall inform all Member States and the undertakings concerned of its decision. It may request the submission of a notification pursuant to Article 4.

The Member State or States having made the request shall no longer apply their national legislation on competition to the concentration.

4   Article 2, Article 4(2) to (3), Articles 5, 6, and 8 to 21 shall apply where the Commission examines a concentration pursuant to paragraph 3. Article 7 shall apply to the extent that the concentration has not been implemented on the date on which the Commission informs the undertakings concerned that a request has been made.

Where a notification pursuant to Article 4 is not required, the period set in Article 10(1) within which proceedings may be initiated shall begin on the working day following that on which the Commission informs the undertakings concerned that it has decided to examine the concentration pursuant to paragraph 3.

5   The Commission may inform one or several Member States that it considers a concentration fulfils the criteria in paragraph 1. In such cases, the Commission may invite that Member State or those Member States to make a request pursuant to paragraph 1.

Article 23

Implementing provisions

1   The Commission shall have the power to lay down in accordance with the procedure referred to in paragraph 2:

(a)   implementing provisions concerning the form, content and other details of notifications and submissions pursuant to Article 4;

(b)   implementing provisions concerning time limits pursuant to Article 4(4), (5) Articles 7, 9, 10 and 22;

(c)   the procedure and time limits for the submission and implementation of commitments pursuant to Article 6(2) and Article 8(2);

(d)   implementing provisions concerning hearings pursuant to Article 18.

2   The Commission shall be assisted by an Advisory Committee, composed of representatives of the Member States.

(a)   Before publishing draft implementing provisions and before adopting such provisions, the Commission shall consult the Advisory Committee.

(b)   Consultation shall take place at a meeting convened at the invitation of and chaired by the Commission. A draft of the implementing provisions to be taken shall be sent with the invitation. The meeting shall take place not less than 10 working days after the invitation has been sent.

(c)   The Advisory Committee shall deliver an opinion on the draft implementing provisions, if necessary by taking a vote. The Commission shall take the utmost account of the opinion delivered by the Committee.

Article 24

Relations with third countries

1   The Member States shall inform the Commission of any general difficulties encountered by their undertakings with concentrations as defined in Article 3 in a third country.

2   Initially not more than one year after the entry into force of this Regulation and, thereafter periodically, the Commission shall draw up a report examining the treatment accorded to undertakings having their seat or their principal fields of activity in the Community, in the terms referred to in paragraphs 3 and 4, as regards concentrations in third countries. The Commission shall submit those reports to the Council, together with any recommendations.

3   Whenever it appears to the Commission, either on the basis of the reports referred to in paragraph 2 or on the basis of other information, that a third country does not grant undertakings having their seat or their principal fields of activity in the Community, treatment comparable to that granted by the Community to undertakings from that country, the Commission may submit proposals to the Council for an appropriate mandate for negotiation with a view to obtaining comparable treatment for undertakings having their seat or their principal fields of activity in the Community.

4   Measures taken under this Article shall comply with the obligations of the Community or of the Member States, without prejudice to Article 307 of the Treaty, under international agreements, whether bilateral or multilateral.

Article 25

Repeal

1   Without prejudice to Article 26(2), Regulations (EEC) No 4064/89 and (EC) No 1310/97 shall be repealed with effect from 1 May 2004.

2   References to the repealed Regulations shall be construed as references to this Regulation and shall be read in accordance with the correlation table in the Annex.

Article 26

Entry into force and transitional provisions

1   This Regulation shall enter into force on the 20th day following that of its publication in the Official Journal of the European Union.

    It shall apply from 1 May 2004.

2   Regulation (EEC) No 4064/89 shall continue to apply to any concentration which was the subject of an agreement or announcement or where control was acquired within the meaning of Article 4(1) of that Regulation before the date of application of this Regulation, subject, in particular, to the provisions governing applicability set out in Article 25(2) and (3) of Regulation (EEC) No 4064/89 and Article 2 of Regulation (EEC) No 1310/97.

3   As regards concentrations to which this Regulation applies by virtue of accession, the date of accession shall be substituted for the date of application of this Regulation.

Commission Regulation (EU) No 330/2010

Article 1

Definitions

1   For the purposes of this Regulation, the following definitions shall apply:

(a)   "vertical agreement" means an agreement or concerted practice entered into between two or more undertakings each of which operates, for the purposes of the agreement or the concerted practice, at a different level of the production or distribution chain, and relating to the conditions under which the parties may purchase, sell or resell certain goods or services;

(b)   "vertical restraint" means a restriction of competition in a vertical agreement falling within the scope of Article 101(1) of the Treaty;

(c)   "competing undertaking" means an actual or potential competitor; "actual competitor" means an undertaking that is active on the same relevant market; "potential competitor" means an undertaking that, in the absence of the vertical agreement, would, on realistic grounds and not just as a mere theoretical possibility, in case of a small but permanent increase in relative prices be likely to undertake, within a short period of time, the necessary additional investments or other necessary switching costs to enter the relevant market;

(d)   "non-compete obligation" means any direct or indirect obligation causing the buyer not to manufacture, purchase, sell or resell goods or services which compete with the contract goods or services, or any direct or indirect obligation on the buyer to purchase from the supplier or from another undertaking designated by the supplier more than 80 % of the buyer's total purchases of the contract goods or services and their substitutes on the relevant market, calculated on the basis of the value or, where such is standard industry practice, the volume of its purchases in the preceding calendar year;

(e)   "selective distribution system" means a distribution system where the supplier undertakes to sell the contract goods or services, either directly or indirectly, only to distributors selected on the basis of specified criteria and where these distributors undertake not to sell such goods or services to unauthorised distributors within the territory reserved by the supplier to operate that system;

(f)   "intellectual property rights" includes industrial property rights, know how, copyright and neighbouring rights;

(g)   "know-how" means a package of non-patented practical information, resulting from experience and testing by the supplier, which is secret, substantial and identified: in this context, "secret" means that the know-how is not generally known or easily accessible; "substantial" means that the know-how is significant and useful to the buyer for the use, sale or resale of the contract goods or services; "identified" means that the know-how is described in a sufficiently comprehensive manner so as to make it possible to verify that it fulfils the criteria of secrecy and substantiality;

(h)   "buyer" includes an undertaking which, under an agreement falling within Article 101(1) of the Treaty, sells goods or services on behalf of another undertaking;

(i)   "customer of the buyer" means an undertaking not party to the agreement which purchases the contract goods or services from a buyer which is party to the agreement.

2   For the purposes of this Regulation, the terms "undertaking", "supplier" and "buyer" shall include their respective connected undertakings.

"Connected undertakings" means:

(a)   undertakings in which a party to the agreement, directly or indirectly:

    (i)   has the power to exercise more than half the voting rights, or

    (ii)   has the power to appoint more than half the members of the supervisory board, board of management or bodies legally representing the undertaking, or

    (iii)   has the right to manage the undertaking's affairs;

(b)   undertakings which directly or indirectly have, over a party to the agreement, the rights or powers listed in point (a);

(c)   undertakings in which an undertaking referred to in point (b) has, directly or indirectly, the rights or powers listed in point (a);

(d)   undertakings in which a party to the agreement together with one or more of the undertakings referred to in points (a), (b) or (c), or in which two or more of the latter undertakings, jointly have the rights or powers listed in point (a);

(e)   undertakings in which the rights or the powers listed in point (a) are jointly held by:

   (i)   parties to the agreement or their respective connected undertakings referred to in points (a) to (d), or

   (ii)   one or more of the parties to the agreement or one or more of their connected undertakings referred to in points (a) to (d) and one or more third parties.

Article 2

Exemption

1   Pursuant to Article 101(3) of the Treaty and subject to the provisions of this Regulation, it is hereby declared that Article 101(1) of the Treaty shall not apply to vertical agreements.

This exemption shall apply to the extent that such agreements contain vertical restraints.

2   The exemption provided for in paragraph 1 shall apply to vertical agreements entered into between an association of undertakings and its members, or between such an association and its suppliers, only if all its members are retailers of goods and if no individual member of the association, together with its connected undertakings, has a total annual turnover exceeding EUR 50 million. Vertical agreements entered into by such associations shall be covered by this Regulation without prejudice to the application of Article 101 of the Treaty to horizontal agreements concluded between the members of the association or decisions adopted by the association.

3   The exemption provided for in paragraph 1 shall apply to vertical agreements con+taining provisions which relate to the assignment to the buyer or use by the buyer of intellectual property rights, provided that those provisions do not constitute the primary object of such agreements and are directly related to the use, sale or resale of goods or services by the buyer or its customers. The exemption applies on condition that, in relation to the contract goods or services, those provisions do not contain restrictions of competition having the same object as vertical restraints which are not exempted under this Regulation.

4   The exemption provided for in paragraph 1 shall not apply to vertical agreements entered into between competing undertakings. However, it shall apply where competing undertakings enter into a non-reciprocal vertical agreement and:

(a)   the supplier is a manufacturer and a distributor of goods, while the buyer is a distributor and not a competing undertaking at the manufacturing level; or

(b)   the supplier is a provider of services at several levels of trade, while the buyer provides its goods or services at the retail level and is not a competing undertaking at the level of trade where it purchases the contract services.

5   This Regulation shall not apply to vertical agreements the subject matter of which falls within the scope of any other block exemption regulation, unless otherwise provided for in such a regulation.

Article 3

Market share threshold

1   The exemption provided for in Article 2 shall apply on condition that the market share held by the supplier does not exceed 30 % of the relevant market on which it sells the contract goods or services and the market share held by the buyer does not exceed 30 % of the relevant market on which it purchases the contract goods or services.

2   For the purposes of paragraph 1, where in a multi party agreement an undertaking buys the contract goods or services from one undertaking party to the agreement and sells the contract goods or services to another undertaking party to the agreement, the market share of the first undertaking must respect the market share threshold provided for in that paragraph both as a buyer and a supplier in order for the exemption provided for in Article 2 to apply.

Article 4

Restrictions that remove the benefit of the block exemption — hardcore restrictions

The exemption provided for in Article 2 shall not apply to vertical agreements which, directly or indirectly, in isolation or in combination with other factors under the control of the parties, have as their object:

(a)   the restriction of the buyer's ability to determine its sale price, without prejudice to the possibility of the supplier to impose a maximum sale price or recommend a sale price, provided that they do not amount to a fixed or minimum sale price as a result of pressure from, or incentives offered by, any of the parties;

(b)   he restriction of the territory into which, or of the customers to whom, a buyer party to the agreement, without prejudice to a restriction on its place of establishment, may sell the contract goods or services, except:

   (i)   the restriction of active sales into the exclusive territory or to an exclusive customer group reserved to the supplier or allocated by the supplier to another buyer, where such a restriction does not limit sales by the customers of the buyer,

   (ii)   the restriction of sales to end users by a buyer operating at the wholesale level of trade,

   (iii)   the restriction of sales by the members of a selective distribution system to unauthorised distributors within the territory reserved by the supplier to operate that system, and

   (iv)   the restriction of the buyer's ability to sell components, supplied for the purposes of incorporation, to customers who would use them to manufacture the same type of goods as those produced by the supplier;

(c)   the restriction of active or passive sales to end users by members of a selective distribution system operating at the retail level of trade, without prejudice to the possibility of prohibiting a member of the system from operating out of an unauthorised place of establishment;

(d)   the restriction of cross-supplies between distributors within a selective distribution system, including between distributors operating at different level of trade;

(e) the restriction, agreed between a supplier of components and a buyer who incorporates those components, of the supplier's ability to sell the components as spare parts to end-users or to repairers or other service providers not entrusted by the buyer with the repair or servicing of its goods.

Article 5

Excluded restrictions

1 The exemption provided for in Article 2 shall not apply to the following obligations contained in vertical agreements:

(a) any direct or indirect non-compete obligation, the duration of which is indefinite or exceeds five years;

(b) any direct or indirect obligation causing the buyer, after termination of the agreement, not to manufacture, purchase, sell or resell goods or services;

(c) any direct or indirect obligation causing the members of a selective distribution system not to sell the brands of particular competing suppliers.

For the purposes of point (a) of the first subparagraph, a non-compete obligation which is tacitly renewable beyond a period of five years shall be deemed to have been concluded for an indefinite duration.

2 By way of derogation from paragraph 1(a), the time limitation of five years shall not apply where the contract goods or services are sold by the buyer from premises and land owned by the supplier or leased by the supplier from third parties not connected with the buyer, provided that the duration of the non-compete obligation does not exceed the period of occupancy of the premises and land by the buyer.

3 By way of derogation from paragraph 1(b), the exemption provided for in Article 2 shall apply to any direct or indirect obligation causing the buyer, after termination of the agreement, not to manufacture, purchase, sell or resell goods or services where the following conditions are fulfilled:

(a) the obligation relates to goods or services which compete with the contract goods or services;

(b) the obligation is limited to the premises and land from which the buyer has operated during the contract period;

(c) the obligation is indispensable to protect know-how transferred by the supplier to the buyer;

(d) the duration of the obligation is limited to a period of one year after termination of the agreement.

Paragraph 1(b) is without prejudice to the possibility of imposing a restriction which is unlimited in time on the use and disclosure of know-how which has not entered the public domain.

Article 6

Non-application of this Regulation

Pursuant to Article 1a of Regulation No 19/65/EEC, the Commission may by regulation declare that, where parallel networks of similar vertical restraints cover more than 50 % of a relevant market, this Regulation shall not apply to vertical agreements containing specific restraints relating to that market.

Article 7

Application of the market share threshold

For the purposes of applying the market share thresholds provided for in Article 3 the following rules shall apply:

(a) the market share of the supplier shall be calculated on the basis of market sales value data and the market share of the buyer shall be calculated on the basis of market purchase value data. If market sales value or market purchase value data are not available, estimates based on other reliable market information, including market sales and purchase volumes, may be used to establish the market share of the undertaking concerned;

(b) the market shares shall be calculated on the basis of data relating to the preceding calendar year;

(c) the market share of the supplier shall include any goods or services supplied to vertically integrated distributors for the purposes of sale;

(d) if a market share is initially not more than 30 % but subsequently rises above that level without exceeding 35 %, the exemption provided for in Article 2 shall continue to apply for a period of two consecutive calendar years following the year in which the 30 % market share threshold was first exceeded;

(e) if a market share is initially not more than 30 % but subsequently rises above 35 %, the exemption provided for in Article 2 shall continue to apply for one calendar year following the year in which the level of 35 % was first exceeded;

(f) the benefit of points (d) and (e) may not be combined so as to exceed a period of two calendar years;

(g) the market share held by the undertakings referred to in point (e) of the second subparagraph of Article 1(2) shall be apportioned equally to each undertaking having the rights or the powers listed in point (a) of the second subparagraph of Article 1(2).

Article 8

Application of the turnover threshold

1 For the purpose of calculating total annual turnover within the meaning of Article 2(2), the turnover achieved during the previous financial year by the relevant party to the vertical agreement and the turnover achieved by its connected undertakings in respect of all goods and services, excluding all taxes and other duties, shall be added together. For this purpose, no account shall be taken of dealings between the party to the vertical agreement and its connected undertakings or between its connected undertakings.

2 The exemption provided for in Article 2 shall remain applicable where, for any period of two consecutive financial years, the total annual turnover threshold is exceeded by no more than 10 %.

Article 9

Transitional period

The prohibition laid down in Article 101(1) of the Treaty shall not apply during the period from 1 June 2010 to 31 May 2011 in respect of agreements already in force on 31 May 2010 which do not satisfy the conditions for exemption provided for in this Regulation but which, on 31 May 2010, satisfied the conditions for exemption provided for in Regulation (EC) No 2790/1999.

SECTION 3 – FREE MOVEMENT OF WORKERS

REGULATION (EEC) No 1612/68 OF THE COUNCIL of 15 October 1968 on freedom of movement for workers within the Community

PART I EMPLOYMENT AND WORKERS' FAMILIES'

TITLE I Eligibility for employment

Article 1

1   Any national of a Member State, shall, irrespective of his place of residence, have the right to take up an activity as an employed person, and to pursue such activity, within the territory of another Member State in accordance with the provisions laid down by law, regulation or administrative action governing the employment of nationals of that State.

2   He shall, in particular, have the right to take up available employment in the territory of another Member State with the same priority as nationals of that State.

Article 2

Any national of a Member State and any employer pursuing an activity in the territory of a Member State may exchange their applications for and offers of employment, and may conclude and perform contracts of employment in accordance with the provisions in force laid down by law, regulation or administrative action, without any discrimination resulting therefrom.

Article 3

1   Under this Regulation, provisions laid down by law, regulation or administrative action or administrative practices of a Member State shall not apply: - where they limit application for and offers of employment, or the right of foreign nationals to take up and pursue employment or subject these to conditions not applicable in respect of their own nationals ; or

▸   where, though applicable irrespective of nationality, their exclusive or principal aim or effect is to keep nationals of other Member States away from the employment offered.

This provision shall not apply to conditions relating to linguistic knowledge required by reason of the nature of the post to be filled.

2   There shall be included in particular among the provisions or practices of a Member State referred to in the first subparagraph of paragraph 1 those which:

(a)   prescribe a special recruitment procedure for foreign nationals;

(b)   limit or restrict the advertising of vacancies in the press or through any other medium or subject it to conditions other than those applicable in respect of employers pursuing their activities in the territory of that Member State;

(c)   subject eligibility for employment to conditions of registration with employment offices or impede recruitment of individual workers, where persons who do not reside in the territory of that State are concerned.

Article 4

1 Provisions laid down by law, regulation or administrative action of the Member States which restrict by number or percentage the employment of foreign nationals in any undertaking, branch of activity or region, or at a national level, shall not apply to nationals of the other Member States.

2 When in a Member State the granting of any benefit to undertakings is subject to a minimum percentage of national workers being employed, nationals of the other Member States shall be counted as national workers, subject to the provisions of the Council Directive of 15 October 1963.2 1 OJ No L 257, 19.10.1968, p. 1. 2 OJ No 159, 2.11.1963, p. 2661/63.

Article 5

A national of a Member State who seeks employment in the territory of another Member State shall receive the same assistance there as that afforded by the employment offices in that State to their own nationals seeking employment.

Article 6

1 The engagement and recruitment of a national of one Member State for a post in another Member State shall not depend on medical, vocational or other criteria which are discriminatory on grounds of nationality by comparison with those applied to nationals of the other Member State who wish to pursue the same activity.

2 Nevertheless, a national who holds an offer in his name from an employer in a Member State other than that of which he is a national may have to undergo a vocational test, if the employer expressly requests this when making his offer of employment.

TITLE II Employment and equality of treatment

Article 7

1 A worker who is a national of a Member State may not, in the territory of another Member State, be treated differently from national workers by reason of his nationality in respect of any conditions of employment and work, in particular as regards remuneration, dismissal, and should he become unemployed, reinstatement or re-employment;

2 He shall enjoy the same social and tax advantages as national workers.

3 He shall also, by virtue of the same right and under the same conditions as national workers, have access to training in vocational schools and retraining centres.

4 Any clause of a collective or individual agreement or of any other collective regulation concerning eligibility for employment, employment, remuneration and other conditions of work or dismissal shall be null and void in so far as it lays down or authorises discriminatory conditions in respect of workers who are nationals of the other Member States.

Article 8

1 A worker who is a national of a Member State and who is employed in the territory of another Member State shall enjoy equality of treatment as regards membership of trade unions and the exercise of rights attaching thereto, including the right to vote ; he may be excluded from taking part in the management of bodies governed by public law and from holding an office governed by public law. Furthermore, he shall have the right of eligibility for workers' representative bodies in the undertaking. The provisions of this

Article shall not affect laws or regulations in certain Member States which grant more extensive rights to workers coming from the other Member States.

2   This Article shall be reviewed by the Council on the basis of a proposal from the Commission which shall be submitted within not more than two years.

Article 9

1   A worker who is a national of a Member State and who is employed in the territory of another Member State shall enjoy all the rights and benefits accorded to national workers in matters of housing, including ownership of the housing he needs.

2   Such worker may, with the same right as nationals, put his name down on the housing lists in the region in which he is employed, where such lists exist ; he shall enjoy the resultant benefits and priorities.

If his family has remained in the country whence he came, they shall be considered for this purpose as residing in the said region, where national workers benefit from a similar presumption.

TITLE III Workers' families

Article 10

1   The following shall, irrespective of their nationality, have the right to install themselves with a worker who is a national of one Member State and who is employed in the territory of another Member State:

   (a)   his spouse and their descendants who are under the age of 21 years or are dependants;

   (b)   dependent relatives in the ascending line of the worker and his spouse.

2   Member States shall facilitate the admission of any member of the family not coming within the provisions of paragraph 1 if dependent on the worker referred to above or living under his roof in the country whence he comes.

3   For the purposes of paragraphs 1 and 2, the worker must have available for his family housing considered as normal for national workers in the region where he is employed ; this provision, however must not give rise to discrimination between national workers and workers from the other Member States.

Article 11

Where a national of a Member State is pursuing an activity as an employed or self-employed person in the territory of another Member State, his spouse and those of the children who are under the age of 21 years or dependent on him shall have the right to take up any activity as an employed person throughout the territory of that same State, even if they are not nationals of any Member State.

Article 12

The children of a national of a Member State who is or has been employed in the territory of another Member State shall be admitted to that State's general educational, apprenticeship and vocational training courses under the same conditions as the nationals of that State, if such children are residing in its territory.

Member States shall encourage all efforts to enable such children to attend these courses under the best possible conditions.

DIRECTIVE 2004/38/EC OF THE EUROPEAN PARLIAMENT AND OF THE COUNCIL

CHAPTER I

General provisions

Article 1

Subject

This Directive lays down:

(a)   the conditions governing the exercise of the right of free movement and residence within the territory of the Member States by Union citizens and their family members;

(b)   the right of permanent residence in the territory of the Member States for Union citizens and their family members;

(c)   the limits placed on the rights set out in (a) and (b) on grounds of public policy, public security or public health.

Article 2

Definitions

For the purposes of this Directive:

(1)   "Union citizen" means any person having the nationality of a Member State;

(2)   "Family member" means:

    (a)   the spouse;

    (b)   the partner with whom the Union citizen has contracted a registered partnership, on the basis of the legislation of a Member State, if the legislation of the host Member State treats registered partnerships as equivalent to marriage and in accordance with the conditions laid down in the relevant legislation of the host Member State;

    (c)   the direct descendants who are under the age of 21 or are dependants and those of the spouse or partner as defined in point (b);

    (d)   the dependent direct relatives in the ascending line and those of the spouse or partner as defined in point (b);

(3)   "Host Member State" means the Member State to which a Union citizen moves in order to exercise his/her right of free movement and residence.

Article 3

Beneficiaries

1   This Directive shall apply to all Union citizens who move to or reside in a Member State other than that of which they are a national, and to their family members as defined in point 2 of Article 2 who accompany or join them.

2   Without prejudice to any right to free movement and residence the persons concerned may have in their own right, the host Member State shall, in accordance with its national legislation, facilitate entry and residence for the following persons:

    (a)   any other family members, irrespective of their nationality, not falling under the definition in point 2 of Article 2 who, in the country from which they have come, are dependants or members of the household of the Union citizen having the primary right of residence, or where serious health grounds strictly require the personal care of the family member by the Union citizen;

    (b)   the partner with whom the Union citizen has a durable relationship, duly attested. The host Member State shall undertake an extensive examination of the personal circumstances and shall justify any denial of entry or residence to these people.

CHAPTER II

Right of exit and entry

Article 4

Right of exit

1   Without prejudice to the provisions on travel documents applicable to national border controls, all Union citizens with a valid identity card or passport and their family members who are not nationals of a Member State and who hold a valid passport shall have the right to leave the territory of a Member State to travel to another Member State.

2   No exit visa or equivalent formality may be imposed on the persons to whom paragraph 1 applies.

3   Member States shall, acting in accordance with their laws, issue to their own nationals, and renew, an identity card or passport stating their nationality.

4   The passport shall be valid at least for all Member States and for countries through which the holder must pass when travelling between Member States. Where the law of a Member State does not provide for identity cards to be issued, the period of validity of any passport on being issued or renewed shall be not less than five years.

Article 5

Right of entry

1   Without prejudice to the provisions on travel documents applicable to national border controls, Member States shall grant Union citizens leave to enter their territory with a valid identity card or passport and shall grant family members who are not nationals of a Member State leave to enter their territory with a valid passport.

    No entry visa or equivalent formality may be imposed on Union citizens.

2   Family members who are not nationals of a Member State shall only be required to have an entry visa in accordance with Regulation (EC) No 539/2001 or, where appropriate, with national law. For the purposes of this Directive, possession of the valid residence card referred to in Article 10 shall exempt such family members from the visa requirement. Member States shall grant such persons every facility to obtain the necessary visas. Such visas shall be issued free of charge as soon as possible and on the basis of an accelerated procedure.

3   The host Member State shall not place an entry or exit stamp in the passport of family members who are not nationals of a Member State provided that they present the residence card provided for in Article 10.

4   Where a Union citizen, or a family member who is not a national of a Member State, does not have the necessary travel documents or, if required, the necessary visas, the Member State concerned shall, before turning them back, give such persons every reasonable opportunity to obtain the necessary documents or have them brought to them within a reasonable period of time or to corroborate or prove by other means that they are covered by the right of free movement and residence.

5   The Member State may require the person concerned to report his/her presence within its territory within a reasonable and non-discriminatory period of time. Failure to comply with this requirement may make the person concerned liable to proportionate and non-discriminatory sanctions.

CHAPTER III

Right of residence

Article 6

Right of residence for up to three months

1   Union citizens shall have the right of residence on the territory of another Member State for a period of up to three months without any conditions or any formalities other than the requirement to hold a valid identity card or passport.

2   The provisions of paragraph 1 shall also apply to family members in possession of a valid passport who are not nationals of a Member State, accompanying or joining the Union citizen.

Article 7

Right of residence for more than three months

1   All Union citizens shall have the right of residence on the territory of another Member State for a period of longer than three months if they:

(a)   are workers or self-employed persons in the host Member State; or

(b)   have sufficient resources for themselves and their family members not to become a burden on the social assistance system of the host Member State during their period of residence and have comprehensive sickness insurance cover in the host Member State; or

(c)   are enrolled at a private or public establishment, accredited or financed by the host Member State on the basis of its legislation or administrative practice, for the principal purpose of following a course of study, including vocational training; and

have comprehensive sickness insurance cover in the host Member State and assure the relevant national authority, by means of a declaration or by such equivalent means as they may choose, that they have sufficient resources for themselves and their family members not to become a burden on the social assistance system of the host Member State during their period of residence; or

(d)   are family members accompanying or joining a Union citizen who satisfies the conditions referred to in points (a), (b) or (c).

2   The right of residence provided for in paragraph 1 shall extend to family members who are not nationals of a Member State, accompanying or joining the Union citizen in the host Member State, provided that such Union citizen satisfies the conditions referred to in paragraph 1(a), (b) or (c).

3   For the purposes of paragraph 1(a), a Union citizen who is no longer a worker or self-employed person shall retain the status of worker or self-employed person in the following circumstances:

(a)   he/she is temporarily unable to work as the result of an illness or accident;

(b)   he/she is in duly recorded involuntary unemployment after having been employed for more than one year and has registered as a job-seeker with the relevant employment office;

(c)   he/she is in duly recorded involuntary unemployment after completing a fixed-term employment contract of less than a year or after having become involuntarily unemployed during the first twelve months and has registered as a job-seeker with the relevant employment office. In this case, the status of worker shall be retained for no less than six months;

(d)   he/she embarks on vocational training. Unless he/she is involuntarily unemployed, the retention of the status of worker shall require the training to be related to the previous employment.

4   By way of derogation from paragraphs 1(d) and 2 above, only the spouse, the registered partner provided for in Article 2(2)(b) and dependent children shall have the right of residence as family members of a Union citizen meeting the conditions under 1(c) above. Article 3(2) shall apply to his/her dependent direct relatives in the ascending lines and those of his/her spouse or registered partner.

Article 8

Administrative formalities for Union citizens

1   Without prejudice to Article 5(5), for periods of residence longer than three months, the host Member State may require Union citizens to register with the relevant authorities.

2   The deadline for registration may not be less than three months from the date of arrival. A registration certificate shall be issued immediately, stating the name and address of the person registering and the date of the registration. Failure to comply with the registration requirement may render the person concerned liable to proportionate and non-discriminatory sanctions.

3   For the registration certificate to be issued, Member States may only require that

▸   Union citizens to whom point (a) of Article 7(1) applies present a valid identity card or passport, a confirmation of engagement from the employer or a certificate of employment, or proof that they are self-employed persons;

▸   Union citizens to whom point (b) of Article 7(1) applies present a valid identity card or passport and provide proof that they satisfy the conditions laid down therein;

▸   Union citizens to whom point (c) of Article 7(1) applies present a valid identity card or passport, provide proof of enrolment at an accredited establishment and of comprehensive sickness insurance cover and the declaration or equivalent means referred to in point (c) of Article 7(1). Member States may not require this declaration to refer to any specific amount of resources.

4   Member States may not lay down a fixed amount which they regard as "sufficient resources", but they must take into account the personal situation of the person concerned. In all cases this amount shall not be higher than the threshold below which nationals of the host Member State become eligible for social assistance, or, where this criterion is not applicable, higher than the minimum social security pension paid by the host Member State.

5   For the registration certificate to be issued to family members of Union citizens, who are themselves Union citizens, Member States may require the following documents to be presented:

(a)   a valid identity card or passport;

(b)   a document attesting to the existence of a family relationship or of a registered partnership;

(c)   where appropriate, the registration certificate of the Union citizen whom they are accompanying or joining;

(d)   in cases falling under points (c) and (d) of Article 2(2), documentary evidence that the conditions laid down therein are met;

(e)   in cases falling under Article 3(2)(a), a document issued by the relevant authority in the country of origin or country from which they are arriving certifying that they are dependants or members of the household of the Union citizen, or proof of the existence of serious health grounds which strictly require the personal care of the family member by the Union citizen;

(f)   in cases falling under Article 3(2)(b), proof of the existence of a durable relationship with the Union citizen.

Article 9

Administrative formalities for family members who are not nationals of a Member State

1   Member States shall issue a residence card to family members of a Union citizen who are not nationals of a Member State, where the planned period of residence is for more than three months.

2   The deadline for submitting the residence card application may not be less than three months from the date of arrival.

3   Failure to comply with the requirement to apply for a residence card may make the person concerned liable to proportionate and non-discriminatory sanctions.

Article 10

Issue of residence cards

1   The right of residence of family members of a Union citizen who are not nationals of a Member State shall be evidenced by the issuing of a document called "Residence card of a family member of a Union citizen" no later than six months from the date on which they submit the application. A certificate of application for the residence card shall be issued immediately.

2   For the residence card to be issued, Member States shall require presentation of the following documents:

(a)   a valid passport;

(b)   a document attesting to the existence of a family relationship or of a registered partnership;

(c)   the registration certificate or, in the absence of a registration system, any other proof of residence in the host Member State of the Union citizen whom they are accompanying or joining;

(d)   in cases falling under points (c) and (d) of Article 2(2), documentary evidence that the conditions laid down therein are met;

(e)   in cases falling under Article 3(2)(a), a document issued by the relevant authority in the country of origin or country from which they are arriving certifying that they are dependants or members of the household of the Union citizen, or proof of the existence of serious health grounds which strictly require the personal care of the family member by the Union citizen;

(f)   in cases falling under Article 3(2)(b), proof of the existence of a durable relationship with the Union citizen.

Article 11

Validity of the residence card

1   The residence card provided for by Article 10(1) shall be valid for five years from the date of issue or for the envisaged period of residence of the Union citizen, if this period is less than five years.

2   The validity of the residence card shall not be affected by temporary absences not exceeding six months a year, or by absences of a longer duration for compulsory military service or by one absence of a maximum of twelve consecutive months for important reasons such as pregnancy and childbirth, serious illness, study or vocational training, or a posting in another Member State or a third country.

Article 12

Retention of the right of residence by family members in the event of death or departure of the Union citizen

1   Without prejudice to the second subparagraph, the Union citizen's death or departure from the host Member State shall not affect the right of residence of his/her family members who are nationals of a Member State.

Before acquiring the right of permanent residence, the persons concerned must meet the conditions laid down in points (a), (b), (c) or (d) of Article 7(1).

2   Without prejudice to the second subparagraph, the Union citizen's death shall not entail loss of the right of residence of his/her family members who are not nationals of a Member State and who have been residing in the host Member State as family members for at least one year before the Union citizen's death.

Before acquiring the right of permanent residence, the right of residence of the persons concerned shall remain subject to the requirement that they are able to show that they are workers or self-employed persons or that they have sufficient resources for themselves and their family members not to become a burden on the social assistance system of the host Member State during their period of residence and have comprehensive sickness insurance cover in the host Member State, or that they are members of the family, already constituted in the host Member State, of a person satisfying these requirements. "Sufficient resources" shall be as defined in Article 8(4).

Such family members shall retain their right of residence exclusively on a personal basis.

3   The Union citizen's departure from the host Member State or his/her death shall not entail loss of the right of residence of his/her children or of the parent who has actual custody of the children, irrespective of nationality, if the children reside in the host Member State and are enrolled at an educational establishment, for the purpose of studying there, until the completion of their studies.

Article 13

Retention of the right of residence by family members in the event of divorce, annulment of marriage or termination of registered partnership

1   Without prejudice to the second subparagraph, divorce, annulment of the Union citizen's marriage or termination of his/her registered partnership, as referred to in point 2(b) of Article 2 shall not affect the right of residence of his/her family members who are nationals of a Member State.

Before acquiring the right of permanent residence, the persons concerned must meet the conditions laid down in points (a), (b), (c) or (d) of Article 7(1).

2   Without prejudice to the second subparagraph, divorce, annulment of marriage or termination of the registered partnership referred to in point 2(b) of Article 2 shall not entail loss of the right of residence of a Union citizen's family members who are not nationals of a Member State where:

   (a)   prior to initiation of the divorce or annulment proceedings or termination of the registered partnership referred to in point 2(b) of Article 2, the marriage or registered partnership has lasted at least three years, including one year in the host Member State; or

   (b)   by agreement between the spouses or the partners referred to in point 2(b) of Article 2 or by court order, the spouse or partner who is not a national of a Member State has custody of the Union citizen's children; or

   (c)   this is warranted by particularly difficult circumstances, such as having been a victim of domestic violence while the marriage or registered partnership was subsisting; or

   (d)   by agreement between the spouses or partners referred to in point 2(b) of Article 2 or by court order, the spouse or partner who is not a national of a Member State has the right of access to a minor child, provided that the court has ruled that such access must be in the host Member State, and for as long as is required.

Before acquiring the right of permanent residence, the right of residence of the persons concerned shall remain subject to the requirement that they are able to show that they are workers or self-employed persons or that they have sufficient resources for themselves and their family members not to become a burden on the social assistance system of the host Member State during their period of residence and have comprehensive sickness insurance cover in the host Member State, or that they are members of the family, already constituted in the host Member State, of a person satisfying these requirements. "Sufficient resources" shall be as defined in Article 8(4).

Such family members shall retain their right of residence exclusively on personal basis.

Article 14

Retention of the right of residence

1   Union citizens and their family members shall have the right of residence provided for in Article 6, as long as they do not become an unreasonable burden on the social assistance system of the host Member State.

2   Union citizens and their family members shall have the right of residence provided for in Articles 7, 12 and 13 as long as they meet the conditions set out therein. In specific cases where there is a reasonable doubt as to whether a Union citizen or his/her family members satisfies the conditions set out in Articles 7, 12 and 13, Member States may verify if these conditions are fulfilled. This verification shall not be carried out systematically.

3   An expulsion measure shall not be the automatic consequence of a Union citizen's or his or her family member's recourse to the social assistance system of the host Member State.

4   By way of derogation from paragraphs 1 and 2 and without prejudice to the provisions of Chapter VI, an expulsion measure may in no case be adopted against Union citizens or their family members if:

   (a)   the Union citizens are workers or self-employed persons, or

   (b)   the Union citizens entered the territory of the host Member State in order to seek employment.

In this case, the Union citizens and their family members may not be expelled for as long as the Union citizens can provide evidence that they are continuing to seek employment and that they have a genuine chance of being engaged.

Article 15

Procedural safeguards

1   The procedures provided for by Articles 30 and 31 shall apply by analogy to all decisions restricting free movement of Union citizens and their family members on grounds other than public policy, public security or public health.

2   Expiry of the identity card or passport on the basis of which the person concerned entered the host Member State and was issued with a registration certificate or residence card shall not constitute a ground for expulsion from the host Member State.

3   The host Member State may not impose a ban on entry in the context of an expulsion decision to which paragraph 1 applies.

CHAPTER IV

Right of permanent residence

Section I

Eligibility

Article 16

General rule for Union citizens and their family members

1   Union citizens who have resided legally for a continuous period of five years in the host Member State shall have the right of permanent residence there. This right shall not be subject to the conditions provided for in Chapter III.

2   Paragraph 1 shall apply also to family members who are not nationals of a Member State and have legally resided with the Union citizen in the host Member State for a continuous period of five years.

3   Continuity of residence shall not be affected by temporary absences not exceeding a total of six months a year, or by absences of a longer duration for compulsory military service, or by one absence of a maximum of twelve consecutive months for important reasons such as pregnancy and childbirth, serious illness, study or vocational training, or a posting in another Member State or a third country.

4   Once acquired, the right of permanent residence shall be lost only through absence from the host Member State for a period exceeding two consecutive years.

Article 17

Exemptions for persons no longer working in the host Member State and their family members

1   By way of derogation from Article 16, the right of permanent residence in the host Member State shall be enjoyed before completion of a continuous period of five years of residence by:

   (a)   workers or self-employed persons who, at the time they stop working, have reached the age laid down by the law of that Member State for entitlement to an old age pension or workers who cease paid employment to take early retirement, provided that they have been working in that Member State for at least the preceding twelve months and have resided there continuously for more than three years.

If the law of the host Member State does not grant the right to an old age pension to certain categories of self-employed persons, the age condition shall be deemed to have been met once the person concerned has reached the age of 60;

(b)   workers or self-employed persons who have resided continuously in the host Member State for more than two years and stop working there as a result of permanent incapacity to work.

If such incapacity is the result of an accident at work or an occupational disease entitling the person concerned to a benefit payable in full or in part by an institution in the host Member State, no condition shall be imposed as to length of residence;

(c)   workers or self-employed persons who, after three years of continuous employment and residence in the host Member State, work in an employed or self-employed capacity in another Member State, while retaining their place of residence in the host Member State, to which they return, as a rule, each day or at least once a week.

For the purposes of entitlement to the rights referred to in points (a) and (b), periods of employment spent in the Member State in which the person concerned is working shall be regarded as having been spent in the host Member State.

Periods of involuntary unemployment duly recorded by the relevant employment office, periods not worked for reasons not of the person's own making and absences from work or cessation of work due to illness or accident shall be regarded as periods of employment.

2   The conditions as to length of residence and employment laid down in point (a) of paragraph 1 and the condition as to length of residence laid down in point (b) of paragraph 1 shall not apply if the worker's or the self-employed person's spouse or partner as referred to in point 2(b) of Article 2 is a national of the host Member State or has lost the nationality of that Member State by marriage to that worker or self-employed person.

3   Irrespective of nationality, the family members of a worker or a self-employed person who are residing with him in the territory of the host Member State shall have the right of permanent residence in that Member State, if the worker or self-employed person has acquired himself the right of permanent residence in that Member State on the basis of paragraph 1.

4   If, however, the worker or self-employed person dies while still working but before acquiring permanent residence status in the host Member State on the basis of paragraph 1, his family members who are residing with him in the host Member State shall acquire the right of permanent residence there, on condition that:

(a)   the worker or self-employed person had, at the time of death, resided continuously on the territory of that Member State for two years; or

(b)   the death resulted from an accident at work or an occupational disease; or

(c)   the surviving spouse lost the nationality of that Member State following marriage to the worker or self-employed person.

Article 18

Acquisition of the right of permanent residence by certain family members who are not nationals of a Member State

Without prejudice to Article 17, the family members of a Union citizen to whom Articles 12(2) and 13(2) apply, who satisfy the conditions laid down therein, shall acquire the right of permanent residence after residing legally for a period of five consecutive years in the host Member State.

Section II

Administrative formalities

Article 19

Document certifying permanent residence for Union citizens

1   Upon application Member States shall issue Union citizens entitled to permanent residence, after having verified duration of residence, with a document certifying permanent residence.

2   The document certifying permanent residence shall be issued as soon as possible.

Article 20

Permanent residence card for family members who are not nationals of a Member State

1   Member States shall issue family members who are not nationals of a Member State entitled to permanent residence with a permanent residence card within six months of the submission of the application. The permanent residence card shall be renewable automatically every ten years.

2   The application for a permanent residence card shall be submitted before the residence card expires. Failure to comply with the requirement to apply for a permanent residence card may render the person concerned liable to proportionate and non-discriminatory sanctions.

3   Interruption in residence not exceeding two consecutive years shall not affect the validity of the permanent residence card.

Article 21

Continuity of residence

For the purposes of this Directive, continuity of residence may be attested by any means of proof in use in the host Member State. Continuity of residence is broken by any expulsion decision duly enforced against the person concerned.

CHAPTER V

Provisions common to the right of residence and the right of permanent residence

Article 22

Territorial scope

The right of residence and the right of permanent residence shall cover the whole territory of the host Member State. Member States may impose territorial restrictions on the right of residence and the right of permanent residence only where the same restrictions apply to their own nationals.

Article 23

Related rights

Irrespective of nationality, the family members of a Union citizen who have the right of residence or the right of permanent residence in a Member State shall be entitled to take up employment or self-employment there.

Article 24

Equal treatment

1   Subject to such specific provisions as are expressly provided for in the Treaty and secondary law, all Union citizens residing on the basis of this Directive in the territory of the host Member State shall enjoy equal treatment with the nationals of that Member State within the scope of the Treaty. The benefit of this right shall be extended to family members who are not nationals of a Member State and who have the right of residence or permanent residence.

2   By way of derogation from paragraph 1, the host Member State shall not be obliged to confer entitlement to social assistance during the first three months of residence or, where appropriate, the longer period provided for in Article 14(4)(b), nor shall it be obliged, prior to acquisition of the right of permanent residence, to grant maintenance aid for studies, including vocational training, consisting in student grants or student loans to persons other than workers, self-employed persons, persons who retain such status and members of their families.

Article 25

General provisions concerning residence documents

1   Possession of a registration certificate as referred to in Article 8, of a document certifying permanent residence, of a certificate attesting submission of an application for a family member residence card, of a residence card or of a permanent residence card, may under no circumstances be made a precondition for the exercise of a right or the completion of an administrative formality, as entitlement to rights may be attested by any other means of proof.

2   All documents mentioned in paragraph 1 shall be issued free of charge or for a charge not exceeding that imposed on nationals for the issuing of similar documents.

Article 26

Checks

Member States may carry out checks on compliance with any requirement deriving from their national legislation for non-nationals always to carry their registration certificate or residence card, provided that the same requirement applies to their own nationals as regards their identity card.

In the event of failure to comply with this requirement, Member States may impose the same sanctions as those imposed on their own nationals for failure to carry their identity card.

CHAPTER VI

Restrictions on the right of entry and the right of residence on grounds of public policy, public security or public health

Article 27

General principles

1   Subject to the provisions of this Chapter, Member States may restrict the freedom of movement and residence of Union citizens and their family members, irrespective of nationality, on grounds of public policy, public security or public health. These grounds shall not be invoked to serve economic ends.

2   Measures taken on grounds of public policy or public security shall comply with the principle of proportionality and shall be based exclusively on the personal conduct of the individual concerned.

Previous criminal convictions shall not in themselves constitute grounds for taking such measures. The personal conduct of the individual concerned must represent a genuine, present and sufficiently serious threat affecting one of the fundamental interests of society. Justifications that are isolated from the particulars of the case or that rely on considerations of general prevention shall not be accepted.

3   In order to ascertain whether the person concerned represents a danger for public policy or public security, when issuing the registration certificate or, in the absence of a registration system, not later than three months from the date of arrival of the person concerned on its territory or from the date of reporting his/her presence within the territory, as provided for in Article 5(5), or when issuing the residence card, the host Member State may, should it consider this essential, request the Member State of origin and, if need be, other Member States to provide information concerning any previous police record the person concerned may have. Such enquiries shall not be made as a matter of routine. The Member State consulted shall give its reply within two months.

4   The Member State which issued the passport or identity card shall allow the holder of the document who has been expelled on grounds of public policy, public security, or public health from another Member State to re-enter its territory without any formality even if the document is no longer valid or the nationality of the holder is in dispute.

Article 28

Protection against expulsion

1   Before taking an expulsion decision on grounds of public policy or public security, the host Member State shall take account of considerations such as how long the individual concerned has resided on its territory, his/her age, state of health, family and economic situation, social and cultural integration into the host Member State and the extent of his/her links with the country of origin.

2   The host Member State may not take an expulsion decision against Union citizens or their family members, irrespective of nationality, who have the right of permanent residence on its territory, except on serious grounds of public policy or public security.

3   An expulsion decision may not be taken against Union citizens, except if the decision is based on imperative grounds of public security, as defined by Member States, if they:

(a)   have resided in the host Member State for the previous ten years; or

(b)   are a minor, except if the expulsion is necessary for the best interests of the child, as provided for in the United Nations Convention on the Rights of the Child of 20 November 1989.

Article 29

Public health

1   The only diseases justifying measures restricting freedom of movement shall be the diseases with epidemic potential as defined by the relevant instruments of the World Health Organisation and other infectious diseases or contagious parasitic diseases if they are the subject of protection provisions applying to nationals of the host Member State.

2   Diseases occurring after a three-month period from the date of arrival shall not constitute grounds for expulsion from the territory.

3   Where there are serious indications that it is necessary, Member States may, within three months of the date of arrival, require persons entitled to the right of residence to undergo, free of charge, a medical

examination to certify that they are not suffering from any of the conditions referred to in paragraph 1. Such medical examinations may not be required as a matter of routine.

Article 30

Notification of decisions

1   The persons concerned shall be notified in writing of any decision taken under Article 27(1), in such a way that they are able to comprehend its content and the implications for them.

2   The persons concerned shall be informed, precisely and in full, of the public policy, public security or public health grounds on which the decision taken in their case is based, unless this is contrary to the interests of State security.

3   The notification shall specify the court or administrative authority with which the person concerned may lodge an appeal, the time limit for the appeal and, where applicable, the time allowed for the person to leave the territory of the Member State. Save in duly substantiated cases of urgency, the time allowed to leave the territory shall be not less than one month from the date of notification.

Article 31

Procedural safeguards

1   The persons concerned shall have access to judicial and, where appropriate, administrative redress procedures in the host Member State to appeal against or seek review of any decision taken against them on the grounds of public policy, public security or public health.

2   Where the application for appeal against or judicial review of the expulsion decision is accompanied by an application for an interim order to suspend enforcement of that decision, actual removal from the territory may not take place until such time as the decision on the interim order has been taken, except:

   ▸   where the expulsion decision is based on a previous judicial decision; or

   ▸   where the persons concerned have had previous access to judicial review; or

   ▸   where the expulsion decision is based on imperative grounds of public security under Article 28(3).

3   The redress procedures shall allow for an examination of the legality of the decision, as well as of the facts and circumstances on which the proposed measure is based. They shall ensure that the decision is not disproportionate, particularly in view of the requirements laid down in Article 28.

4   Member States may exclude the individual concerned from their territory pending the redress procedure, but they may not prevent the individual from submitting his/her defence in person, except when his/her appearance may cause serious troubles to public policy or public security or when the appeal or judicial review concerns a denial of entry to the territory.

Article 32

Duration of exclusion orders

1   Persons excluded on grounds of public policy or public security may submit an application for lifting of the exclusion order after a reasonable period, depending on the circumstances, and in any event after three years from enforcement of the final exclusion order which has been validly adopted in accordance with Community law, by putting forward arguments to establish that there has been a material change in the circumstances which justified the decision ordering their exclusion.

The Member State concerned shall reach a decision on this application within six months of its submission.

2   The persons referred to in paragraph 1 shall have no right of entry to the territory of the Member State concerned while their application is being considered.

Article 33

Expulsion as a penalty or legal consequence

1   Expulsion orders may not be issued by the host Member State as a penalty or legal consequence of a custodial penalty, unless they conform to the requirements of Articles 27, 28 and 29.

2   If an expulsion order, as provided for in paragraph 1, is enforced more than two years after it was issued, the Member State shall check that the individual concerned is currently and genuinely a threat to public policy or public security and shall assess whether there has been any material change in the circumstances since the expulsion order was issued.

CHAPTER VII

Final provisions

Article 34

Publicity

Member States shall disseminate information concerning the rights and obligations of Union citizens and their family members on the subjects covered by this Directive, particularly by means of awareness-raising campaigns conducted through national and local media and other means of communication.

Article 35

Abuse of rights

Member States may adopt the necessary measures to refuse, terminate or withdraw any right conferred by this Directive in the case of abuse of rights or fraud, such as marriages of convenience.

Any such measure shall be proportionate and subject to the procedural safeguards provided for in Articles 30 and 31.

Article 36

Sanctions

Member States shall lay down provisions on the sanctions applicable to breaches of national rules adopted for the implementation of this Directive and shall take the measures required for their application. The sanctions laid down shall be effective and proportionate. Member States shall notify the Commission of these provisions not later than ......* and as promptly as possible in the case of any subsequent changes.

Article 37

More favourable national provisions

The provisions of this Directive shall not affect any laws, regulations or administrative provisions laid down by a Member State which would be more favourable to the persons covered by this Directive.

Article 38

Repeals

1   Articles 10 and 11 of Regulation (EEC) No 1612/68 shall be repealed with effect from … *.

2   Directives 64/221/EEC, 68/360/EEC, 72/194/EEC, 73/148/EEC, 75/34/EEC, 75/35/EEC, 90/364/EEC, 90/365/EEC and 93/96/EEC shall be repealed with effect from …. *.

      * Two years from the date of entry into force of this Directive.

3   References made to the repealed provisions and Directives shall be construed as being made to this Directive.

Article 39

Report

No later than…..* the Commission shall submit a report on the application of this Directive to the European Parliament and the Council, together with any necessary proposals, notably on the opportunity to extend the period of time during which Union citizens and their family members may reside in the territory of the host Member State without any conditions. The Member States shall provide the Commission with the information needed to produce the report.

Article 40

Transposition

1   Member States shall bring into force the laws, regulations and administrative provisions necessary to comply with this Directive by ……**.

When Member States adopt those measures, they shall contain a reference to this Directive or shall be accompanied by such a reference on the occasion of their official publication. The methods of making such reference shall be laid down by the Member States.

SECTION 4 – SEX DISCRIMINATION

COUNCIL DIRECTIVE of 10 February 1975 on the approximation of the laws of the Member States relating to the application of the principle of equal pay for men and women (75/117/EEC)

Article 1

The principle of equal pay for men and women outlined in Article 119 of the Treaty, hereinafter called "principle of equal pay", means, for the same work or for work to which equal value is attributed, the elimination of all discrimination on grounds of sex with regard to all aspects and conditions of remuneration.

In particular, where a job classification system is used for determining pay, it must be based on the same criteria for both men and women and so drawn up as to exclude any discrimination on grounds of sex.

Article 2

Member States shall introduce into their national legal systems such measures as are necessary to enable all employees who consider themselves wronged by failure to apply the principle of equal pay to pursue their claims by judicial process after possible recourse to other competent authorities.

Article 3

Member States shall abolish all discrimination between men and women arising from laws, regulations or administrative provisions which is contrary to the principle of equal pay.

Article 4

Member States shall take the necessary measures to ensure that provisions appearing in collective agreements, wage scales, wage agreements or individual contracts of employment which are contrary to the principle of equal pay shall be, or may be declared, null and void or may be amended.

Article 5

Member States shall take the necessary measures to protect employees against dismissal by the employer as a reaction to a complaint within the undertaking or to any legal proceedings aimed at enforcing compliance with the principle of equal pay.

Article 6

Member States shall, in accordance with their national circumstances and legal systems, take the measures necessary to ensure that the priciple of equal pay is applied. They shall see that effective means are available to take care that this principle is observed.

Article 7

Member States shall take care that the provisions adopted pursuant to this Directive, together with the relevant provisions already in force, are brought to the attention of employees by all appropriate means, for example at their place of employment.

Article 8

1   Member States shall put into force the laws, regulations and administrative provisions necessary in order to comply with this Directive within one year of its notification and shall immediately inform the Commission thereof.

2   Member States shall communicate to the Commission the texts of the laws, regulations and administrative provisions which they adopt in the field covered by this Directive.

Article 9

Within two years of the expiry of the one-year period referred to in Article 8, Member States shall forward all necessary information to the Commission to enable it to draw up a report on the application of this Directive for submission to the Council.

79/7/EEC Arts 1–2 COUNCIL DIRECTIVE 79/7 (EEC)

Article 1

The purpose of this Directive is the progressive implementation, in the field of social secure and other elements of social protection provided for in Article 3, of the principle of equal treatment for men and women in matters of social security, hereinafter referred to as 'the principle of equal treatment'.

Article 2

This Directive shall apply to the working population - including self-employed persons, workers and self-employed persons whose activity is interrupted by illness, accident or involuntary unemployment and persons seeking employment - and to retired or invalid workers and self-employed persons.

Article 3

1   This Directive shall apply to:

    (a)   statutory schemes which provide protection against the following risks;

        ▶   sickness,

        ▶   invalidity,

        ▶   old age,

        ▶   accidents at work and occupational diseases,

        ▶   unemployment;

    (b)   social assistance, in so far as it is intended to supplement or replace the schemes referred to in (a).

2   This Directive shall not apply tot he provisions concerning survivors' benefits nor to those concerning family benefits, except in the case of family benefits granted by way of increases of benefits due in respect of the risks referred to in paragraph 1(a).

3   With a view to ensuring implementation of the principle of equal treatment in occupational schemes, the Council, acting on a proposal from the Commission will adopt provisions defining its substance, its scope and the arrangements for its application.

Article 4

1   The principle of equal treatment means that there shall be no discrimination whatsoever on ground of sex either directly, or indirectly by reference in particular to marital or family status, in particular or concerns;

        ▶   the scope of the schemes and the conditions of access thereto,

        ▶   the obligation to contribute and the calculation of contributions,

        ▶   the calculation of benefits including increases due in respect of a spouse and for dependants and the conditions governing the duration and retention of entitlement to benefits.

2   The principle of equal treatment shall be without prejudice to the provisions relating tot he protection of women on the grounds of maternity.

Article 5

Member States shall take the measures necessary to ensure that any laws, regulations and administrative provisions contrary to the principle of equal treatment are abolished.

Article 6

Member States shall introduce into their national legal systems such measures as are necessary to enable all persons who consider themselves wronged by failure to apply the principle of equal treatment to pursue their claims by judicial process, possibly after recourse to other competent authorities.

Article 7

1   This Directive shall be without prejudice to the right of Member States to exclude from its scope:

   (a)   the determination of pensionable age for the purposes of granting old age and retirement pensions and the possible consequences thereof for other benefits;

   (b)   advantages in respect of old-age pension schemes granted to persons who have brought up children; the acquisition of benefit entitlements following periods of interruption of employment due to the bringing up of children;

   Supplement No. 9 [Dec 89] The Law Relating to Social Security 9.6553

   79/7/EEC Arts 7–10 COUNCIL DIRECTIVE 79/7 (EEC)

   (c)   the granting of old-age or invalidity benefit entitlements by virtue of the derived entitlements of a wife;

   (d)   the granting of increases of long-term invalidity, old-age, accidents at work and occupational disease benefits for a dependent wife;

   (e)   the consequences of the exercise, before the adoption of this Directive, of a right of option not to acquire rights or incur obligations under a statutory scheme.

2   Member States shall periodically examine matters excluded under paragraph 1 in order to ascertain, in the light of social developments in the matter concerned, whether there is justification for maintaining the exclusions concerned.

Article 8

1   Member States shall bring into force the laws, regulations and administrative provisions necessary to comply with this Directive within six years of its notification. They shall immediately inform the Commission thereof.

2   Member States shall communicate to the Commission the text of laws, regulations and administrative provisions which they adopt in the field covered by this Directive, including measures adopted pursuant to Article 7(2).

   They shall inform the Commission of their reasons for maintaining any existing provisions on the matters referred to in Article 7(1) and of the possibilities for reviewing them at a later date.

Article 9

Within seven years of notification of this Directive, Member States shall forward all information necessary to the Commission to enable it to draw up a report on the application of this Directive for submission to the Council and to propose such further measures as may be required for the implementation of the principle of equal treatment.

COUNCIL DIRECTIVE 92/85/EEC

SECTION I

PURPOSE AND DEFINITIONS

Article 1

Purpose

1   The purpose of this Directive, which is the tenth individual Directive within the meaning of Article 16 (1) of Directive 89/391/EEC, is to implement measures to encourage improvements in the safety and health at work of pregnant workers and workers who have recently given birth or who are breastfeeding.

2   The provisions of Directive 89/391/EEC, except for Article 2 (2) thereof, shall apply in full to the whole area covered by paragraph 1, without prejudice to any more stringent and/or specific provisions contained in this Directive.

3   This Directive may not have the effect of reducing the level of protection afforded to pregnant workers, workers who have recently given birth or who are breastfeeding as compared with the situation which exists in each Member State on the date on which this Directive is adopted.

Article 2

Definitions

For the purposes of this Directive:

(a)   pregnant worker shall mean a pregnant worker who informs her employer of her condition, in accordance with national legislation and/or national practice;

(b)   worker who has recently given birth shall mean a worker who has recently given birth within the meaning of national legislation and/or national practice and who informs her employer of her condition, in accordance with that legislation and/or practice;

(c)   worker who is breastfeeding shall mean a worker who is breastfeeding within the meaning of national legislation and/or national practice and who informs her employer of her condition, in accordance with that legislation and/or practice.

SECTION II

GENERAL PROVISIONS

Article 3

Guidelines

1   In consultation with the Member States and assisted by the Advisory Committee on Safety, Hygiene and Health Protection at Work, the Commission shall draw up guidelines on the assessment of the chemical, physical and biological agents and industrial processes considered hazardous for the safety or health of workers within the meaning of Article 2.

The guidelines referred to in the first subparagraph shall also cover movements and postures, mental and physical fatigue and other types of physical and mental stress connected with the work done by workers within the meaning of Article 2.

2   The purpose of the guidelines referred to in paragraph 1 is to serve as a basis for the assessment referred to in Article 4 (1).

To this end, Member States shall bring these guidelines to the attention of all employers and all female workers and/or their representatives in the respective Member State.

Article 4

Assessment and information

1   For all activities liable to involve a specific risk of exposure to the agents, processes or working conditions of which a non-exhaustive list is given in Annex I, the employer shall assess the nature, degree and duration of exposure, in the undertaking and/or establishment concerned, of workers within the meaning of Article 2, either directly or by way of the protective and preventive services referred to in Article 7 of Directive 89/391/EEC, in order to:

–   assess any risks to the safety or health and any possible effect on the pregnancys or breastfeeding of workers within the meaning of Article 2,

–   decide what measures should be taken.

2   Without prejudice to Article 10 of Directive 89/391/EEC, workers within the meaning of Article 2 and workers likely to be in one of the situations referred to in Article 2 in the undertaking and/or establishment concerned and/or their representatives shall be informed of the results of the assessment referred to in paragraph 1 and of all measures to be taken concerning health and safety at work.

Article 5

Action further to the results of the assessment

1   Without prejudice to Article 6 of Directive 89/391/EEC, if the results of the assessment referred to in Article 4 (1) reveal a risk to the safety or health or an effect on the pregnancy or breastfeeding of a worker within the meaning of Article 2, the employer shall take the necessary measures to ensure that, by temporarily adjusting the working conditions and/or the working hours of the worker concerned, the exposure of that worker to such risks is avoided.

2   If the adjustment of her working conditions and/or working hours is not technically and/or objectively feasible, or cannot reasonably be required on duly substantiated grounds, the employer shall take the necessary measures to move the worker concerned to another job.

3   If moving her to another job is not technically and/or objectively feasible or cannot reasonably be required on duly substantiated grounds, the worker concerned shall be granted leave in accordance with national legislation and/or national practice for the whole of the period necessary to protect her safety or health.

4   The provisions of this Article shall apply mutatis mutandis to the case where a worker pursuing an activity which is forbidden pursuant to Article 6 becomes pregnant or starts breastfeeding and informs her employer thereof.

Article 6

Cases in which exposure is prohibited

In addition to the general provisions concerning the protection of workers, in particular those relating to the limit values for occupational exposure:

1   pregnant workers within the meaning of Article 2 (a) may under no circumstances be obliged to perform duties for which the assessment has revealed a risk of exposure, which would jeopardize safety or health, to the agents and working conditions listed in Annex II, Section A;

2   workers who are breastfeeding, within the meaning of Article 2 (c), may under no circumstances be obliged to perform duties for which the assessment has revealed a risk of exposure, which would jeopardize safety or health, to the agents and working conditions listed in Annex II, Section B.

Article 7

Night work

1   Member States shall take the necessary measures to ensure that workers referred to in Article 2 are not obliged to perform night work during their pregnancy and for a period following childbirth which shall be determined by the national authority competent for safety and health, subject to submission, in accordance with the procedures laid down by the Member States, of a medical certificate stating that this is necessary for the safety or health of the worker concerned.

2   The measures referred to in paragraph 1 must entail the possibility, in accordance with national legislation and/or national practice, of:

(a)   transfer to daytime work; or

(b)   leave from work or extension of maternity leave where such a transfer is not technically and/or objectively feasible or cannot reasonably by required on duly substantiated grounds.

Article 8

Maternity leave

1   Member States shall take the necessary measures to ensure that workers within the meaning of Article 2 are entitled to a continuous period of maternity leave of a least 14 weeks allocated before and/or after confinement in accordance with national legislation and/or practice.

2   The maternity leave stipulated in paragraph 1 must include compulsory maternity leave of at least two weeks allocated before and/or after confinement in accordance with national legislation and/or practice.

Article 9

Time off for ante-natal examinations

Member States shall take the necessary measures to ensure that pregnant workers within the meaning of Article 2 (a) are entitled to, in accordance with national legislation and/or practice, time off, without loss of pay, in order to attend ante-natal examinations, if such examinations have to take place during working hours.

Article 10

Prohibition of dismissal

In order to guarantee workers, within the meaning of Article 2, the exercise of their health and safety protection rights as recognized under this Article, it shall be provided that:

1   Member States shall take the necessary measures to prohibit the dismissal of workers, within the meaning of Article 2, during the period from the beginning of their pregnancy to the end of the maternity leave referred to in Article 8 (1), save in exceptional cases not connected with their condition which are permitted under national legislation and/or practice and, where applicable, provided that the competent authority has given its consent;

2 if a worker, within the meaning of Article 2, is dismissed during the period referred to in point 1, the employer must cite duly substantiated grounds for her dismissal in writing;

3 Member States shall take the necessary measures to protect workers, within the meaning of Article 2, from consequences of dismissal which is unlawful by virtue of point 1.

Article 11

Employment rights

In order to guarantee workers within the meaning of Article 2 the exercise of their health and safety protection rights as recognized in this Article, it shall be provided that:

1 in the cases referred to in Articles 5, 6 and 7, the employment rights relating to the employment contract, including the maintenance of a payment to, and/or entitlement to an adequate allowance for, workers within the meaning of Article 2, must be ensured in accordance with national legislation and/or national practice;

2 in the case referred to in Article 8, the following must be ensured:

 (a) the rights connected with the employment contract of workers within the meaning of Article 2, other than those referred to in point (b) below;

 (b) maintenance of a payment to, and/or entitlement to an adequate allowance for, workers within the meaning of Article 2;

3 the allowance referred to in point 2 (b) shall be deemed adequate if it guarantees income at least equivalent to that which the worker concerned would receive in the event of a break in her activities on grounds connected with her state of health, subject to any ceiling laid down under national legislation;

4 Member States may make entitlement to pay or the allowance referred to in points 1 and 2 (b) conditional upon the worker concerned fulfilling the conditions of eligibilty for such benefits laid down under national legislation.

These conditions may under no circumstances provide for periods of previous employment in excess of 12 months immediately prior to the presumed date of confinement.

Article 12

Defence of rights

Member States shall introduce into their national legal systems such measures as are necessary to enable all workers who should themselves wronged by failure to comply with the obligations arising from this Directive to pursue their claims by judicial process (and/or, in accordance with national laws and/or practices) by recourse to other competent authorities.

Article 13

Amendments to the Annexes

1 Strictly technical adjustments to Annex I as a result of technical progress, changes in international regulations or specifications and new findings in the area covered by this Directive shall be adopted in accordance with the procedure laid down in Article 17 of Directive 89/391/EEC.

2 Annex II may be amended only in accordance with the procedure laid down in Article 118a of the Treaty.

Article 14

Final provisions

1   Member States shall bring into force the laws, regulations and administrative provisions necessary to comply with this Directive not later than two years after the adoption thereof or ensure, at the latest two years after adoption of this Directive, that the two sides of industry introduce the requisite privisions by means of collective agreements, with Member States being required to make all the necessary provisions to enable them at all times to guarantee the results laid down by this Directive. They shall forthwith inform the Commission thereof.

2   When Member States adopt the measures referred to in paragraph 1, they shall contain a reference of this Directive or shall be accompanied by such reference on the occasion of their official publication. The methods of making such a reference shall be laid down by the Member States.

3   Member States shall communicate to the Commission the texts of the essential provisions of national law which they have already adopted or adopt in the field governed by this Directive.

4   Member States shall report to the Commission every five years on the practical implementation of the provisions of this Directive, indicating the points of view of the two sides of industry.

However, Member States shall report for the first time to the Commission on the practical implementation of the provisions of this Directive, indicating the points of view of the two sides of industry, four years after its adoption.

The Commission shall inform the European Parliament, the Council, the Economic and Social Committee and the Advisory Committee on Safety, Hygiene and Health Protection at Work.

5   The Commission shall periodically submit to the European Parliament, the Council and the Economic and Social Committee a report on the implementation of this Directive, taking into account paragraphs 1, 2 and 3.

6   The Council will re-examine this Directive, on the basis of an assessment carried out on the basis of the reports referred to in the second subparagraph of paragraph 4 and, should the need arise, of a proposal, to be submitted by the Commission at the latest five years after adoption of the Directive.

DIRECTIVE 2006/54/EC OF THE EUROPEAN PARLIAMENT AND OF THE COUNCIL

TITLE I

GENERAL PROVISIONS

Article 1

Purpose

The purpose of this Directive is to ensure the implementation of the principle of equal opportunities and equal treatment of men and women in matters of employment and occupation. To that end, it contains provisions to implement the principle of equal treatment in relation to:

(a)   access to employment, including promotion, and to vocational training;

(b)   working conditions, including pay;

(c)   occupational social security schemes.

It also contains provisions to ensure that such implementation is made more effective by the establishment of appropriate procedures.

Article 2

Definitions

1   For the purposes of this Directive, the following definitions shall apply:

(a)   'direct discrimination': where one person is treated less favourably on grounds of sex than another is, has been or would be treated in a comparable situation;

(b)   'indirect discrimination': where an apparently neutral provision, criterion or practice would put persons of one sex at a particular disadvantage compared with persons of the other sex, unless that provision, criterion or practice is objectively justified by a legitimate aim, and the means of achieving that aim are appropriate and necessary;

(c)   'harassment': where unwanted conduct related to the sex of a person occurs with the purpose or effect of violating the dignity of a person, and of creating an intimidating, hostile, degrading, humiliating or offensive environment; L 204/26 EN Official Journal of the European Union 26.7.2006 (1) OJ C 321, 31.12.2003, p. 1.

(d)   'sexual harassment': where any form of unwanted verbal, non-verbal or physical conduct of a sexual nature occurs, with the purpose or effect of violating the dignity of a person, in particular when creating an intimidating, hostile, degrading, humiliating or offensive environment;

(e)   'pay': the ordinary basic or minimum wage or salary and any other consideration, whether in cash or in kind, which the worker receives directly or indirectly, in respect of his/ her employment from his/her employer;

(f)   'occupational social security schemes': schemes not governed by Council Directive 79/7/EEC of 19 December 1978 on the progressive implementation of the principle of equal treatment for men and women in matters of social security (1) whose purpose is to provide workers, whether employees or self-employed, in an undertaking or group of undertakings, area of economic activity, occupational sector or group of sectors with benefits intended to supplement the benefits provided by statutory social security schemes or to replace them, whether membership of such schemes is compulsory or optional.

2   For the purposes of this Directive, discrimination includes:

(a)   harassment and sexual harassment, as well as any less favourable treatment based on a person's rejection of or submission to such conduct;

(b)   instruction to discriminate against persons on grounds of sex;

(c)   any less favourable treatment of a woman related to pregnancy or maternity leave within the meaning of Directive 92/85/EEC.

Article 3

Positive action

Member States may maintain or adopt measures within the meaning of Article 141(4) of the Treaty with a view to ensuring full equality in practice between men and women in working life.

TITLE II

SPECIFIC PROVISIONS

CHAPTER 1

Equal pay

Article 4

Prohibition of discrimination

For the same work or for work to which equal value is attributed, direct and indirect discrimination on grounds of sex with regard to all aspects and conditions of remuneration shall be eliminated. In particular, where a job classification system is used for determining pay, it shall be based on the same criteria for both men and women and so drawn up as to exclude any discrimination on grounds of sex.

CHAPTER 2

Equal treatment in occupational social security schemes

Article 5

Prohibition of discrimination

Without prejudice to Article 4, there shall be no direct or indirect discrimination on grounds of sex in occupational social security schemes, in particular as regards:

(a)   the scope of such schemes and the conditions of access to them;

(b)   the obligation to contribute and the calculation of contributions;

(c)   the calculation of benefits, including supplementary benefits due in respect of a spouse or dependants, and the conditions governing the duration and retention of entitlement to benefits.

Article 6

Personal scope

This Chapter shall apply to members of the working population, including self-employed persons, persons whose activity is interrupted by illness, maternity, accident or involuntary unemployment and persons seeking employment and to retired and disabled workers, and to those claiming under them, in accordance with national law and/or practice.

Article 7

Material scope

1   This Chapter applies to:

(a)   occupational social security schemes which provide protection against the following risks:

(i)   sickness,

(ii)   invalidity,

(iii)   old age, including early retirement,

(iv)   industrial accidents and occupational diseases,

(v)   unemployment;

(b)   occupational social security schemes which provide for other social benefits, in cash or in kind, and in particular survivors' benefits and family allowances, if such benefits constitute a consideration paid by the employer to the worker by reason of the latter's employment.

2   This Chapter also applies to pension schemes for a particular category of worker such as that of public servants if the benefits payable under the scheme are paid by reason of the employment relationship with the public employer. The fact that such a scheme forms part of a general statutory scheme shall be without prejudice in that respect.

Article 8

Exclusions from the material scope

1   This Chapter does not apply to:

(a)   individual contracts for self-employed persons;

(b)   single-member schemes for self-employed persons;

(c)   insurance contracts to which the employer is not a party, in the case of workers;

(d)   optional provisions of occupational social security schemes offered to participants individually to guarantee them:

(i)   either additional benefits,

(ii)   or a choice of date on which the normal benefits for self-employed persons will start, or a choice between several benefits;

(e)   occupational social security schemes in so far as benefits are financed by contributions paid by workers on a voluntary basis.

2   This Chapter does not preclude an employer granting to persons who have already reached the retirement age for the purposes of granting a pension by virtue of an occupational social security scheme, but who have not yet reached the retirement age for the purposes of granting a statutory retirement pension, a pension supplement, the aim of which is to make equal or more nearly equal the overall amount of benefit paid to these persons in relation to the amount paid to persons of the other sex in the same situation who have already reached the statutory retirement age, until the persons benefiting from the supplement reach the statutory retirement age.

Article 9

Examples of discrimination

1   Provisions contrary to the principle of equal treatment shall include those based on sex, either directly or indirectly, for:

(a)   determining the persons who may participate in an occupational social security scheme;

(b)   fixing the compulsory or optional nature of participation in an occupational social security scheme;

(c)   laying down different rules as regards the age of entry into the scheme or the minimum period of employment or membership of the scheme required to obtain the benefits thereof;

(d) laying down different rules, except as provided for in points (h) and (j), for the reimbursement of contributions when a worker leaves a scheme without having fulfilled the conditions guaranteeing a deferred right to long-term benefits;

(e) setting different conditions for the granting of benefits or restricting such benefits to workers of one or other of the sexes;

(f) fixing different retirement ages;

(g) suspending the retention or acquisition of rights during periods of maternity leave or leave for family reasons which are granted by law or agreement and are paid by the employer;

(h) setting different levels of benefit, except in so far as may be necessary to take account of actuarial calculation factors which differ according to sex in the case of definedcontribution schemes; in the case of funded defined-benefit schemes, certain elements may be unequal where the inequality of the amounts results from the effects of the use of actuarial factors differing according to sex at the time when the scheme's funding is implemented; L 204/28 EN Official Journal of the European Union 26.7.2006

(i) setting different levels for workers' contributions;

(j) setting different levels for employers' contributions, except:

(i) in the case of defined-contribution schemes if the aim is to equalise the amount of the final benefits or to make them more nearly equal for both sexes,

(ii) in the case of funded defined-benefit schemes where the employer's contributions are intended to ensure the adequacy of the funds necessary to cover the cost of the benefits defined;

(k) laying down different standards or standards applicable only to workers of a specified sex, except as provided for in points (h) and (j), as regards the guarantee or retention of entitlement to deferred benefits when a worker leaves a scheme.

2 Where the granting of benefits within the scope of this Chapter is left to the discretion of the scheme's management bodies, the latter shall comply with the principle of equal treatment.

Article 10

Implementation as regards self-employed persons

1 Member States shall take the necessary steps to ensure that the provisions of occupational social security schemes for selfemployed persons contrary to the principle of equal treatment are revised with effect from 1 January 1993 at the latest or for Member States whose accession took place after that date, at the date that Directive 86/378/EEC became applicable in their territory.

2 This Chapter shall not preclude rights and obligations relating to a period of membership of an occupational social security scheme for self-employed persons prior to revision of that scheme from remaining subject to the provisions of the scheme in force during that period.

Article 11

Possibility of deferral as regards self-employed persons

As regards occupational social security schemes for selfemployed persons, Member States may defer compulsory application of the principle of equal treatment with regard to:

(a)   determination of pensionable age for the granting of oldage or retirement pensions, and the possible implications for other benefits:

    (i)   either until the date on which such equality is achieved in statutory schemes,

    (ii) or, at the latest, until such equality is prescribed by a directive;

(b)   survivors' pensions until Community law establishes the principle of equal treatment in statutory social security schemes in that regard;

(c)   the application of Article 9(1)(i) in relation to the use of actuarial calculation factors, until 1 January 1999 or for Member States whose accession took place after that date until the date that Directive 86/378/EEC became applicable in their territory.

Article 12

Retroactive effect

1   Any measure implementing this Chapter, as regards workers, shall cover all benefits under occupational social security schemes derived from periods of employment subsequent to 17 May 1990 and shall apply retroactively to that date, without prejudice to workers or those claiming under them who have, before that date, initiated legal proceedings or raised an equivalent claim under national law. In that event, the implementation measures shall apply retroactively to 8 April 1976 and shall cover all the benefits derived from periods of employment after that date. For Member States which acceded to the Community after 8 April 1976, and before 17 May 1990, that date shall be replaced by the date on which Article 141 of the Treaty became applicable in their territory.

2   The second sentence of paragraph 1 shall not prevent national rules relating to time limits for bringing actions under national law from being relied on against workers or those claiming under them who initiated legal proceedings or raised an equivalent claim under national law before 17 May 1990, provided that they are not less favourable for that type of action than for similar actions of a domestic nature and that they do not render the exercise of rights conferred by Community law impossible in practice.

3   For Member States whose accession took place after 17 May 1990 and which were on 1 January 1994 Contracting Parties to the Agreement on the European Economic Area, the date of 17 May 1990 in the first sentence of paragraph 1 shall be replaced by 1 January 1994.

4   For other Member States whose accession took place after 17 May 1990, the date of 17 May 1990 in paragraphs 1 and 2 shall be replaced by the date on which Article 141 of the Treaty became applicable in their territory.

Article 13

Flexible pensionable age

Where men and women may claim a flexible pensionable age under the same conditions, this shall not be deemed to be incompatible with this Chapter.

26.7.2006 EN Official Journal of the European Union L 204/29

CHAPTER 3

Equal treatment as regards access to employment, vocational training and promotion and working conditions

Article 14

Prohibition of discrimination

1   There shall be no direct or indirect discrimination on grounds of sex in the public or private sectors, including public bodies, in relation to:

   (a)   conditions for access to employment, to self-employment or to occupation, including selection criteria and recruitment conditions, whatever the branch of activity and at all levels of the professional hierarchy, including promotion;

   (b)   access to all types and to all levels of vocational guidance, vocational training, advanced vocational training and retraining, including practical work experience;

   (c)   employment and working conditions, including dismissals, as well as pay as provided for in Article 141 of the Treaty;

   (d)   membership of, and involvement in, an organisation of workers or employers, or any organisation whose members carry on a particular profession, including the benefits provided for by such organisations.

2   Member States may provide, as regards access to employment including the training leading thereto, that a difference of treatment which is based on a characteristic related to sex shall not constitute discrimination where, by reason of the nature of the particular occupational activities concerned or of the context in which they are carried out, such a characteristic constitutes a genuine and determining occupational requirement, provided that its objective is legitimate and the requirement is proportionate.

Article 15

Return from maternity leave

A woman on maternity leave shall be entitled, after the end of her period of maternity leave, to return to her job or to an equivalent post on terms and conditions which are no less favourable to her and to benefit from any improvement in working conditions to which she would have been entitled during her absence.

Article 16

Paternity and adoption leave

This Directive is without prejudice to the right of Member States to recognise distinct rights to paternity and/or adoption leave. Those Member States which recognise such rights shall take the necessary measures to protect working men and women against dismissal due to exercising those rights and ensure that, at the end of such leave, they are entitled to return to their jobs or to equivalent posts on terms and conditions which are no less favourable to them, and to benefit from any improvement in working conditions to which they would have been entitled during their absence.

TITLE III
HORIZONTAL PROVISIONS
CHAPTER 1
Remedies and enforcement

Section 1

Remedies

Article 17

Defence of rights

1   Member States shall ensure that, after possible recourse to other competent authorities including where they deem it appropriate conciliation procedures, judicial procedures for the enforcement of obligations under this Directive are available to all persons who consider themselves wronged by failure to apply the principle of equal treatment to them, even after the relationship in which the discrimination is alleged to have occurred has ended.

2   Member States shall ensure that associations, organisations or other legal entities which have, in accordance with the criteria laid down by their national law, a legitimate interest in ensuring that the provisions of this Directive are complied with, may engage, either on behalf or in support of the complainant, with his/her approval, in any judicial and/or administrative procedure provided for the enforcement of obligations under this Directive.

3   Paragraphs 1 and 2 are without prejudice to national rules relating to time limits for bringing actions as regards the principle of equal treatment.

Article 18

Compensation or reparation

Member States shall introduce into their national legal systems such measures as are necessary to ensure real and effective compensation or reparation as the Member States so determine for the loss and damage sustained by a person injured as a result of discrimination on grounds of sex, in a way which is dissuasive and proportionate to the damage suffered. Such compensation or reparation may not be restricted by the fixing of a prior upper limit, except in cases where the employer can prove that the only damage suffered by an applicant as a result of discrimination within the meaning of this Directive is the refusal to take his/her job application into consideration.

L 204/30 EN Official Journal of the European Union 26.7.2006

Section 2

Burden of proof

Article 19

Burden of proof

1   Member States shall take such measures as are necessary, in accordance with their national judicial systems, to ensure that, when persons who consider themselves wronged because the principle of equal treatment has not been applied to them establish, before a court or other competent authority, facts from

which it may be presumed that there has been direct or indirect discrimination, it shall be for the respondent to prove that there has been no breach of the principle of equal treatment.

2   Paragraph 1 shall not prevent Member States from introducing rules of evidence which are more favourable to plaintiffs.

3   Member States need not apply paragraph 1 to proceedings in which it is for the court or competent body to investigate the facts of the case.

4   Paragraphs 1, 2 and 3 shall also apply to:

(a)   the situations covered by Article 141 of the Treaty and, insofar as discrimination based on sex is concerned, by Directives 92/85/EEC and 96/34/EC;

(b)   any civil or administrative procedure concerning the public or private sector which provides for means of redress under national law pursuant to the measures referred to in (a) with the exception of out-of-court procedures of a voluntary nature or provided for in national law.

5   This Article shall not apply to criminal procedures, unless otherwise provided by the Member States.

CHAPTER 2

Promotion of equal treatment — dialogue

Article 20

Equality bodies

1   Member States shall designate and make the necessary arrangements for a body or bodies for the promotion, analysis, monitoring and support of equal treatment of all persons without discrimination on grounds of sex. These bodies may form part of agencies with responsibility at national level for the defence of human rights or the safeguard of individuals' rights.

2   Member States shall ensure that the competences of these bodies include:

(a)   without prejudice to the right of victims and of associations, organisations or other legal entities referred to in Article 17(2), providing independent assistance to victims of discrimination in pursuing their complaints about discrimination;

(b)   conducting independent surveys concerning discrimination;

(c)   publishing independent reports and making recommendations on any issue relating to such discrimination;

(d)   at the appropriate level exchanging available information with corresponding European bodies such as any future European Institute for Gender Equality.

Article 21

Social dialogue

1   Member States shall, in accordance with national traditions and practice, take adequate measures to promote social dialogue between the social partners with a view to fostering equal treatment, including, for example, through the monitoring of practices in the workplace, in access to employment, vocational training and promotion, as well as through the monitoring of collective agreements, codes of conduct, research or exchange of experience and good practice.

2   Where consistent with national traditions and practice, Member States shall encourage the social partners, without prejudice to their autonomy, to promote equality between men and women, and flexible working arrangements, with the aim of facilitating the reconciliation of work and private life, and to conclude, at the appropriate level, agreements laying down antidiscrimination rules in the fields referred to in Article 1 which fall within the scope of collective bargaining. These agreements shall respect the provisions of this Directive and the relevant national implementing measures.

3   Member States shall, in accordance with national law, collective agreements or practice, encourage employers to promote equal treatment for men and women in a planned and systematic way in the workplace, in access to employment, vocational training and promotion.

4   To this end, employers shall be encouraged to provide at appropriate regular intervals employees and/or their representatives with appropriate information on equal treatment for men and women in the undertaking.

Such information may include an overview of the proportions of men and women at different levels of the organisation; their pay and pay differentials; and possible measures to improve the situation in cooperation with employees' representatives.

Article 22

Dialogue with non-governmental organisations

Member States shall encourage dialogue with appropriate nongovernmental organisations which have, in accordance with their national law and practice, a legitimate interest in contributing to 26.7.2006 EN Official Journal of the European Union L 204/31 the fight against discrimination on grounds of sex with a view to promoting the principle of equal treatment.

CHAPTER 3

General horizontal provisions

Article 23

Compliance

Member States shall take all necessary measures to ensure that:

(a)   any laws, regulations and administrative provisions contrary to the principle of equal treatment are abolished;

(b)   provisions contrary to the principle of equal treatment in individual or collective contracts or agreements, internal rules of undertakings or rules governing the independent occupations and professions and workers' and employers' organisations or any other arrangements shall be, or may be, declared null and void or are amended;

(c)   occupational social security schemes containing such provisions may not be approved or extended by administrative measures.

Article 24

Victimisation

Member States shall introduce into their national legal systems such measures as are necessary to protect employees, including those who are employees' representatives provided for by national laws and/or practices, against dismissal or other adverse treatment by the employer as a reaction to a complaint within the undertaking or to any legal proceedings aimed at enforcing compliance with the principle of equal treatment.

Article 25

Penalties

Member States shall lay down the rules on penalties applicable to infringements of the national provisions adopted pursuant to this Directive, and shall take all measures necessary to ensure that they are applied. The penalties, which may comprise the payment of compensation to the victim, must be effective, proportionate and dissuasive. The Member States shall notify those provisions to the Commission by 5 October 2005 at the latest and shall notify it without delay of any subsequent amendment affecting them.

Article 26

Prevention of discrimination

Member States shall encourage, in accordance with national law, collective agreements or practice, employers and those responsible for access to vocational training to take effective measures to prevent all forms of discrimination on grounds of sex, in particular harassment and sexual harassment in the workplace, in access to employment, vocational training and promotion.

Article 27

Minimum requirements

1   Member States may introduce or maintain provisions which are more favourable to the protection of the principle of equal treatment than those laid down in this Directive.

2   Implementation of this Directive shall under no circumstances be sufficient grounds for a reduction in the level of protection of workers in the areas to which it applies, without prejudice to the Member States' right to respond to changes in the situation by introducing laws, regulations and administrative provisions which differ from those in force on the notification of this Directive, provided that the provisions of this Directive are complied with.

Article 28

Relationship to Community and national provisions

1   This Directive shall be without prejudice to provisions concerning the protection of women, particularly as regards pregnancy and maternity.

2   This Directive shall be without prejudice to the provisions of Directive 96/34/EC and Directive 92/85/EEC.

Article 29

Gender mainstreaming

Member States shall actively take into account the objective of equality between men and women when formulating and implementing laws, regulations, administrative provisions, policies and activities in the areas referred to in this Directive.

Article 30

Dissemination of information

Member States shall ensure that measures taken pursuant to this Directive, together with the provisions already in force, are brought to the attention of all the persons concerned by all suitable means and, where appropriate, at the workplace.

TITLE IV

FINAL PROVISIONS

Article 31

Reports

1   By 15 February 2011, the Member States shall communicate to the Commission all the information necessary for the Commission to draw up a report to the European Parliament and the Council on the application of this Directive.

2   Without prejudice to paragraph 1, Member States shall communicate to the Commission, every four years, the texts of any measures adopted pursuant to Article 141(4) of the Treaty, as well as reports on these measures and their implementation. On the basis of that information, the Commission will adopt and publish every four years a report establishing a comparative assessment of any measures in the light of Declaration No 28 annexed to the Final Act of the Treaty of Amsterdam.

3   Member States shall assess the occupational activities referred to in Article 14(2), in order to decide, in the light of social developments, whether there is justification for maintaining the exclusions concerned. They shall notify the Commission of the results of this assessment periodically, but at least every 8 years.

Article 32

Review

By 15 February 2011 at the latest, the Commission shall review the operation of this Directive and if appropriate, propose any amendments it deems necessary.

Article 33

Implementation

Member States shall bring into force the laws, regulations and administrative provisions necessary to comply with this Directive by 15 August 2008 at the latest or shall ensure, by that date, that management and labour introduce the requisite provisions by way of agreement. Member States may, if necessary to take account of particular difficulties, have up to one additional year to comply with this Directive.

Member States shall take all necessary steps to be able to guarantee the results imposed by this Directive. They shall forthwith communicate to the Commission the texts of those measures.

When Member States adopt these measures, they shall contain a reference to this Directive or be accompanied by such reference on the occasion of their official publication. They shall also include a statement that references in existing laws, regulations and administrative provisions to the Directives repealed by this Directive shall be construed as references to this Directive.

Member States shall determine how such reference is to be made and how that statement is to be formulated. The obligation to transpose this Directive into national law shall be confined to those provisions which represent a substantive change as compared with the earlier Directives. The obligation to transpose the provisions which are substantially unchanged arises under the earlier Directives.

Member States shall communicate to the Commission the text of the main provisions of national law which they adopt in the field covered by this Directive.

SECTION 5 – FREEDOM OF ESTABLISHMENT AND PROVISION OF SERVICES

Directive 98/5/EC OF the European Parliament and of the Council

of 16 February 1998 to facilitate practice of the profession of lawyer on a permanent basis in a Member State

Article 1

Object, scope and definitions

1   The purpose of this Directive is to facilitate practice of the profession of lawyer on a permanent basis in a self-employed or salaried capacity in a Member State other than that in which the professional qualification was obtained.

2   For the purposes of this Directive:

(a)   'lawyer` means any person who is a national of a Member State and who is authorised to pursue his professional activities under one of the following professional titles:

(b)   'home Member State` means the Member State in which a lawyer acquired the right to use one of the professional titles referred to in (a) before practising the profession of lawyer in another Member State;

(c)   'host Member State` means the Member State in which a lawyer practises pursuant to this Directive;

(d)   'home-country professional title` means the professional title used in the Member State in which a lawyer acquired the right to use that title before practising the profession of lawyer in the host Member State;

(e)   'grouping` means any entity, with or without legal personality, formed under the law of a Member State, within which lawyers pursue their professional activities jointly under a joint name;

(f)   'relevant professional title` or 'relevant profession` means the professional title or profession governed by the competent authority with whom a lawyer has registered under Article 3, and 'competent authority` means that authority.

3   This Directive shall apply both to lawyers practising in a self-employed capacity and to lawyers practising in a salarial capacity in the home Member State and, subject to Article 8, in the host Member State.

4   Practice of the profession of lawyer within the meaning of this Directive shall not include the provision of services, which is covered by Directive 77/249/EEC.

Article 2

Right to practise under the home-country professional title

Any lawyer shall be entitled to pursue on a permanent basis, in any other Member State under his home-country professional title, the activities specified in Article 5.

Integration into the profession of lawyer in the host Member State shall be subject to Article 10.

Article 3

Registration with the competent authority

1   A lawyer who wishes to practise in a Member State other than that in which he obtained his professional qualification shall register with the competent authority in that State.

2   The competent authority in the host Member State shall register the lawyer upon presentation of a certificate attesting to his registration with the competent authority in the home Member State. It may require that, when presented by the competent authority of the home Member State, the certificate be not more than three months old. It shall inform the competent authority in the home Member State of the registration.

3   For the purpose of applying paragraph 1:

> ▶   in the United Kingdom and Ireland, lawyers practising under a professional title other than those used in the United Kingdom or Ireland shall register either with the authority responsible for the profession of barrister or advocate or with the authority responsible for the profession of solicitor,

> ▶   in the United Kingdom, the authority responsible for a barrister from Ireland shall be that responsible for the profession of barrister or advocate, and the authority responsible for a solicitor from Ireland shall be that responsible for the profession of solicitor,

> ▶   in Ireland, the authority responsible for a barrister or an advocate from the United Kingdom shall be that responsible for the profession of barrister, and the authority responsible for a solicitor from the United Kingdom shall be that responsible for the profession of solicitor.

4   Where the relevant competent authority in a host Member State publishes the names of lawyers registered with it, it shall also publish the names of lawyers registered pursuant to this Directive.

Article 4

Practice under the home-country professional title

1   A lawyer practising in a host Member State under his home-country professional title shall do so under that title, which must be expressed in the official language or one of the official languages of his home Member State, in an intelligible manner and in such a way as to avoid confusion with the professional title of the host Member State.

2   For the purpose of applying paragraph 1, a host Member State may require a lawyer practising under his home-country professional title to indicate the professional body of which he is a member in his home Member State or the judicial authority before which he is entitled to practise pursuant to the laws of his home Member State. A host Member State may also require a lawyer practising under his home-country professional title to include a reference to his registration with the competent authority in that State.

Article 5

Area of activity

1   Subject to paragraphs 2 and 3, a lawyer practising under his home-country professional title carries on the same professional activities as a lawyer practising under the relevant professional title used in the host Member State and may, inter alia, give advice on the law of his home Member State, on Community law, on international law and on the law of the host Member State. He shall in any event comply with the rules of procedure applicable in the national courts.

2   Member States which authorise in their territory a prescribed category of lawyers to prepare deeds for obtaining title to administer estates of deceased persons and for creating or transferring interests in land which, in other Member States, are reserved for professions other than that of lawyer may exclude from such activities lawyers practising under a home-country professional title conferred in one of the latter Member States.

3   For the pursuit of activities relating to the representation or defence of a client in legal proceedings and insofar as the law of the host Member State reserves such activities to lawyers practising under the professional title of that State, the latter may require lawyers practising under their home-country professional titles to work in conjunction with a lawyer who practises before the judicial authority in question and who would, where necessary, be answerable to that authority or with an 'avoué` practising before it.

Nevertheless, in order to ensure the smooth operation of the justice system, Member States may lay down specific rules for access to supreme courts, such as the use of specialist lawyers.

Article 6

Rules of professional conduct applicable

1   Irrespective of the rules of professional conduct to which he is subject in his home Member State, a lawyer practising under his home-country professional title shall be subject to the same rules of professional conduct as lawyers practising under the relevant professional title of the host Member State in respect of all the activities he pursues in its territory.

2   Lawyers practising under their home-country professional titles shall be granted appropriate representation in the professional associations of the host Member State. Such representation shall involve at least the right to vote in elections to those associations' governing bodies.

3   The host Member State may require a lawyer practising under his home-country professional title either to take out professional indemnity insurance or to become a member of a professional guarantee fund in accordance with the rules which that State lays down for professional activities pursued in its territory. Nevertheless, a lawyer practising under his home-country professional title shall be exempted from that requirement if he can prove that he is covered by insurance taken out or a guarantee provided in accordance with the rules of his home Member State, insofar as such insurance or guarantee is equivalent in terms of the conditions and extent of cover. Where the equivalence is only partial, the competent authority in the host Member State may require that additional insurance or an additional guarantee be contracted to cover the elements which are not already covered by the insurance or guarantee contracted in accordance with the rules of the home Member State.

Article 7

Disciplinary proceedings

1   In the event of failure by a lawyer practising under his home-country professional title to fulfil the obligations in force in the host Member State, the rules of procedure, penalties and remedies provided for in the host Member State shall apply.

2   Before initiating disciplinary proceedings against a lawyer practising under his home-country professional title, the competent authority in the host Member State shall inform the competent authority in the home Member State as soon as possible, furnishing it with all the relevant details.

The first subparagraph shall apply mutatis mutandis where disciplinary proceedings are initiated by the competent authority of the home Member State, which shall inform the competent authority of the host Member State(s) accordingly.

3   Without prejudice to the decision-making power of the competent authority in the host Member State, that authority shall cooperate throughout the disciplinary proceedings with the competent authority in the home Member State. In particular, the host Member State shall take the measures necessary to ensure that the competent authority in the home Member State can make submissions to the bodies responsible for hearing any appeal.

4   The competent authority in the home Member State shall decide what action to take, under its own procedural and substantive rules, in the light of a decision of the competent authority in the host Member State concerning a lawyer practising under his home-country professional title.

5   Although it is not a prerequisite for the decision of the competent authority in the host Member State, the temporary or permanent withdrawal by the competent authority in the home Member State of the authorisation to practise the profession shall automatically lead to the lawyer concerned being temporarily or permanently prohibited from practising under his home-country professional title in the host Member State.

Article 8

Salaried practice

A lawyer registered in a host Member State under his home-country professional title may practise as a salaried lawyer in the employ of another lawyer, an association or firm of lawyers, or a public or private enterprise to the extent that the host Member State so permits for lawyers registered under the professional title used in that State.

Article 9

Statement of reasons and remedies

Decisions not to effect the registration referred to in Article 3 or to cancel such registration and decisions imposing disciplinary measures shall state the reasons on which they are based.

A remedy shall be available against such decisions before a court or tribunal in accordance with the provisions of domestic law.

Article 10

Like treatment as a lawyer of the host Member State

1   A lawyer practising under his home-country professional title who has effectively and regularly pursued for a period of at least three years an activity in the host Member State in the law of that State including Community law shall, with a view to gaining admission to the profession of lawyer in the host Member State, be exempted from the conditions set out in Article 4(1)(b) of Directive 89/48/EEC, 'Effective and regular pursuit' means actual exercise of the activity without any interruption other than that resulting from the events of everyday life.

It shall be for the lawyer concerned to furnish the competent authority in the host Member State with proof of such effective regular pursuit for a period of at least three years of an activity in the law of the host Member State. To that end:

(a)   the lawyer shall provide the competent authority in the host Member State with any relevant information and documentation, notably on the number of matters he has dealt with and their nature;

(b)   the competent authority of the host Member State may verify the effective and regular nature of the activity pursued and may, if need be, request the lawyer to provide, orally or in writing, clarification of or further details on the information and documentation mentioned in point (a).

Reasons shall be given for a decision by the competent authority in the host Member State not to grant an exemption where proof is not provided that the requirements laid down in the first subparagraph have been fulfilled, and the decision shall be subject to appeal under domestic law.

2　A lawyer practising under his home-country professional title in a host Member State may, at any time, apply to have his diploma recognised in accordance with Directive 89/48/EEC with a view to gaining admission to the profession of lawyer in the host Member State and practising it under the professional title corresponding to the profession in that Member State.

3　A lawyer practising under his home-country professional title who has effectively and regularly pursued a professional activity in the host Member State for a period of at least three years but for a lesser period in the law of that Member State may obtain from the competent authority of that State admission to the profession of lawyer in the host Member State and the right to practise it under the professional title corresponding to the profession in that Member State, without having to meet the conditions referred to in Article 4(1)(b) of Directive 89/48/EEC, under the conditions and in accordance with the procedures set out below:

(a)　The competent authority of the host Member State shall take into account the effective and regular professional activity pursued during the abovementioned period and any knowledge and professional experience of the law of the host Member State, and any attendance at lectures or seminars on the law of the host Member State, including the rules regulating professional practice and conduct.

(b)　The lawyer shall provide the competent authority of the host Member State with any relevant information and documentation, in particular on the matters he has dealt with. Assessment of the lawyer's effective and regular activity in the host Member State and assessment of his capacity to continue the activity he has pursued there shall be carried out by means of an interview with the competent authority of the host Member State in order to verify the regular and effective nature of the activity pursued.

Reasons shall be given for a decision by the competent authority in the host Member State not to grant authorisation where proof is not provided that the requirements laid down in the first subparagraph have been fulfilled, and the decision shall be subject to appeal under domestic law.

4　The competent authority of the host Member State may, by reasoned decision subject to appeal under domestic law, refuse to allow the lawyer the benefit of the provisions of this Article if it considers that this would be against public policy, in a particular because of disciplinary proceedings, complaints or incidents of any kind.

5　The representatives of the competent authority entrusted with consideration of the application shall preserve the confidentiality of any information received.

6　A lawyer who gains admission to the profession of lawyer in the host Member State in accordance with paragraphs 1, 2 and 3 shall be entitled to use his home-country professional title, expressed in the official language or one of the official languages of his home Member State, alongside the professional title corresponding to the profession of lawyer in the host Member State.

Article 11

Joint practice

Where joint practise is authorised in respect of lawyers carrying on their activities under the relevant professional title in the host Member State, the following provisions shall apply in respect of lawyers wishing to carry on activities under that title or registering with the competent authority:

(1) One or more lawyers who belong to the same grouping in their home Member State and who practise under their home-country professional title in a host Member State may pursue their professional activities in a branch or agency of their grouping in the host Member State. However, where the fundamental rules governing that grouping in the home Member State are incompatible with the fundamental rules laid down by law, regulation or administrative action in the host Member State, the latter rules shall prevail insofar as compliance therewith is justified by the public interest in protecting clients and third parties.

(2) Each Member State shall afford two or more lawyers from the same grouping or the same home Member State who practise in its territory under their home-country professional titles access to a form of joint practice. If the host Member State gives its lawyers a choice between several forms of joint practice, those same forms shall also be made available to the aforementioned lawyers. The manner in which such lawyers practise jointly in the host Member State shall be governed by the laws, regulations and administrative provisions of that State.

(3) The host Member State shall take the measures necessary to permit joint practice also between:

(a) several lawyers from different Member States practising under their home-country professional titles;

(b) one or more lawyers covered by point (a) and one or more lawyers from the host Member State.

The manner in which such lawyers practice jointly in the host Member State shall be governed by the laws, regulations and administrative provisions of that State.

(4) A lawyer who wishes to practise under his home-country professional title shall inform the competent authority in the host Member State of the fact that he is a member of a grouping in his home Member State and furnish any relevant information on that grouping.

(5) Notwithstanding points 1 to 4, a host Member State, insofar as it prohibits lawyers practising under its own relevant professional title from practising the profession of lawyer within a grouping in which some persons are not members of the profession, may refuse to allow a lawyer registered under his home-country professional title to practice in its territory in his capacity as a member of his grouping. The grouping is deemed to include persons who are not members of the profession if

▶ the capital of the grouping is held entirely or partly, or

▶ the name under which it practises is used, or

▶ the decision-making power in that grouping is exercised, de facto or de jure, by persons who do not have the status of lawyer within the meaning of Article 1(2).

Where the fundamental rules governing a grouping of lawyers in the home Member State are incompatible with the rules in force in the host Member State or with the provisions of the first subparagraph, the host Member State may oppose the opening of a branch or agency within its territory without the restrictions laid down in point (1).

Article 12

Name of the grouping

Whatever the manner in which lawyers practise under their home-country professional titles in the host Member State, they may employ the name of any grouping to which they belong in their home Member State.

The host Member State may require that, in addition to the name referred to in the first subparagraph, mention be made of the legal form of the grouping in the home Member State and/or of the names of any members of the grouping practising in the host Member State.

Article 13

Cooperation between the competent authorities in the home and host Member States and confidentiality

In order to facilitate the application of this Directive and to prevent its provisions from being misapplied for the sole purpose of circumventing the rules applicable in the host Member State, the competent authority in the host Member State and the competent authority in the home Member State shall collaborate closely and afford each other mutual assistance.

They shall preserve the confidentiality of the information they exchange.

Article 14

Designation of the competent authorities

Member States shall designate the competent authorities empowered to receive the applications and to take the decisions referred to in this Directive by 14 March 2000. They shall communicate this information to the other Member States and to the Commission.

Article 15

Report by the Commission

Ten years at the latest from the entry into force of this Directive, the Commission shall report to the European Parliament and to the Council on progress in the implementation of the Directive.

After having held all the necessary consultations, it shall on that occasion present its conclusions and any amendments which could be made to the existing system.

Article 16

Implementation

1   Member States shall bring into force the laws, regulations and administrative provisions necessary to comply with this Directive by 14 March 2000. They shall forthwith inform the Commission thereof.

When Member States adopt these measures, they shall contain a reference to this Directive or shall be accompanied by such reference on the occasion of their official publication. The methods of making such reference shall be adopted by Member States.

2   Member States shall communicate to the Commission the texts of the main provisions of domestic law which they adopt in the field covered by this Directive.

DIRECTIVE 2005/36/EC OF THE EUROPEAN PARLIAMENT AND OF THE COUNCIL

TITLE I

GENERAL PROVISIONS

Article 1

Purpose

This Directive establishes rules according to which a Member State which makes access to or pursuit of a regulated profession in its territory contingent upon possession of specific professional qualifications (referred to hereinafter as the host Member State) shall recognise professional qualifications obtained in one or more other

Member States (referred to hereinafter as the home Member State) and which allow the holder of the said qualifications to pursue the same profession there, for access to and pursuit of that profession.

Article 2

Scope

1   This Directive shall apply to all nationals of a Member State wishing to pursue a regulated profession in a Member State, including those belonging to the liberal professions, other than that in which they obtained their professional qualifications, on either a self-employed or employed basis.

2   Each Member State may permit Member State nationals in possession of evidence of professional qualifications not obtained in a Member State to pursue a regulated profession within the meaning of Article 3(1)(a) on its territory in accordance with its rules. In the case of professions covered by Title III, Chapter III, this initial recognition shall respect the minimum training conditions laid down in that Chapter.

3   Where, for a given regulated profession, other specific arrangements directly related to the recognition of professional qualifications are established in a separate instrument of Community law, the corresponding provisions of this Directive shall not apply.

Article 3

Definitions

1   For the purposes of this Directive, the following definitions apply:

(a)   'regulated profession': a professional activity or group of professional activities, access to which, the pursuit of which, or one of the modes of pursuit of which is subject, directly or indirectly, by virtue of legislative, regulatory or administrative provisions to the possession of specific professional qualifications; in particular, the use of a professional title limited by legislative, regulatory or administrative provisions to holders of a given professional qualification shall constitute a mode of pursuit. Where the first sentence of this definition does not apply, a profession referred to in paragraph 2 shall be treated as a regulated profession;

(b)   'professional qualifications': qualifications attested by evidence of formal qualifications, an attestation of competence referred to in Article 11, point (a) (i) and/or professional experience;

(c)   'evidence of formal qualifications': diplomas, certificates and other evidence issued by an authority in a Member State designated pursuant to legislative, regulatory or administrative provisions of that Member State and certifying successful completion of professional training obtained mainly in the Community. Where the first sentence of this definition does not apply, evidence of formal qualifications referred to in paragraph 3 shall be treated as evidence of formal qualifications;

(d)   'competent authority': any authority or body empowered by a Member State specifically to issue or receive training diplomas and other documents or information and to receive the applications, and take the decisions, referred to in this Directive;

(e)   'regulated education and training': any training which is specifically geared to the pursuit of a given profession and which comprises a course or courses complemented, where appropriate, by professional training, or probationary or professional practice. The structure and level of the professional training, probationary or professional practice shall be determined by the laws, regulations or administrative provisions of the Member State concerned or monitored or approved by the authority designated for that purpose;

(f)   'professional experience': the actual and lawful pursuit of the profession concerned in a Member State;

(g)   'adaptation period': the pursuit of a regulated profession in the host Member State under the responsibility of a qualified member of that profession, such period of supervised practice possibly being accompanied by further training. This period of supervised practice shall be the subject of an assessment. The detailed rules governing the adaptation period and its assessment as well as the status of a migrant under supervision shall be laid down by the competent authority in the host Member State. The status enjoyed in the host Member State by the person undergoing the period of supervised practice, in particular in the matter of right of residence as well as obligations, social rights and benefits, allowances and remuneration, shall be established by the competent authorities in that Member State in accordance with applicable Community law;

(h)   'aptitude test': a test limited to the professional knowledge of the applicant, made by the competent authorities of the host Member State with the aim of assessing the ability of the applicant to pursue a regulated profession in that Member State. In order to permit this test to be carried out, the competent authorities shall draw up a list of subjects which, on the basis of a comparison of the education and training required in the Member State and that received by the applicant, are not covered by the diploma or other evidence of formal qualifications possessed by the applicant. The aptitude test must take account of the fact that the applicant is a qualified professional in the home Member State or the Member State from which he comes. It shall cover subjects to be selected from those on the list, knowledge of which is essential in order to be able to pursue the profession in the host Member State. The test may also include knowledge of the professional rules applicable to the activities in question in the host Member State. The detailed application of the aptitude test and the status, in the host Member State, of the applicant who wishes to prepare himself for the aptitude test in that State shall be determined by the competent authorities in that Member State;

(i)   'manager of an undertaking': any person who in an undertaking in the occupational field in question has pursued an activity:

   (i)   as a manager of an undertaking or a manager of a branch of an undertaking; or

   (ii)   as a deputy to the proprietor or the manager of an undertaking where that post involves responsibility equivalent to that of the proprietor or manager represented; or

   (iii)   in a managerial post with duties of a commercial and/ or technical nature and with responsibility for one or more departments of the undertaking.

2   A profession practised by the members of an association or organisation listed in Annex I shall be treated as a regulated profession.

The purpose of the associations or organisations referred to in the first subparagraph is, in particular, to promote and maintain a high standard in the professional field concerned. To that end they are recognised in a special form by a Member State and award evidence of formal qualifications to their members, ensure that their members respect the rules of professional conduct which they prescribe, and confer on them the right to use a title or designatory letters or to benefit from a status corresponding to those formal qualifications. On each occasion that a Member State grants recognition to an association or organisation referred to in the first subparagraph, it shall inform the Commission, which shall publish an appropriate notification in the Official Journal of the European Union.

3   Evidence of formal qualifications issued by a third country shall be regarded as evidence of formal qualifications if the holder has three years' professional experience in the profession concerned on the territory of the Member State which recognised that evidence of formal qualifications in accordance with Article 2(2), certified by that Member State.

Article 4

Effects of recognition

1   The recognition of professional qualifications by the host Member State allows the beneficiary to gain access in that Member State to the same profession as that for which he is qualified in the home Member State and to pursue it in the host Member State under the same conditions as its nationals.

2   For the purposes of this Directive, the profession which the applicant wishes to pursue in the host Member State is the same as that for which he is qualified in his home Member State if the activities covered are comparable.

TITLE II

FREE PROVISION OF SERVICES

Article 5

Principle of the free provision of services

1   Without prejudice to specific provisions of Community law, as well as to Articles 6 and 7 of this Directive, Member States shall not restrict, for any reason relating to professional qualifications, the free provision of services in another Member State:

(a)   if the service provider is legally established in a Member State for the purpose of pursuing the same profession there (hereinafter referred to as the Member State of establishment), and

(b)   where the service provider moves, if he has pursued that profession in the Member State of establishment for at least two years during the 10 years preceding the provision of services when the profession is not regulated in that Member State. The condition requiring two years' pursuit shall not apply when either the profession or the education and training leading to the profession is regulated.

2   The provisions of this title shall only apply where the service provider moves to the territory of the host Member State to pursue, on a temporary and occasional basis, the profession referred to in paragraph 1.

The temporary and occasional nature of the provision of services shall be assessed case by case, in particular in relation to its duration, its frequency, its regularity and its continuity.

3   Where a service provider moves, he shall be subject to professional rules of a professional, statutory or administrative nature which are directly linked to professional qualifications, such as the definition of the profession, the use of titles and serious professional malpractice which is directly and specifically linked to consumer protection and safety, as well as disciplinary provisions which are applicable in the host Member State to professionals who pursue the same profession in that Member State.

Article 6

Exemptions

Pursuant to Article 5(1), the host Member State shall exempt service providers established in another Member State from the requirements which it places on professionals established in its territory relating to:

(a)   authorisation by, registration with or membership of a professional organisation or body. In order to facilitate the application of disciplinary provisions in force on their territory according to Article 5(3), Member States may provide either for automatic temporary registration with or for pro forma membership of such a professional organisation or body, provided that such registration or membership does not delay or complicate in any way the provision of services and does not entail any additional costs for the service provider. A copy of the declaration and, where applicable, of the renewal referred to in Article 7(1), accompanied, for professions which have implications for public health and safety referred to in Article 7(4) or which benefit from automatic recognition under Title III Chapter III, by a copy of the documents referred to in Article 7(2) shall be sent by the competent authority to the relevant professional organisation or body, and this shall constitute automatic temporary registration or pro forma membership for this purpose;

(b) registration with a public social security body for the purpose of settling accounts with an insurer relating to activities pursued for the benefit of insured persons. The service provider shall, however, inform in advance or, in an urgent case, afterwards, the body referred to in point (b) of the services which he has provided.

Article 7

Declaration to be made in advance, if the service provider moves

1 Member States may require that, where the service provider first moves from one Member State to another in order to provide services, he shall inform the competent authority in the host Member State in a written declaration to be made in advance including the details of any insurance cover or other means of personal or collective protection with regard to professional liability. Such declaration shall be renewed once a year if the service provider intends to provide temporary or occasional services in that Member State during that year. The service provider may supply the declaration by any means.

2 Moreover, for the first provision of services or if there is a material change in the situation substantiated by the documents, Member States may require that the declaration be accompanied by the following documents:

(a) proof of the nationality of the service provider;

(b) an attestation certifying that the holder is legally established in a Member State for the purpose of pursuing the activities concerned and that he is not prohibited from practising, even temporarily, at the moment of delivering the attestation;

(c) evidence of professional qualifications;

(d) for cases referred to in Article 5(1)(b), any means of proof that the service provider has pursued the activity concerned for at least two years during the previous ten years; (e) for professions in the security sector, where the Member State so requires for its own nationals, evidence of no criminal convictions.

3 The service shall be provided under the professional title of the Member State of establishment, in so far as such a title exists in that Member State for the professional activity in question. That title shall be indicated in the official language or one of the official languages of the Member State of establishment in such a way as to avoid any confusion with the professional title of the host Member State. Where no such professional title exists in the Member State of establishment, the service provider shall indicate his formal qualification in the official language or one of the official languages of that Member State.

By way of exception, the service shall be provided under the professional title of the host Member State for cases referred to in Title III Chapter III.

4 For the first provision of services, in the case of regulated professions having public health or safety implications, which do not benefit from automatic recognition under Title III Chapter III, the competent authority of the host Member State may check the professional qualifications of the service provider prior to the first provision of services. Such a prior check shall be possible only where the purpose of the check is to avoid serious damage to the health or safety of the service recipient due to a lack of professional

qualification of the service provider and where this does not go beyond what is necessary for that purpose. Within a maximum of one month of receipt of the declaration and accompanying documents, the competent authority shall endeavour to inform the service provider either of its decision not to check his qualifications or of the outcome of such check. Where there is a difficulty which would result in delay, the competent authority shall notify the service provider within the first month of the reason for the delay and the timescale for a decision, which must be finalised within the second month of receipt of completed documentation. Where there is a substantial difference between the professional qualifications of the service provider and the training required in the host Member State, to the extent that that difference is such as to be harmful to public health or safety, the host Member State shall give the service provider the opportunity to show, in particular by means of an aptitude test, that he has acquired the knowledge or competence lacking. In any case, it must be possible to provide the service within one month of a decision being taken in accordance with the previous subparagraph.

In the absence of a reaction of the competent authority within the deadlines set in the previous subparagraphs, the service may be provided.

In cases where qualifications have been verified under this paragraph, the service shall be provided under the professional title of the host Member State.

Article 8

Administrative cooperation

1   The competent authorities of the host Member State may ask the competent authorities of the Member State of establishment, for each provision of services, to provide any information relevant to the legality of the service provider's establishment and his good conduct, as well as the absence of any disciplinary or criminal sanctions of a professional nature. The competent authorities of the Member State of establishment shall provide this information in accordance with the provisions of Article 56.

2   The competent authorities shall ensure the exchange of all information necessary for complaints by a recipient of a service against a service provider to be correctly pursued. Recipients shall be informed of the outcome of the complaint.

Article 9

Information to be given to the recipients of the service

In cases where the service is provided under the professional title of the Member State of establishment or under the formal qualification of the service provider, in addition to the other requirements relating to information contained in Community law, the competent authorities of the host Member State may require the service provider to furnish the recipient of the service with any or all of the following information:

(a)   if the service provider is registered in a commercial register or similar public register, the register in which he is registered, his registration number, or equivalent means of identification contained in that register;

(b)   if the activity is subject to authorisation in the Member State of establishment, the name and address of the competent supervisory authority;

(c)   any professional association or similar body with which the service provider is registered;

(d)   the professional title or, where no such title exists, the formal qualification of the service provider and the Member State in which it was awarded;

(e)   if the service provider performs an activity which is subject to VAT, the VAT identification number referred to in Article 22(1) of the sixth Council Directive 77/388/EEC of 17 May 1977 on the harmonisation of the laws of the Member States relating to turnover taxes - Common system of value added tax: uniform basis of assessment (1);

(f)   details of any insurance cover or other means of personal or collective protection with regard to professional liability.

TITLE III

FREEDOM OF ESTABLISHMENT

CHAPTER I

General system for the recognition of evidence of training

Article 10

Scope

This Chapter applies to all professions which are not covered by Chapters II and III of this Title and in the following cases in which the applicant, for specific and exceptional reasons, does not satisfy the conditions laid down in those Chapters:

(a)   for activities listed in Annex IV, when the migrant does not meet the requirements set out in Articles 17, 18 and 19;

(b)   for doctors with basic training, specialised doctors, nurses responsible for general care, dental practitioners, specialised dental practitioners, veterinary surgeons, midwives, pharmacists and architects, when the migrant does not meet the requirements of effective and lawful professional practice referred to in Articles 23, 27, 33, 37, 39, 43 and 49;

(c)   for architects, when the migrant holds evidence of formal qualification not listed in Annex V, point 5.7;

(d)   without prejudice to Articles 21(1), 23 and 27, for doctors, nurses, dental practitioners, veterinary surgeons, midwives, pharmacists and architects holding evidence of formal qualifications as a specialist, which must follow the training leading to the possession of a title listed in Annex V, points 5.1.1, 5.2.2, 5.3.2, 5.4.2, 5.5.2, 5.6.2 and 5.7.1, and solely for the purpose of the recognition of the relevant specialty;

(e)   for nurses responsible for general care and specialised nurses holding evidence of formal qualifications as a specialist which follows the training leading to the possession of a title listed in Annex V, point 5.2.2, when the migrant seeks recognition in another Member State where the relevant professional activities are pursued by specialised nurses without training as general care nurse;

(f)   for specialised nurses without training as general care nurse, when the migrant seeks recognition in another Member State where the relevant professional activities are pursued by nurses responsible for general care, specialised nurses without training as general care nurse or specialised nurses holding evidence of formal qualifications as a specialist which follows the training leading to the possession of the titles listed in Annex V, point 5.2.2;

(g)   for migrants meeting the requirements set out in Article 3(3).

Article 11

Levels of qualification

For the purpose of applying Article 13, the professional qualifications are grouped under the following levels as described below:

(a)   an attestation of competence issued by a competent authority in the home Member State designated pursuant to legislative, regulatory or administrative provisions of that Member State, on the basis of:

    (i)   either a training course not forming part of a certificate or diploma within the meaning of points (b), (c), (d) or (e), or a specific examination without prior training, or full-time pursuit of the profession in a Member State for three consecutive years or for an equivalent duration on a part-time basis during the previous 10 years,

    (ii)   or general primary or secondary education, attesting that the holder has acquired general knowledge;

(b)   a certificate attesting to a successful completion of a secondary course,

    (i)   either general in character, supplemented by a course of study or professional training other than those referred to in point (c) and/or by the probationary or professional practice required in addition to that course,

    (ii)   or technical or professional in character, supplemented where appropriate by a course of study or professional training as referred to in point (i), and/or by the probationary or professional practice required in addition to that course;

(c)   a diploma certifying successful completion of

    (i)   either training at post-secondary level other than that referred to in points (d) and (e) of a duration of at least one year or of an equivalent duration on a part-time basis, one of the conditions of entry of which is, as a general rule, the successful completion of the secondary course required to obtain entry to university or higher education or the completion of equivalent school education of the second secondary level, as well as the professional training which may be required in addition to that post-secondary course; or

    (ii)   in the case of a regulated profession, training with a special structure, included in Annex II, equivalent to the level of training provided for under (i), which provides a comparable professional standard and which prepares the trainee for a comparable level of responsibilities and functions. The list in Annex II may be amended in accordance with the procedure referred to in Article 58(2) in order to take account of training which meets the requirements provided for in the previous sentence;

(d)   a diploma certifying successful completion of training at post-secondary level of at least three and not more than four years' duration, or of an equivalent duration on a parttime basis, at a university or establishment of higher education or another establishment providing the same level of training, as well as the professional training which may be required in addition to that post-secondary course;

(e)   a diploma certifying that the holder has successfully completed a post-secondary course of at least four years' duration, or of an equivalent duration on a part-time basis, at a university or establishment of higher education or another establishment of equivalent level and, where appropriate, that he has successfully completed the professional training required in addition to the post-secondary course.

Article 12

Equal treatment of qualifications

Any evidence of formal qualifications or set of evidence of formal qualifications issued by a competent authority in a Member State, certifying successful completion of training in the Community which is recognised by that Member State as being of an equivalent level and which confers on the holder the same rights of access to or pursuit of a profession or prepares for the pursuit of that profession, shall be treated as evidence of formal qualifications of the type covered by Article 11, including the level in question. Any professional qualification which, although not satisfying the requirements contained in the legislative, regulatory or administrative provisions in force in the home Member State for access to or the pursuit of a profession, confers on the holder acquired rights by virtue of these provisions, shall also be treated as such evidence of formal qualifications under the same conditions as set out in the first subparagraph. This applies in particular if the home Member State raises the level of training required for admission to a profession and for its exercise, and if an individual who has undergone former training, which does not meet the requirements of the new qualification, benefits from acquired rights by virtue of national legislative, regulatory or administrative provisions; in such case this former training is considered by the host Member State, for the purposes of the application of Article 13, as corresponding to the level of the new training.

Article 13

Conditions for recognition

1   If access to or pursuit of a regulated profession in a host Member State is contingent upon possession of specific professional qualifications, the competent authority of that Member State shall permit access to and pursuit of that profession, under the same conditions as apply to its nationals, to applicants possessing the attestation of competence or evidence of formal qualifications required by another Member State in order to gain access to and pursue that profession on its territory. Attestations of competence or evidence of formal qualifications shall satisfy the following conditions:

     (a)   they shall have been issued by a competent authority in a Member State, designated in accordance with the legislative, regulatory or administrative provisions of that Member State;

     (b)   they shall attest a level of professional qualification at least equivalent to the level immediately prior to that which is required in the host Member State, as described in Article 11.

2   Access to and pursuit of the profession, as described in paragraph 1, shall also be granted to applicants who have pursued the profession referred to in that paragraph on a fulltime basis for two years during the previous 10 years in another Member State which does not regulate that profession, providing they possess one or more attestations of competence or documents providing evidence of formal qualifications. Attestations of competence and evidence of formal qualifications shall satisfy the following conditions:

     (a)   they shall have been issued by a competent authority in a Member State, designated in accordance with the legislative, regulatory or administrative provisions of that Member State;

     (b)   they shall attest a level of professional qualification at least equivalent to the level immediately prior to that required in the host Member State, as described in Article 11;

     (c)   they shall attest that the holder has been prepared for the pursuit of the profession in question.

The two years' professional experience referred to in the first subparagraph may not, however, be required if the evidence of formal qualifications which the applicant possesses certifies regulated education and training within the meaning of Article 3(1)(e) at the levels of qualifications described in Article 11, points (b), (c), (d) or (e). The regulated education and training listed in Annex III shall be considered as such regulated education and training at the level described in Article 11, point (c). The list in Annex III may be amended in accordance with the procedure referred to in Article 58(2) in order to take account of regulated education and training which provides a comparable professional standard and which prepares the trainee for a comparable level of responsibilities and functions.

3   By way of derogation from paragraph 1, point (b) and to paragraph 2, point (b), the host Member State shall permit access and pursuit of a regulated profession where access to this profession is contingent in its territory upon possession of a qualification certifying successful completion of higher or university education of four years' duration, and where the applicant possesses a qualification referred to in Article 11, point (c).

Article 14

Compensation measures

1   Article 13 does not preclude the host Member State from requiring the applicant to complete an adaptation period of up to three years or to take an aptitude test if:

   (a)   the duration of the training of which he provides evidence under the terms of Article 13, paragraph 1 or 2, is at least one year shorter than that required by the host Member State;

   (b)   the training he has received covers substantially different matters than those covered by the evidence of formal qualifications required in the host Member State;

   (c)   the regulated profession in the host Member State comprises one or more regulated professional activities which do not exist in the corresponding profession in the applicant's home Member State within the meaning of Article 4(2), and that difference consists in specific training which is required in the host Member State and which covers substantially different matters from those covered by the applicant's attestation of competence or evidence of formal qualifications.

2   If the host Member State makes use of the option provided for in paragraph 1, it must offer the applicant the choice between an adaptation period and an aptitude test. Where a Member State considers, with respect to a given profession, that it is necessary to derogate from the requirement, set out in the previous subparagraph, that it give the applicant a choice between an adaptation period and an aptitude test, it shall inform the other Member States and the Commission in advance and provide sufficient justification for the derogation.

If, after receiving all necessary information, the Commission considers that the derogation referred to in the second subparagraph is inappropriate or that it is not in accordance with Community law, it shall, within three months, ask the Member State in question to refrain from taking the envisaged measure.

In the absence of a response from the Commission within the abovementioned deadline, the derogation may be applied.

3   By way of derogation from the principle of the right of the applicant to choose, as laid down in paragraph 2, for professions whose pursuit requires precise knowledge of national law and in respect of which the provision of advice and/or assistance concerning national law is an essential and constant aspect of the professional activity, the host Member State may stipulate either an adaptation period or an aptitude test.

This applies also to the cases provided for in Article 10 points (b) and (c), in Article 10 point (d) concerning doctors and dental practitioners, in Article 10 point (f) when the migrant seeks recognition in another Member State where the relevant professional activities are pursued by nurses responsible for general care or specialised nurses holding evidence of formal qualifications as a specialist which follows the training leading to the possession of the titles listed in Annex V, point 5.2.2 and in Article 10 point (g).

In the cases covered by Article 10 point (a), the host Member State may require an adaptation period or an aptitude test if the migrant envisages pursuing professional activities in a selfemployed capacity or as a manager of an undertaking which require the knowledge and the application of the specific national rules in force, provided that knowledge and application of those rules are required by the competent authorities of the host Member State for access to such activities by its own nationals.

4   For the purpose of applying paragraph 1 points (b) and (c), 'substantially different matters' means matters of which knowledge is essential for pursuing the profession and with regard to which the training received by the migrant shows important differences in terms of duration or content from the training required by the host Member State.

5   Paragraph 1 shall be applied with due regard to the principle of proportionality. In particular, if the host Member State intends to require the applicant to complete an adaptation period or take an aptitude test, it must first ascertain whether the knowledge acquired by the applicant in the course of his professional experience in a Member State or in a third country, is of a nature to cover, in full or in part, the substantial difference referred to in paragraph 4.

Article 15

Waiving of compensation measures on the basis of common platforms

1   For the purpose of this Article, 'common platforms' is defined as a set of criteria of professional qualifications which are suitable for compensating for substantial differences which have been identified between the training requirements existing in the various Member States for a given profession. These substantial differences shall be identified by comparison between the duration and contents of the training in at least two thirds of the Member States, including all Member States which regulate this profession. The differences in the contents of the training may result from substantial differences in the scope of the professional activities.

2   Common platforms as defined in paragraph 1 may be submitted to the Commission by Member States or by professional associations or organisations which are representative at national and European level. If the Commission, after consulting the Member States, is of the opinion that a draft common platform facilitates the mutual recognition of professional qualifications, it may present draft measures with a view to their adoption in accordance with the procedure referred to in Article 58(2).

3   Where the applicant's professional qualifications satisfy the criteria established in the measure adopted in accordance with paragraph 2, the host Member State shall waive the application of compensation measures under Article 14.

4   Paragraphs 1 to 3 shall not affect the competence of Member States to decide the professional qualifications required for the pursuit of professions in their territory as well as the contents and the organisation of their systems of education and professional training.

5   If a Member State considers that the criteria established in a measure adopted in accordance with paragraph 2 no longer offer adequate guarantees with regard to professional qualifications, it shall inform the Commission accordingly, which shall, if appropriate, present a draft measure in accordance with the procedure referred to in Article 58(2).

6   The Commission shall, by 20 October 2010, submit to the European Parliament and the Council a report on the operation of this Article and, if necessary, appropriate proposals for amending this Article.

CHAPTER II

Recognition of professional experience

Article 16

Requirements regarding professional experience

If, in a Member State, access to or pursuit of one of the activities listed in Annex IV is contingent upon possession of general, commercial or professional knowledge and aptitudes, that Member State shall recognise previous pursuit of the activity in another Member State as sufficient proof of such knowledge and aptitudes. The activity must have been pursued in accordance with Articles 17, 18 and 19.

CHAPTER III

Recognition on the basis of coordination of minimum training conditions

Section 1

General Provisions

Article 21

Principle of automatic recognition

1   Each Member State shall recognise evidence of formal qualifications as doctor giving access to the professional activities of doctor with basic training and specialised doctor, as nurse responsible for general care, as dental practitioner, as specialised dental practitioner, as veterinary surgeon, as pharmacist and as architect, listed in Annex V, points 5.1.1, 5.1.2, 5.2.2, 5.3.2, 5.3.3, 5.4.2, 5.6.2 and 5.7.1 respectively, which satisfy the minimum training conditions referred to in Articles 24, 25, 31, 34, 35, 38, 44 and 46 respectively, and shall, for the purposes of access to and pursuit of the professional activities, give such evidence the same effect on its territory as the evidence of formal qualifications which it itself issues. Such evidence of formal qualifications must be issued by the competent bodies in the Member States and accompanied, where appropriate, by the certificates listed in Annex V, points 5.1.1, 5.1.2, 5.2.2, 5.3.2, 5.3.3, 5.4.2, 5.6.2 and 5.7.1 respectively.

The provisions of the first and second subparagraphs do not affect the acquired rights referred to in Articles 23, 27, 33, 37, 39 and 49.

2   Each Member State shall recognise, for the purpose of pursuing general medical practice in the framework of its national social security system, evidence of formal qualifications listed in Annex V, point 5.1.4 and issued to nationals of the Member States by the other Member States in accordance with the minimum training conditions laid down in Article 28. The provisions of the previous subparagraph do not affect the acquired rights referred to in Article 30.

3   Each Member State shall recognise evidence of formal qualifications as a midwife, awarded to nationals of Member States by the other Member States, listed in Annex V, point 5.5.2, which complies with the minimum training conditions referred to in Article 40 and satisfies the criteria set out in Article 41, and shall, for the purposes of access to and pursuit of the professional activities, give such evidence the same effect on its territory as the evidence of formal qualifications which it itself issues. This provision does not affect the acquired rights referred to in Articles 23 and 43.

4   Member States shall not be obliged to give effect to evidence of formal qualifications referred to in Annex V, point 5.6.2, for the setting up of new pharmacies open to the public. For the purposes of this paragraph, pharmacies which have been open for less than three years shall also be considered as new pharmacies.

5   Evidence of formal qualifications as an architect referred to in Annex V, point 5.7.1, which is subject to automatic recognition pursuant to paragraph 1, proves completion of a course of training which began not earlier than during the academic reference year referred to in that Annex.

6   Each Member State shall make access to and pursuit of the professional activities of doctors, nurses responsible for general care, dental practitioners, veterinary surgeons, midwives and pharmacists subject to possession of evidence of formal qualifications referred to in Annex V, points 5.1.1, 5.1.2, 5.1.4, 5.2.2, 5.3.2, 5.3.3, 5.4.2, 5.5.2 and 5.6.2 respectively, attesting that the person concerned has acquired, over the duration of his training, and where appropriate, the knowledge and skills referred to in Articles 24(3), 31(6), 34(3), 38(3), 40(3) and 44(3).

The knowledge and skills referred to in Articles 24(3), 31(6), 34(3), 38(3), 40(3) and 44(3) may be amended in accordance with the procedure referred to in Article 58(2) with a view to adapting them to scientific and technical progress. Such updates shall not entail, for any Member State, an amendment of its existing legislative principles regarding the structure of professions as regards training and conditions of access by natural persons.

7   Each Member State shall notify the Commission of the legislative, regulatory and administrative provisions which it adopts with regard to the issuing of evidence of formal qualifications in the area covered by this Chapter. In addition, for evidence of formal qualifications in the area referred to in Section 8, this notification shall be addressed to the other Member States.

The Commission shall publish an appropriate communication in the Official Journal of the European Union, indicating the titles adopted by the Member States for evidence of formal qualifications and, where appropriate, the body which issues the evidence of formal qualifications, the certificate which accompanies it and the corresponding professional title referred to in Annex V, points 5.1.1, 5.1.2, 5.1.4, 5.2.2, 5.3.2, 5.3.3, 5.4.2, 5.5.2, 5.6.2 and 5.7.1 respectively.

Article 22

Common provisions on training

With regard to the training referred to in Articles 24, 25, 28, 31, 34, 35, 38, 40, 44 and 46:

(a)   Member States may authorise part-time training under conditions laid down by the competent authorities; those authorities shall ensure that the overall duration, level and quality of such training is not lower than that of continuous full-time training;

(b)   in accordance with the procedures specific to each Member State, continuing education and training shall ensure that persons who have completed their studies are able to keep abreast of professional developments to the extent necessary to maintain safe and effective practice.

Article 23

Acquired rights

1   Without prejudice to the acquired rights specific to the professions concerned, in cases where the evidence of formal qualifications as doctor giving access to the professional activities of doctor with basic training and specialised doctor, as nurse responsible for general care, as dental practitioner, as specialised dental practitioner, as veterinary surgeon, as midwife and as pharmacist held by Member States nationals does not satisfy all the training requirements referred to in Articles 24, 25, 31, 34, 35,

38, 40 and 44, each Member State shall recognise as sufficient proof evidence of formal qualifications issued by those Member States insofar as such evidence attests successful completion of training which began before the reference dates laid down in Annex V, points 5.1.1, 5.1.2, 5.2.2, 5.3.2, 5.3.3, 5.4.2, 5.5.2 and 5.6.2 and is accompanied by a certificate stating that the holders have been effectively and lawfully engaged in the activities in question for at least three consecutive years during the five years preceding the award of the certificate.

2   The same provisions shall apply to evidence of formal qualifications as doctor giving access to the professional activities of doctor with basic training and specialised doctor, as nurse responsible for general care, as dental practitioner, as specialised dental practitioner, as veterinary surgeon, as midwife and as pharmacist, obtained in the territory of the former German Democratic Republic, which does not satisfy all the minimum training requirements laid down in Articles 24, 25, 31, 34, 35, 38, 40 and 44 if such evidence certifies successful completion of training which began before:

(a)   3 October 1990 for doctors with basic training, nurses responsible for general care, dental practitioners with basic training, specialised dental practitioners, veterinary surgeons, midwives and pharmacists, and

(b)   3 April 1992 for specialised doctors. The evidence of formal qualifications referred to in the first subparagraph confers on the holder the right to pursue professional activities throughout German territory under the same conditions as evidence of formal qualifications issued by the competent German authorities referred to in Annex V, points 5.1.1, 5.1.2, 5.2.2, 5.3.2, 5.3.3, 5.4.2, 5.5.2 and 5.6.2.

3   Without prejudice to the provisions of Article 37(1), each Member State shall recognise evidence of formal qualifications as doctor giving access to the professional activities of doctor with basic training and specialised doctor, as nurse responsible for general care, as veterinary surgeon, as midwife, as pharmacist and as architect held by Member States nationals and issued by the former Czechoslovakia, or whose training commenced, for the Czech Republic and Slovakia, before 1 January 1993, where the authorities of either of the two aforementioned Member States attest that such evidence of formal qualifications has the same legal validity within their territory as the evidence of formal qualifications which they issue and, with respect to architects, as the evidence of formal qualifications specified for those Member States in Annex VI, point 6, as regards access to the professional activities of doctor with basic training, specialised doctor, nurse responsible for general care, veterinary surgeon, midwife, pharmacist with respect to the activities referred to in Article 45(2), and architect with respect to the activities referred to in Article 48, and the pursuit of such activities.

Such an attestation must be accompanied by a certificate issued by those same authorities stating that such persons have effectively and lawfully been engaged in the activities in question within their territory for at least three consecutive years during the five years prior to the date of issue of the certificate.

4   Each Member State shall recognise evidence of formal qualifications as doctor giving access to the professional activities of doctor with basic training and specialised doctor, as nurse responsible for general care, as dental practitioner, as specialised dental practitioner, as veterinary surgeon, as midwife, as pharmacist and as architect held by nationals of the Member States and issued by the former Soviet Union, or whose training commenced

(a)   for Estonia, before 20 August 1991,

(b)   for Latvia, before 21 August 1991,

(c)   for Lithuania, before 11 March 1990,

where the authorities of any of the three aforementioned Member States attest that such evidence has the same legal validity within their territory as the evidence which they issue and, with respect to architects, as the evidence of formal qualifications specified for those Member States in Annex VI, point 6, as regards access to the professional activities of doctor with basic training, specialised doctor, nurse responsible for general care, dental practitioner, specialised dental practitioner, veterinary surgeon, midwife, pharmacist with respect to the activities referred to in Article 45(2), and architect with respect to the activities referred to in Article 48, and the pursuit of such activities.

Such an attestation must be accompanied by a certificate issued by those same authorities stating that such persons have effectively and lawfully been engaged in the activities in question within their territory for at least three consecutive years during the five years prior to the date of issue of the certificate.

With regard to evidence of formal qualifications as veterinary surgeons issued by the former Soviet Union or in respect of which training commenced, for Estonia, before 20 August 1991, the attestation referred to in the preceding subparagraph must be accompanied by a certificate issued by the Estonian authorities stating that such persons have effectively and lawfully been engaged in the activities in question within their territory for at least five consecutive years during the seven years prior to the date of issue of the certificate.

5   Each Member State shall recognise evidence of formal qualifications as doctor giving access to the professional activities of doctor with basic training and specialised doctor, as nurse responsible for general care, as dental practitioner, as specialised dental practitioner, as veterinary surgeon, as midwife, as pharmacist and as architect held by nationals of the Member States and issued by the former Yugoslavia, or whose training commenced, for Slovenia, before 25 June 1991, where the authorities of the aforementioned Member State attest that such evidence has the same legal validity within their territory as the evidence which they issue and, with respect to architects, as the evidence of formal qualifications specified for those Member States in Annex VI, point 6, as regards access to the professional activities of doctor with basic training, specialised doctor, nurse responsible for general care, dental practitioner, specialised dental practitioner, veterinary surgeon, midwife, pharmacist with respect to the activities referred to in Article 45(2), and architect with respect to the activities referred to in Article 48, and the pursuit of such activities.

Such an attestation must be accompanied by a certificate issued by those same authorities stating that such persons have effectively and lawfully been engaged in the activities in question within their territory for at least three consecutive years during the five years prior to the date of issue of the certificate.

6   Each Member State shall recognise as sufficient proof for Member State nationals whose evidence of formal qualifications as a doctor, nurse responsible for general care, dental practitioner, veterinary surgeon, midwife and pharmacist does not correspond to the titles given for that Member State in Annex V, points 5.1.1, 5.1.2, 5.1.3, 5.1.4, 5.2.2, 5.3.2, 5.3.3, 5.4.2, 5.5.2 and 5.6.2, evidence of formal qualifications issued by those Member States accompanied by a certificate issued by the competent authorities or bodies. The certificate referred to in the first subparagraph shall state that the evidence of formal qualifications certifies successful completion of training in accordance with Articles 24, 25, 28, 31, 34, 35, 38, 40 and 44 respectively and is treated by the Member State which issued it in the same way as the qualifications whose titles are listed in Annex V, points 5.1.1, 5.1.2, 5.1.3, 5.1.4, 5.2.2, 5.3.2, 5.3.3, 5.4.2, 5.5.2 and 5.6.2.

Section 2

Doctors of medicine

Article 24

Basic medical training

1   Admission to basic medical training shall be contingent upon possession of a diploma or certificate providing access, for the studies in question, to universities.

2   Basic medical training shall comprise a total of at least six years of study or 5 500 hours of theoretical and practical training provided by, or under the supervision of, a university. For persons who began their studies before 1 January 1972, the course of training referred to in the first subparagraph may comprise six months of full-time practical training at university level under the supervision of the competent authorities.

3   Basic medical training shall provide an assurance that the person in question has acquired the following knowledge and skills:

(a)   adequate knowledge of the sciences on which medicine is based and a good understanding of the scientific methods including the principles of measuring biological functions, the evaluation of scientifically established facts and the analysis of data;

(b)   sufficient understanding of the structure, functions and behaviour of healthy and sick persons, as well as relations between the state of health and physical and social surroundings of the human being;

(c)   adequate knowledge of clinical disciplines and practices, providing him with a coherent picture of mental and physical diseases, of medicine from the points of view of prophylaxis, diagnosis and therapy and of human reproduction;

(d)   suitable clinical experience in hospitals under appropriate supervision.

Article 25

Specialist medical training

1   Admission to specialist medical training shall be contingent upon completion and validation of six years of study as part of a training programme referred to in Article 24 in the course of which the trainee has acquired the relevant knowledge of basic medicine.

2   Specialist medical training shall comprise theoretical and practical training at a university or medical teaching hospital or, where appropriate, a medical care establishment approved for that purpose by the competent authorities or bodies. The Member States shall ensure that the minimum duration of specialist medical training courses referred to in Annex V, point 5.1.3 is not less than the duration provided for in that point. Training shall be given under the supervision of the competent authorities or bodies. It shall include personal participation of the trainee specialised doctor in the activity and responsibilities entailed by the services in question.

3   Training shall be given on a full-time basis at specific establishments which are recognised by the competent authorities. It shall entail participation in the full range of medical activities of the department where the training is given, including duty on call, in such a way that the trainee specialist devotes all his professional activity to his practical and theoretical training throughout the entire working week and throughout the year, in accordance with the procedures laid down by the competent authorities. Accordingly, these posts shall be the subject of appropriate remuneration.

4   The Member States shall make the issuance of evidence of specialist medical training contingent upon possession of evidence of basic medical training referred to in Annex V, point 5.1.1.

5   The minimum periods of training referred to in Annex V, point 5.1.3 may be amended in accordance with the procedure referred to in Article 58(2) with a view to adapting them to scientific and technical progress.

Article 26

Types of specialist medical training

Evidence of formal qualifications as a specialised doctor referred to in Article 21 is such evidence awarded by the competent authorities or bodies referred to in Annex V, point 5.1.2 as corresponds, for the specialised training in question, to the titles in use in the various Member States and referred to in Annex V, point 5.1.3. The inclusion in Annex V, point 5.1.3 of new medical specialties common to at least two fifths of the Member States may be decided on in accordance with the procedure referred to in Article 58(2) with a view to updating this Directive in the light of changes in national legislation.

Article 27

Acquired rights specific to specialised doctors

1   A host Member State may require of specialised doctors whose part-time specialist medical training was governed by legislative, regulatory and administrative provisions in force as of 20 June 1975 and who began their specialist training no later than 31 December 1983 that their evidence of formal qualifications be accompanied by a certificate stating that they have been effectively and lawfully engaged in the relevant activities for at least three consecutive years during the five years preceding the award of that certificate.

2   Every Member State shall recognise the qualification of specialised doctors awarded in Spain to doctors who completed their specialist training before 1 January 1995, even if that training does not satisfy the minimum training requirements provided for in Article 25, in so far as that qualification is accompanied by a certificate issued by the competent Spanish authorities and attesting that the person concerned has passed the examination in specific professional competence held in the context of exceptional measures concerning recognition laid down in Royal Decree 1497/99, with a view to ascertaining that the person concerned possesses a level of knowledge and skill comparable to that of doctors who possess a qualification as a specialised doctor defined for Spain in Annex V, points 5.1.2 and 5.1.3.

3   Every Member State which has repealed its legislative, regulatory or administrative provisions relating to the award of evidence of formal qualifications as a specialised doctor referred to in Annex V, points 5.1.2 and 5.1.3 and which has adopted measures relating to acquired rights benefiting its nationals, shall grant nationals of other Member States the right to benefit from those measures, in so far as such evidence of formal qualifications was issued before the date on which the host Member State ceased to issue such evidence for the specialty in question.

The dates on which these provisions were repealed are set out in Annex V, point 5.1.3.

Article 28

Specific training in general medical practice

1   Admission to specific training in general medical practice shall be contingent on the completion and validation of six years of study as part of a training programme referred to in Article 24.

2   The specific training in general medical practice leading to the award of evidence of formal qualifications issued before 1 January 2006 shall be of a duration of at least two years on a full-time basis. In the case of evidence of formal qualifications issued after that date, the training shall be of a duration of at least

three years on a full-time basis. Where the training programme referred to in Article 24 comprises practical training given by an approved hospital possessing appropriate general medical equipment and services or as part of an approved general medical practice or an approved centre in which doctors provide primary medical care, the duration of that practical training may, up to a maximum of one year, be included in the duration provided for in the first subparagraph for certificates of training issued on or after 1 January 2006.

The option provided for in the second subparagraph shall be available only for Member States in which the specific training in general medical practice lasted two years as of 1 January 2001.

3   The specific training in general medical practice shall be carried out on a full-time basis, under the supervision of the competent authorities or bodies. It shall be more practical than theoretical. The practical training shall be given, on the one hand, for at least six months in an approved hospital possessing appropriate equipment and services and, on the other hand, for at least six months as part of an approved general medical practice or an approved centre at which doctors provide primary health care. The practical training shall take place in conjunction with other health establishments or structures concerned with general medicine. Without prejudice to the minimum periods laid down in the second subparagraph, however, the practical training may be given during a period of not more than six months in other approved establishments or health structures concerned with general medicine.

The training shall require the personal participation of the trainee in the professional activity and responsibilities of the persons with whom he is working.

4   Member States shall make the issuance of evidence of formal qualifications in general medical practice subject to possession of evidence of formal qualifications in basic medical training referred to in Annex V, point 5.1.1.

5   Member States may issue evidence of formal qualifications referred to in Annex V, point 5.1.4 to a doctor who has not completed the training provided for in this Article but who has completed a different, supplementary training, as attested by evidence of formal qualifications issued by the competent authorities in a Member State. They may not, however, award evidence of formal qualifications unless it attests knowledge of a level qualitatively equivalent to the knowledge acquired from the training provided for in this Article.

Member States shall determine, inter alia, the extent to which the complementary training and professional experience already acquired by the applicant may replace the training provided for in this Article.

The Member States may only issue the evidence of formal qualifications referred to in Annex V, point 5.1.4 if the applicant has acquired at least six months' experience of general medicine in a general medical practice or a centre in which doctors provide primary health care of the types referred to in paragraph 3.

Article 29

Pursuit of the professional activities of general practitioners

Each Member State shall, subject to the provisions relating to acquired rights, make the pursuit of the activities of a general practitioner in the framework of its national social security system contingent upon possession of evidence of formal qualifications referred to in Annex V, point 5.1.4.

Member States may exempt persons who are currently undergoing specific training in general medicine from this condition.

Article 30

Acquired rights specific to general practitioners

1   Each Member State shall determine the acquired rights. It shall, however, confer as an acquired right the right to pursue the activities of a general practitioner in the framework of its national social security system, without the evidence of formal qualifications referred to in Annex V, point 5.1.4, on all doctors who enjoy this right as of the reference date stated in that point by virtue of provisions applicable to the medical profession giving access to the professional activities of doctor with basic training and who are established as of that date on its territory, having benefited from the provisions of Articles 21 or 23.

   The competent authorities of each Member State shall, on demand, issue a certificate stating the holder's right to pursue the activities of general practitioner in the framework of their national social security systems, without the evidence of formal qualifications referred to in Annex V, point 5.1.4, to doctors who enjoy acquired rights pursuant to the first subparagraph.

2   Every Member State shall recognise the certificates referred to in paragraph 1, second subparagraph, awarded to nationals of Member States by the other Member States, and shall give such certificates the same effect on its territory as evidence of formal qualifications which it awards and which permit the pursuit of the activities of a general practitioner in the framework of its national social security system.

Section 3

Nurses responsible for general care

Article 31

Training of nurses responsible for general care

1   Admission to training for nurses responsible for general care shall be contingent upon completion of general education of 10 years, as attested by a diploma, certificate or other evidence issued by the competent authorities or bodies in a Member State or by a certificate attesting success in an examination, of an equivalent level, for admission to a school of nursing.

2   Training of nurses responsible for general care shall be given on a full-time basis and shall include at least the programme described in Annex V, point 5.2.1. The content listed in Annex V, point 5.2.1 may be amended in accordance with the procedure referred to in Article 58(2) with a view to adapting it to scientific and technical progress. Such updates may not entail, for any Member State, any amendment of its existing legislative principles relating to the structure of professions as regards training and the conditions of access by natural persons.

3   The training of nurses responsible for general care shall comprise at least three years of study or 4 600 hours of theoretical and clinical training, the duration of the theoretical training representing at least one-third and the duration of the clinical training at least one half of the minimum duration of the training. Member States may grant partial exemptions to persons who have received part of their training on courses which are of at least an equivalent level.

   The Member States shall ensure that institutions providing nursing training are responsible for the coordination of theoretical and clinical training throughout the entire study programme.

4   Theoretical training is that part of nurse training from which trainee nurses acquire the professional knowledge, insights and skills necessary for organising, dispensing and evaluating overall health care. The training shall be given by teachers of nursing care and by other competent persons, in nursing schools and other training establishments selected by the training institution.

5   Clinical training is that part of nurse training in which trainee nurses learn, as part of a team and in direct contact with a healthy or sick individual and/or community, to organise, dispense and evaluate the required comprehensive nursing care, on the basis of the knowledge and skills which they have acquired. The trainee nurse shall learn not only how to work in a team, but also how to lead a team and organise overall nursing care, including health education for individuals and small groups, within the health institute or in the community. This training shall take place in hospitals and other health institutions and in the community, under the responsibility of nursing teachers, in cooperation with and assisted by other qualified nurses. Other qualified personnel may also take part in the teaching process.

Trainee nurses shall participate in the activities of the department in question insofar as those activities are appropriate to their training, enabling them to learn to assume the responsibilities involved in nursing care.

6   Training for nurses responsible for general care shall provide an assurance that the person in question has acquired the following knowledge and skills:

(a)   adequate knowledge of the sciences on which general nursing is based, including sufficient understanding of the structure, physiological functions and behaviour of healthy and sick persons, and of the relationship between the state of health and the physical and social environment of the human being;

(b)   sufficient knowledge of the nature and ethics of the profession and of the general principles of health and nursing;

(c)   adequate clinical experience; such experience, which should be selected for its training value, should be gained under the supervision of qualified nursing staff and in places where the number of qualified staff and equipment are appropriate for the nursing care of the patient;

(d)   the ability to participate in the practical training of health personnel and experience of working with such personnel;

(e)   experience of working with members of other professions in the health sector.

Article 32

Pursuit of the professional activities of nurses responsible for general care

For the purposes of this Directive, the professional activities of nurses responsible for general care are the activities pursued on a professional basis and referred to in Annex V, point 5.2.2.

Article 33

Acquired rights specific to nurses responsible for general care

1   Where the general rules of acquired rights apply to nurses responsible for general care, the activities referred to in Article 23 must have included full responsibility for the planning, organisation and administration of nursing care delivered to the patient.

2   As regards the Polish qualification of nurse responsible for general care, only the following acquired rights provisions shall apply. In the case of nationals of the Member States whose evidence of formal qualifications as nurse responsible for general care was awarded by, or whose training started in, Poland before 1 May 2004 and who do not satisfy the minimum training requirements laid down in Article 31, Member States shall recognise the following evidence of formal qualifications as nurse responsible for general care as being sufficient proof if accompanied by a certificate stating that those Member State nationals have effectively and lawfully been engaged in the activities of a nurse responsible for general care in Poland for the period specified below:

(a) evidence of formal qualifications as a nurse at degree level (dyplom licencjata pielęgniarstwa) — at least three consecutive years during the five years prior to the date of issue of the certificate,

(b) evidence of formal qualifications as a nurse certifying completion of post-secondary education obtained from a medical vocational school (dyplom pielęgniarki albo pielęgniarki dyplomowanej) — at least five consecutive years during the seven years prior to the date of issue of the certificate.

The said activities must have included taking full responsibility for the planning, organisation and administration of nursing care delivered to the patient.

3 Member States shall recognise evidence of formal qualifications in nursing awarded in Poland, to nurses who completed training before 1 May 2004, which did not comply with the minimum training requirements laid down in Article 31, attested by the diploma 'bachelor' which has been obtained on the basis of a special upgrading programme contained in Article 11 of the Act of 20 April 2004 on the amendment of the Act on professions of nurse and midwife and on some other legal acts (Official Journal of the Republic of Poland of 30 April 2004 No 92, pos. 885), and the Regulation of the Minister of Health of 11 May 2004 on the detailed conditions of delivering studies for nurses and midwives, who hold a certificate of secondary school (final examination — matura) and are graduates of medical lyceum and medical vocational schools teaching in a profession of a nurse and a midwife (Official Journal of the Republic of Poland of 13 May 2004 No 110, pos. 1170), with the aim of verifying that the person concerned has a level of knowledge and competence comparable to that of nurses holding the qualifications which, in the case of Poland, are defined in Annex V, point 5.2.2.

Section 4

Dental practitioners

Article 34

Basic dental training

1 Admission to basic dental training presupposes possession of a diploma or certificate giving access, for the studies in question, to universities or higher institutes of a level recognised as equivalent, in a Member State.

2 Basic dental training shall comprise a total of at least five years of full-time theoretical and practical study, comprising at least the programme described in Annex V, point 5.3.1 and given in a university, in a higher institute providing training recognised as being of an equivalent level or under the supervision of a university.

The content listed in Annex V, point 5.3.1 may be amended in accordance with the procedure referred to in Article 58(2) with a view to adapting it to scientific and technical progress. Such updates may not entail, for any Member State, any amendment of its existing legislative principles relating to the system of professions as regards training and the conditions of access by natural persons.

3 Basic dental training shall provide an assurance that the person in question has acquired the following knowledge and skills:

(a) adequate knowledge of the sciences on which dentistry is based and a good understanding of scientific methods, including the principles of measuring biological functions, the evaluation of scientifically established facts and the analysis of data;

(b)   adequate knowledge of the constitution, physiology and behaviour of healthy and sick persons as well as the influence of the natural and social environment on the state of health of the human being, in so far as these factors affect dentistry;

(c)   adequate knowledge of the structure and function of the teeth, mouth, jaws and associated tissues, both healthy and diseased, and their relationship to the general state of health and to the physical and social well-being of the patient;

(d)   adequate knowledge of clinical disciplines and methods, providing the dentist with a coherent picture of anomalies, lesions and diseases of the teeth, mouth, jaws and associated tissues and of preventive, diagnostic and therapeutic dentistry;

(e)   suitable clinical experience under appropriate supervision. This training shall provide him with the skills necessary for carrying out all activities involving the prevention, diagnosis and treatment of anomalies and diseases of the teeth, mouth, jaws and associated tissues.

Article 35

Specialist dental training

1   Admission to specialist dental training shall entail the completion and validation of five years of theoretical and practical instruction within the framework of the training referred to in Article 34, or possession of the documents referred to in Articles 23 and 37.

2   Specialist dental training shall comprise theoretical and practical instruction in a university centre, in a treatment teaching and research centre or, where appropriate, in a health establishment approved for that purpose by the competent authorities or bodies. Full-time specialist dental courses shall be of a minimum of three years' duration supervised by the competent authorities or bodies. It shall involve the personal participation of the dental practitioner training to be a specialist in the activity and in the responsibilities of the establishment concerned.

The minimum period of training referred to in the second subparagraph may be amended in accordance with the procedure referred to in Article 58(2) with a view to adapting it to scientific and technical progress.

3   The Member States shall make the issuance of evidence of specialist dental training contingent upon possession of evidence of basic dental training referred to in Annex V, point 5.3.2.

Article 36

Pursuit of the professional activities of dental practitioners

1   For the purposes of this Directive, the professional activities of dental practitioners are the activities defined in paragraph 3 and pursued under the professional qualifications listed in Annex V, point 5.3.2.

2   The profession of dental practitioner shall be based on dental training referred to in Article 34 and shall constitute a specific profession which is distinct from other general or specialised medical professions. Pursuit of the activities of a dental practitioner requires the possession of evidence of formal qualifications referred to in Annex V, point 5.3.2. Holders of such evidence of formal qualifications shall be treated in the same way as those to whom Articles 23 or 37 apply.

3   The Member States shall ensure that dental practitioners are generally able to gain access to and pursue the activities of prevention, diagnosis and treatment of anomalies and diseases affecting the teeth, mouth, jaws and adjoining tissue, having due regard to the regulatory provisions and rules of professional ethics on the reference dates referred to in Annex V, point 5.3.2.

Article 37

Acquired rights specific to dental practitioners

1   Every Member State shall, for the purposes of the pursuit of the professional activities of dental practitioners under the qualifications listed in Annex V, point 5.3.2, recognise evidence of formal qualifications as a doctor issued in Italy, Spain, Austria, the Czech Republic and Slovakia to persons who began their medical training on or before the reference date stated in that Annex for the Member State concerned, accompanied by a certificate issued by the competent authorities of that Member State.

The certificate must show that the two following conditions are met:

(a)   that the persons in question have been effectively, lawfully and principally engaged in that Member State in the activities referred to in Article 36 for at least three consecutive years during the five years preceding the award of the certificate;

(b)   that those persons are authorised to pursue the said activities under the same conditions as holders of evidence of formal qualifications listed for that Member State in Annex V, point 5.3.2.

Persons who have successfully completed at least three years of study, certified by the competent authorities in the Member State concerned as being equivalent to the training referred to in Article 34, shall be exempt from the three-year practical work experience referred to in the second subparagraph, point (a).

With regard to the Czech Republic and Slovakia, evidence of formal qualifications obtained in the former Czechoslovakia shall be accorded the same level of recognition as Czech and Slovak evidence of formal qualifications and under the same conditions as set out in the preceding subparagraphs.

2   Each Member State shall recognise evidence of formal qualifications as a doctor issued in Italy to persons who began their university medical training after 28 January 1980 and no later than 31 December 1984, accompanied by a certificate issued by the competent Italian authorities.

The certificate must show that the three following conditions are met:

(a)   that the persons in question passed the relevant aptitude test held by the competent Italian authorities with a view to establishing that those persons possess a level of knowledge and skills comparable to that of persons possessing evidence of formal qualifications listed for Italy in Annex V, point 5.3.2;

(b)   that they have been effectively, lawfully and principally engaged in the activities referred to in Article 36 in Italy for at least three consecutive years during the five years preceding the award of the certificate;

(c)   that they are authorised to engage in or are effectively, lawfully and principally engaged in the activities referred to in Article 36, under the same conditions as the holders of evidence of formal qualifications listed for Italy in Annex V, point 5.3.2.

Persons who have successfully completed at least three years of study certified by the competent authorities as being equivalent to the training referred to in Article 34 shall be exempt from the aptitude test referred to in the second subparagraph, point (a).

Persons who began their university medical training after 31 December 1984 shall be treated in the same way as those referred to above, provided that the abovementioned three years of study began before 31 December 1994.

Section 5

Veterinary surgeons

Article 38

The training of veterinary surgeons

1   The training of veterinary surgeons shall comprise a total of at least five years of full-time theoretical and practical study at a university or at a higher institute providing training recognised as being of an equivalent level, or under the supervision of a university, covering at least the study programme referred to in Annex V, point 5.4.1.

   The content listed in Annex V, point 5.4.1 may be amended in accordance with the procedure referred to in Article 58(2) with a view to adapting it to scientific and technical progress. Such updates may not entail, for any Member State, any amendment of its existing legislative principles relating to the structure of professions as regards training and conditions of access by natural persons.

2   Admission to veterinary training shall be contingent upon possession of a diploma or certificate entitling the holder to enter, for the studies in question, university establishments or institutes of higher education recognised by a Member State to be of an equivalent level for the purpose of the relevant study.

3   Training as a veterinary surgeon shall provide an assurance that the person in question has acquired the following knowledge and skills:

   (a)   adequate knowledge of the sciences on which the activities of the veterinary surgeon are based;

   (b)   adequate knowledge of the structure and functions of healthy animals, of their husbandry, reproduction and hygiene in general, as well as their feeding, including the technology involved in the manufacture and preservation of foods corresponding to their needs;

   (c)   adequate knowledge of the behaviour and protection of animals;

   (d)   adequate knowledge of the causes, nature, course, effects, diagnosis and treatment of the diseases of animals, whether considered individually or in groups, including a special knowledge of the diseases which may be transmitted to humans;

   (e)   adequate knowledge of preventive medicine;

   (f)   adequate knowledge of the hygiene and technology involved in the production, manufacture and putting into circulation of animal foodstuffs or foodstuffs of animal origin intended for human consumption;

   (g)   adequate knowledge of the laws, regulations and administrative provisions relating to the subjects listed above;

   (h)   adequate clinical and other practical experience under appropriate supervision.

Article 39

Acquired rights specific to veterinary surgeons

Without prejudice to Article 23(4), with regard to nationals of Member States whose evidence of formal qualifications as a veterinary surgeon was issued by, or whose training commenced in, Estonia before 1 May 2004, Member States shall recognise such evidence of formal qualifications as a veterinary surgeon if it is accompanied by a certificate stating that such persons have effectively and lawfully been engaged in the activities in question in Estonia for at least five consecutive years during the seven years prior to the date of issue of the certificate.

Section 6

Midwives

Article 40

The training of midwives

1   The training of midwives shall comprise a total of at least:

   (a)   specific full-time training as a midwife comprising at least three years of theoretical and practical study (route I) comprising at least the programme described in Annex V, point 5.5.1, or

   (b)   specific full-time training as a midwife of 18 months' duration (route II), comprising at least the study programme described in Annex V, point 5.5.1, which was not the subject of equivalent training of nurses responsible for general care.

The Member States shall ensure that institutions providing midwife training are responsible for coordinating theory and practice throughout the programme of study. The content listed in Annex V, point 5.5.1 may be amended in accordance with the procedure referred to in Article 58(2) with a view to adapting it to scientific and technical progress.

Such updates must not entail, for any Member State, any amendment of existing legislative principles relating to the structure of professions as regards training and the conditions of access by natural persons.

2   Access to training as a midwife shall be contingent upon one of the following conditions:

   (a)   completion of at least the first 10 years of general school education for route I, or

   (b)   possession of evidence of formal qualifications as a nurse responsible for general care referred to in Annex V, point 5.2.2 for route II.

3   Training as a midwife shall provide an assurance that the person in question has acquired the following knowledge and skills:

   (a)   adequate knowledge of the sciences on which the activities of midwives are based, particularly obstetrics and gynaecology;

   (b)   adequate knowledge of the ethics of the profession and the professional legislation;

   (c)   detailed knowledge of biological functions, anatomy and physiology in the field of obstetrics and of the newly born, and also a knowledge of the relationship between the state of health and the physical and social environment of the human being, and of his behaviour;

   (d)   adequate clinical experience gained in approved institutions under the supervision of staff qualified in midwifery and obstetrics;

   (e)   adequate understanding of the training of health personnel and experience of working with such.

Article 41

Procedures for the recognition of evidence of formal qualifications as a midwife

1   The evidence of formal qualifications as a midwife referred to in Annex V, point 5.5.2 shall be subject to automatic recognition pursuant to Article 21 in so far as they satisfy one of the following criteria:

(a) full-time training of at least three years as a midwife:

(i) either made contingent upon possession of a diploma, certificate or other evidence of qualification giving access to universities or higher education institutes, or otherwise guaranteeing an equivalent level of knowledge; or

(ii) followed by two years of professional practice for which a certificate has been issued in accordance with paragraph 2;

(b) full-time training as a midwife of at least two years or 3 600 hours, contingent upon possession of evidence of formal qualifications as a nurse responsible for general care referred to in Annex V, point 5.2.2;

(c) full-time training as a midwife of at least 18 months or 3 000 hours, contingent upon possession of evidence of formal qualifications as a nurse responsible for general care referred to in Annex V, point 5.2.2 and followed by one year's professional practice for which a certificate has been issued in accordance with paragraph 2.

2 The certificate referred to in paragraph 1 shall be issued by the competent authorities in the home Member State. It shall certify that the holder, after obtaining evidence of formal qualifications as a midwife, has satisfactorily pursued all the activities of a midwife for a corresponding period in a hospital or a health care establishment approved for that purpose.

Article 42

Pursuit of the professional activities of a midwife

1 The provisions of this section shall apply to the activities of midwives as defined by each Member State, without prejudice to paragraph 2, and pursued under the professional titles set out in Annex V, point 5.5.2.

2 The Member States shall ensure that midwives are able to gain access to and pursue at least the following activities:

(a) provision of sound family planning information and advice;

(b) diagnosis of pregnancies and monitoring normal pregnancies; carrying out the examinations necessary for the monitoring of the development of normal pregnancies;

(c) prescribing or advising on the examinations necessary for the earliest possible diagnosis of pregnancies at risk;

(d) provision of programmes of parenthood preparation and complete preparation for childbirth including advice on hygiene and nutrition;

(e) caring for and assisting the mother during labour and monitoring the condition of the foetus in utero by the appropriate clinical and technical means;

(f) conducting spontaneous deliveries including where required episiotomies and in urgent cases breech deliveries;

(g) recognising the warning signs of abnormality in the mother or infant which necessitate referral to a doctor and assisting the latter where appropriate; taking the necessary emergency measures in the doctor's absence, in particular the manual removal of the placenta, possibly followed by manual examination of the uterus;

(h)   examining and caring for the new-born infant; taking all initiatives which are necessary in case of need and carrying out where necessary immediate resuscitation;

(i)   caring for and monitoring the progress of the mother in the post-natal period and giving all necessary advice to the mother on infant care to enable her to ensure the optimum progress of the new-born infant;

(j)   carrying out treatment prescribed by doctors;

(k)   drawing up the necessary written reports.

Article 43

Acquired rights specific to midwives

1   Every Member State shall, in the case of Member State nationals whose evidence of formal qualifications as a midwife satisfies all the minimum training requirements laid down in Article 40 but, by virtue of Article 41, is not recognised unless it is accompanied by a certificate of professional practice referred to in Article 41(2), recognise as sufficient proof evidence of formal qualifications issued by those Member States before the reference date referred to in Annex V, point 5.5.2, accompanied by a certificate stating that those nationals have been effectively and lawfully engaged in the activities in question for at least two consecutive years during the five years preceding the award of the certificate.

2   The conditions laid down in paragraph 1 shall apply to the nationals of Member States whose evidence of formal qualifications as a midwife certifies completion of training received in the territory of the former German Democratic Republic and satisfying all the minimum training requirements laid down in Article 40 but where the evidence of formal qualifications, by virtue of Article 41, is not recognised unless it is accompanied by the certificate of professional experience referred to in Article 41(2), where it attests a course of training which began before 3 October 1990.

3   As regards the Polish evidence of formal qualifications as a midwife, only the following acquired rights provisions shall apply.

In the case of Member States nationals whose evidence of formal qualifications as a midwife was awarded by, or whose training commenced in, Poland before 1 May 2004, and who do not satisfy the minimum training requirements as set out in Article 40, Member States shall recognise the following evidence of formal qualifications as a midwife if accompanied by a certificate stating that such persons have effectively and lawfully been engaged in the activities of a midwife for the period specified below:

(a)   evidence of formal qualifications as a midwife at degree level (dyplom licencjata położnictwa): at least three consecutive years during the five years prior to the date of issue of the certificate,

(b)   evidence of formal qualifications as a midwife certifying completion of post-secondary education obtained from a medical vocational school (dyplom położnej): at least five consecutive years during the seven years prior to the date of issue of the certificate.

4   Member States shall recognise evidence of formal qualifications in midwifery awarded in Poland, to midwives who completed training before 1 May 2004, which did not comply with the minimum training requirements laid down in Article 40, attested by the diploma 'bachelor' which has been obtained on the basis of a special upgrading programme contained in Article 11 of the Act of 20 April 2004 on the amendment of the Act on professions of nurse and midwife and on some other legal acts (Official Journal of the Republic of Poland of 30 April 2004 No 92, pos. 885), and the Regulation of the Minister of Health of 11 May 2004 on the detailed conditions of delivering studies for nurses and midwives, who hold a certificate of secondary school (final examination — matura) and are graduates of medical lyceum and medical vocational schools teaching in a profession of a nurse and a midwife (Official Journal of the Republic of Poland of 13 May 2004 No 110, pos 1170), with the aim of verifying that the person

concerned has a level of knowledge and competence comparable to that of midwives holding the qualifications which, in the case of Poland, are defined in Annex V, point 5.5.2.

Section 7

Pharmacist

Article 44

Training as a pharmacist

1   Admission to a course of training as a pharmacist shall be contingent upon possession of a diploma or certificate giving access, in a Member State, to the studies in question, at universities or higher institutes of a level recognised as equivalent.

2   Evidence of formal qualifications as a pharmacist shall attest to training of at least five years' duration, including at least:

(a)   four years of full-time theoretical and practical training at a university or at a higher institute of a level recognised as equivalent, or under the supervision of a university;

(b)   six-month traineeship in a pharmacy which is open to the public or in a hospital, under the supervision of that hospital's pharmaceutical department.

That training cycle shall include at least the programme described in Annex V, point 5.6.1. The contents listed in Annex V, point 5.6.1 may be amended in accordance with the procedure referred to in Article 58(2) with a view to adapting them to scientific and technical progress.

Such updates must not entail, for any Member State, any amendment of existing legislative principles relating to the structure of professions as regards training and the conditions of access by natural persons.

3   Training for pharmacists shall provide an assurance that the person concerned has acquired the following knowledge and skills:

(a)   adequate knowledge of medicines and the substances used in the manufacture of medicines;

(b)   adequate knowledge of pharmaceutical technology and the physical, chemical, biological and microbiological testing of medicinal products;

(c)   adequate knowledge of the metabolism and the effects of medicinal products and of the action of toxic substances, and of the use of medicinal products;

(d)   adequate knowledge to evaluate scientific data concerning medicines in order to be able to supply appropriate information on the basis of this knowledge;

(e)   adequate knowledge of the legal and other requirements associated with the pursuit of pharmacy.

Article 45

Pursuit of the professional activities of a pharmacist

1   For the purposes of this Directive, the activities of a pharmacist are those, access to which and pursuit of which are contingent, in one or more Member States, upon professional qualifications and which are open to holders of evidence of formal qualifications of the types listed in Annex V, point 5.6.2.

2   The Member States shall ensure that the holders of evidence of formal qualifications in pharmacy at university level or a level deemed to be equivalent, which satisfies the provisions of Article 44, are able to

gain access to and pursue at least the following activities, subject to the requirement, where appropriate, of supplementary professional experience:

(a)   preparation of the pharmaceutical form of medicinal products;

(b)   manufacture and testing of medicinal products;

(c)   testing of medicinal products in a laboratory for the testing of medicinal products;

(d)   storage, preservation and distribution of medicinal products at the wholesale stage;

(e)   preparation, testing, storage and supply of medicinal products in pharmacies open to the public;

(f)   preparation, testing, storage and dispensing of medicinal products in hospitals;

(g)   provision of information and advice on medicinal products.

3   If a Member State makes access to or pursuit of one of the activities of a pharmacist contingent upon supplementary professional experience, in addition to possession of evidence of formal qualifications referred to in Annex V, point 5.6.2, that Member State shall recognise as sufficient proof in this regard a certificate issued by the competent authorities in the home Member State stating that the person concerned has been engaged in those activities in the home Member State for a similar period.

4   The recognition referred to in paragraph 3 shall not apply with regard to the two-year period of professional experience required by the Grand Duchy of Luxembourg for the grant of a State public pharmacy concession.

5   If, on 16 September 1985, a Member State had a competitive examination in place designed to select from among the holders referred to in paragraph 2, those who are to be authorised to become owners of new pharmacies whose creation has been decided on as part of a national system of geographical division, that Member State may, by way of derogation from paragraph 1, proceed with that examination and require nationals of Member States who possess evidence of formal qualifications as a pharmacist referred to in Annex V, point 5.6.2 or who benefit from the provisions of Article 23 to take part in it.

Section 8

Architect

Article 46

Training of architects

1   Training as an architect shall comprise a total of at least four years of full-time study or six years of study, at least three years of which on a full-time basis, at a university or comparable teaching institution. The training must lead to successful completion of a university-level examination. That training, which must be of university level, and of which architecture is the principal component, must maintain a balance between theoretical and practical aspects of architectural training and guarantee the acquisition of the following knowledge and skills:

(a)   ability to create architectural designs that satisfy both aesthetic and technical requirements;

(b)   adequate knowledge of the history and theories of architecture and the related arts, technologies and human sciences;

(c)   knowledge of the fine arts as an influence on the quality of architectural design;

(d)   adequate knowledge of urban design, planning and the skills involved in the planning process;

(e)   understanding of the relationship between people and buildings, and between buildings and their environment, and of the need to relate buildings and the spaces between them to human needs and scale;

(f)   understanding of the profession of architecture and the role of the architect in society, in particular in preparing briefs that take account of social factors;

(g)   understanding of the methods of investigation and preparation of the brief for a design project;

(h)   understanding of the structural design, constructional and engineering problems associated with building design;

(i)   adequate knowledge of physical problems and technologies and of the function of buildings so as to provide them with internal conditions of comfort and protection against the climate;

(j)   the necessary design skills to meet building users' requirements within the constraints imposed by cost factors and building regulations;

(k)   adequate knowledge of the industries, organisations, regulations and procedures involved in translating design concepts into buildings and integrating plans into overall planning.

2   The knowledge and skills listed in paragraph 1 may be amended in accordance with the procedure referred to in Article 58(2) with a view to adapting them to scientific and technical progress.

Such updates must not entail, for any Member State, any amendment of existing legislative principles relating to the structure of professions as regards training and the conditions of access by natural persons.

Article 47

Derogations from the conditions for the training of architects

1   By way of derogation from Article 46, the following shall also be recognised as satisfying Article 21: training existing as of 5 August 1985, provided by 'Fachhochschulen' in the Federal Republic of Germany over a period of three years, satisfying the requirements referred to in Article 46 and giving access to the activities referred to in Article 48 in that Member State under the professional title of 'architect', in so far as the training was followed by a four-year period of professional experience in the Federal Republic of Germany, as attested by a certificate issued by the professional association in whose roll the name of the architect wishing to benefit from the provisions of this Directive appears. The professional association must first ascertain that the work performed by the architect concerned in the field of architecture represents convincing application of the full range of knowledge and skills listed in Article 46(1). That certificate shall be awarded in line with the same procedure as that applying to registration in the professional association's roll.

2   By way of derogation from Article 46, the following shall also be recognised as satisfying Article 21: training as part of social betterment schemes or part-time university studies which satisfies the requirements referred to in Article 46, as attested by an examination in architecture passed by a person who has been working for seven years or more in the field of architecture under the supervision of an architect or architectural bureau. The examination must be of university level and be equivalent to the final examination referred to in Article 46(1), first subparagraph.

Article 48

Pursuit of the professional activities of architects

1   For the purposes of this Directive, the professional activities of an architect are the activities regularly carried out under the professional title of 'architect'.

2   Nationals of a Member State who are authorised to use that title pursuant to a law which gives the competent authority of a Member State the power to award that title to Member States nationals who are especially distinguished by the quality of their work in the field of architecture shall be deemed to satisfy the conditions required for the pursuit of the activities of an architect, under the professional title of 'architect'. The architectural nature of the activities of the persons concerned shall be attested by a certificate awarded by their home Member State.

Article 49

Acquired rights specific to architects

1   Each Member State shall accept evidence of formal qualifications as an architect listed in Annex VI, point 6, awarded by the other Member States, and attesting a course of training which began no later than the reference academic year referred to in that Annex, even if they do not satisfy the minimum requirements laid down in Article 46, and shall, for the purposes of access to and pursuit of the professional activities of an architect, give such evidence the same effect on its territory as evidence of formal qualifications as an architect which it itself issues.

Under these circumstances, certificates issued by the competent authorities of the Federal Republic of Germany attesting that evidence of formal qualifications issued on or after 8 May 1945 by the competent authorities of the German Democratic Republic is equivalent to such evidence listed in that Annex, shall be recognised.

2   Without prejudice to paragraph 1, every Member State shall recognise the following evidence of formal qualifications and shall, for the purposes of access to and pursuit of the professional activities of an architect performed, give them the same effect on its territory as evidence of formal qualifications which it itself issues: certificates issued to nationals of Member States by the Member States which have enacted rules governing the access to and pursuit of the activities of an architect as of the following dates:

(a)   1 January 1995 for Austria, Finland and Sweden;

(b)   1 May 2004 for the Czech Republic, Estonia, Cyprus, Latvia, Lithuania, Hungary, Malta, Poland, Slovenia and Slovakia;

(c)   5 August 1987 for the other Member States.

The certificates referred to in paragraph 1 shall certify that the holder was authorised, no later than the respective date, to use the professional title of architect, and that he has been effectively engaged, in the context of those rules, in the activities in question for at least three consecutive years during the five years preceding the award of the certificate.

CHAPTER IV

Common provisions on establishment

Article 50

Documentation and formalities

1   Where the competent authorities of the host Member State decide on an application for authorisation to pursue the regulated profession in question by virtue of this Title, those authorities may demand the documents and certificates listed in Annex VII.

The documents referred to in Annex VII, point 1(d), (e) and (f), shall not be more than three months old by the date on which they are submitted. The Member States, bodies and other legal persons shall guarantee the confidentiality of the information which they receive.

2   In the event of justified doubts, the host Member State may require from the competent authorities of a Member State confirmation of the authenticity of the attestations and evidence of formal qualifications awarded in that other Member State, as well as, where applicable, confirmation of the fact that the beneficiary fulfils, for the professions referred to in Chapter III of this Title, the minimum training conditions set out respectively in Articles 24, 25, 28, 31, 34, 35, 38, 40, 44 and 46.

3   In cases of justified doubt, where evidence of formal qualifications, as defined in Article 3(1)(c), has been issued by a competent authority in a Member State and includes training received in whole or in part in an establishment legally established in the territory of another Member State, the host Member State shall be entitled to verify with the competent body in the Member State of origin of the award:

(a)   whether the training course at the establishment which gave the training has been formally certified by the educational establishment based in the Member State of origin of the award;

(b)   whether the evidence of formal qualifications issued is the same as that which would have been awarded if the course had been followed entirely in the Member State of origin of the award; and

(c)   whether the evidence of formal qualifications confers the same professional rights in the territory of the Member State of origin of the award.

4   Where a host Member State requires its nationals to swear a solemn oath or make a sworn statement in order to gain access to a regulated profession, and where the wording of that oath or statement cannot be used by nationals of the other Member States, the host Member State shall ensure that the persons concerned can use an appropriate equivalent wording.

Article 51

Procedure for the mutual recognition of professional qualifications

1   The competent authority of the host Member State shall acknowledge receipt of the application within one month of receipt and inform the applicant of any missing document.

2   The procedure for examining an application for authorisation to practise a regulated profession must be completed as quickly as possible and lead to a duly substantiated decision by the competent authority in the host Member State in any case within three months after the date on which the applicant's complete file was submitted. However, this deadline may be extended by one month in cases falling under Chapters I and II of this Title.

3   The decision, or failure to reach a decision within the deadline, shall be subject to appeal under national law.

Article 52

Use of professional titles

1   If, in a host Member State, the use of a professional title relating to one of the activities of the profession in question is regulated, nationals of the other Member States who are authorised to practise a regulated profession on the basis of Title III shall use the professional title of the host Member State, which corresponds to that profession in that Member State, and make use of any associated initials.

2   Where a profession is regulated in the host Member State by an association or organisation within the meaning of Article 3(2), nationals of Member States shall not be authorised to use the professional title issued by that organisation or association, or its abbreviated form, unless they furnish proof that they are

members of that association or organisation. If the association or organisation makes membership contingent upon certain qualifications, it may do so, only under the conditions laid down in this Directive, in respect of nationals of other Member States who possess professional qualifications.

TITLE IV

DETAILED RULES FOR PURSUING THE PROFESSION

Article 53

Knowledge of languages

Persons benefiting from the recognition of professional qualifications shall have a knowledge of languages necessary for practising the profession in the host Member State.

Article 54

Use of academic titles

Without prejudice to Articles 7 and 52, the host Member State shall ensure that the right shall be conferred on the persons concerned to use academic titles conferred on them in the home Member State, and possibly an abbreviated form thereof, in the language of the home Member State. The host Member State may require that title to be followed by the name and address of the establishment or examining board which awarded it. Where an academic title of the home Member State is liable to be confused in the host Member State with a title which, in the latter Member State, requires supplementary training not acquired by the beneficiary, the host Member State may require the beneficiary to use the academic title of the home Member State in an appropriate form, to be laid down by the host Member State.

Article 55

Approval by health insurance funds

Without prejudice to Article 5(1) and Article 6, first subparagraph, point (b), Member States which require persons who acquired their professional qualifications in their territory to complete a preparatory period of in-service training and/or a period of professional experience in order to be approved by a health insurance fund, shall waive this obligation for the holders of evidence of professional qualifications of doctor and dental practitioner acquired in other Member States.

TITLE V

ADMINISTRATIVE COOPERATION AND RESPONSIBILITY FOR IMPLEMENTATION

Article 56

Competent authorities

1   The competent authorities of the host Member State and of the home Member State shall work in close collaboration and shall provide mutual assistance in order to facilitate application of this Directive. They shall ensure the confidentiality of the information which they exchange.

2   The competent authorities of the host and home Member States shall exchange information regarding disciplinary action or criminal sanctions taken or any other serious, specific circumstances which are likely

to have consequences for the pursuit of activities under this Directive, respecting personal data protection legislation provided for in Directives 95/46/EC of the European Parliament and of the Council of 24 October 1995 on the protection of individuals with regard to the processing of personal data and on the free movement of such data (1) and 2002/58/EC of the European Parliament and of the Council of 12 July 2002 concerning the processing of personal data and the protection of privacy in the electronic communications sector (Directive on privacy and electronic communications) (2).

The home Member State shall examine the veracity of the circumstances and its authorities shall decide on the nature and scope of the investigations which need to be carried out and shall inform the host Member State of the conclusions which it draws from the information available to it.

3   Each Member State shall, no later than 20 October 2007, designate the authorities and bodies competent to award or receive evidence of formal qualifications and other documents or information, and those competent to receive applications and take the decisions referred to in this Directive, and shall forthwith inform the other Member States and the Commission thereof.

4   Each Member State shall designate a coordinator for the activities of the authorities referred to in paragraph 1 and shall inform the other Member States and the Commission thereof. The coordinators' remit shall be:

(a)   to promote uniform application of this Directive;

(b)   to collect all the information which is relevant for application of this Directive, such as on the conditions for access to regulated professions in the Member States.

For the purpose of fulfilling the remit described in point (b), the coordinators may solicit the help of the contact points referred to in Article 57.

Article 57

Contact points

Each Member State shall designate, no later than 20 October 2007, a contact point whose remit shall be:

(a)   to provide the citizens and contact points of the other Member States with such information as is necessary concerning the recognition of professional qualifications provided for in this Directive, such as information on the national legislation governing the professions and the pursuit of those professions, including social legislation, and, where appropriate, the rules of ethics;

(b)   to assist citizens in realising the rights conferred on them by this Directive, in cooperation, where appropriate, with the other contact points and the competent authorities in the host Member State.

At the Commission's request, the contact points shall inform the Commission of the result of enquiries with which they are dealing pursuant to the provisions of point (b) within two months of receiving them.

Article 58

Committee on the recognition of professional qualifications

1   The Commission shall be assisted by a Committee on the recognition of professional qualifications, hereinafter referred to as 'the Committee', made up of representatives of the Member States and chaired by a representative of the Commission.

2   Where reference is made to this paragraph, Articles 5 and 7 of Decision 1999/468/EC shall apply, having due regard to the provisions of Article 8 thereof.

The period laid down in Article 5(6) of Decision 1999/468/EC shall be set at two months.

3   The Committee shall adopt its rules of procedure.

Article 59

Consultation

The Commission shall ensure the consultation of experts from the professional groups concerned in an appropriate manner in particular in the context of the work of the committee referred to in Article 58 and shall provide a reasoned report on these consultations to that committee.

DIRECTIVE 2006/123/EC OF THE EUROPEAN PARLIAMENT AND OF THE COUNCIL

Article 1

Subject matter

1   This Directive establishes general provisions facilitating the exercise of the freedom of establishment for service providers and the free movement of services, while maintaining a high quality of services.

2   This Directive does not deal with the liberalisation of services of general economic interest, reserved to public or private entities, nor with the privatisation of public entities providing services.

3   This Directive does not deal with the abolition of monopolies providing services nor with aids granted by Member States which are covered by Community rules on competition. This Directive does not affect the freedom of Member States to define, in conformity with Community law, what they consider to be services of general economic interest, how those services should be organised and financed, in compliance with the State aid rules, and what specific obligations they should be subject to.

4   This Directive does not affect measures taken at Community level or at national level, in conformity with Community law, to protect or promote cultural or linguistic diversity or media pluralism.

    (1)   OJ L 184, 17.7.1999, p. 23. Decision as amended by Decision 2006/512/EC (OJ L 200, 22.7.2006, p. 11).

    (2)   OJ C 321, 31.12.2003, p. 1. L 376/50 EN Official Journal of the European Union 27.12.2006

5   This Directive does not affect Member States' rules of criminal law. However, Member States may not restrict the freedom to provide services by applying criminal law provisions which specifically regulate or affect access to or exercise of a service activity in circumvention of the rules laid down in this Directive.

6   This Directive does not affect labour law, that is any legal or contractual provision concerning employment conditions, working conditions, including health and safety at work and the relationship between employers and workers, which Member States apply in accordance with national law which respects Community law. Equally, this Directive does not affect the social security legislation of the Member States.

7   This Directive does not affect the exercise of fundamental rights as recognised in the Member States and by Community law. Nor does it affect the right to negotiate, conclude and enforce collective agreements and to take industrial action in accordance with national law and practices which respect Community law.

Article 2

Scope

1   This Directive shall apply to services supplied by providers established in a Member State.

2   This Directive shall not apply to the following activities:

    (a)   non-economic services of general interest;

(b) financial services, such as banking, credit, insurance and re-insurance, occupational or personal pensions, securities, investment funds, payment and investment advice, including the services listed in Annex I to Directive 2006/48/EC;

(c) electronic communications services and networks, and associated facilities and services, with respect to matters covered by Directives 2002/19/EC, 2002/20/EC, 2002/21/EC, 2002/22/EC and 2002/58/EC;

(d) services in the field of transport, including port services, falling within the scope of Title V of the Treaty;

(e) services of temporary work agencies;

(f) healthcare services whether or not they are provided via healthcare facilities, and regardless of the ways in which they are organised and financed at national level or whether they are public or private;

(g) audiovisual services, including cinematographic services, whatever their mode of production, distribution and transmission, and radio broadcasting;

(h) gambling activities which involve wagering a stake with pecuniary value in games of chance, including lotteries, gambling in casinos and betting transactions;

(i) activities which are connected with the exercise of official authority as set out in Article 45 of the Treaty;

(j) social services relating to social housing, childcare and support of families and persons permanently or temporarily in need which are provided by the State, by providers mandated by the State or by charities recognised as such by the State;

(k) private security services;

(l) services provided by notaries and bailiffs, who are appointed by an official act of government.

3 This Directive shall not apply to the field of taxation.

Article 3

Relationship with other provisions of Community law

1 If the provisions of this Directive conflict with a provision of another Community act governing specific aspects of access to or exercise of a service activity in specific sectors or for specific professions, the provision of the other Community act shall prevail and shall apply to those specific sectors or professions. These include:

(a) Directive 96/71/EC;

(b) Regulation (EEC) No 1408/71;

(c) Council Directive 89/552/EEC of 3 October 1989 on the coordination of certain provisions laid down by law, regulation or administrative action in Member States concerning the pursuit of television broadcasting activities (1);

(d) Directive 2005/36/EC.

2 This Directive does not concern rules of private international law, in particular rules governing the law applicable to contractual and non contractual obligations, including those which guarantee that consumers benefit from the protection granted to them by the consumer protection rules laid down in the consumer legislation in force in their Member State.

(1)   OJ L 298, 17.10.1989, p. 23. Directive as amended by Directive 97/36/EC of the European Parliament and of the Council (OJ L 202, 30.7.1997, p. 60). 27.12.2006 EN Official Journal of the European Union L 376/51

3   Member States shall apply the provisions of this Directive in compliance with the rules of the Treaty on the right of establishment and the free movement of services.

Article 4

Definitions

For the purposes of this Directive, the following definitions shall apply:

(1)   'service' means any self-employed economic activity, normally provided for remuneration, as referred to in Article 50 of the Treaty;

(2)   'provider' means any natural person who is a national of a Member State, or any legal person as referred to in Article 48 of the Treaty and established in a Member State, who offers or provides a service;

(3)   'recipient' means any natural person who is a national of a Member State or who benefits from rights conferred upon him by Community acts, or any legal person as referred to in Article 48 of the Treaty and established in a Member State, who, for professional or non-professional purposes, uses, or wishes to use, a service;

(4)   'Member State of establishment' means the Member State in whose territory the provider of the service concerned is established;

(5)   'establishment' means the actual pursuit of an economic activity, as referred to in Article 43 of the Treaty, by the provider for an indefinite period and through a stable infrastructure from where the business of providing services is actually carried out;

(6)   'authorisation scheme' means any procedure under which a provider or recipient is in effect required to take steps in order to obtain from a competent authority a formal decision, or an implied decision, concerning access to a service activity or the exercise thereof;

(7)   'requirement' means any obligation, prohibition, condition or limit provided for in the laws, regulations or administrative provisions of the Member States or in consequence of case-law, administrative practice, the rules of professional bodies, or the collective rules of professional associations or other professional organisations, adopted in the exercise of their legal autonomy; rules laid down in collective agreements negotiated by the social partners shall not as such be seen as requirements within the meaning of this Directive;

(8)   'overriding reasons relating to the public interest' means reasons recognised as such in the case law of the Court of Justice, including the following grounds: public policy; public security; public safety; public health; preserving the financial equilibrium of the social security system; the protection of consumers, recipients of services and workers; fairness of trade transactions; combating fraud; the protection of the environment and the urban environment; the health of animals; intellectual property; the conservation of the national historic and artistic heritage; social policy objectives and cultural policy objectives;

(9)   'competent authority' means any body or authority which has a supervisory or regulatory role in a Member State in relation to service activities, including, in particular, administrative authorities, including courts acting as such, professional bodies, and those professional associations or other professional organisations which, in the exercise of their legal autonomy, regulate in a collective manner access to service activities or the exercise thereof;

(10)   'Member State where the service is provided' means the Member State where the service is supplied by a provider established in another Member State;

(11)   'regulated profession' means a professional activity or a group of professional activities as referred to in Article 3(1)(a) of Directive 2005/36/EC;

(12)   'commercial communication' means any form of communication designed to promote, directly or indirectly, the goods, services or image of an undertaking, organisation or person engaged in commercial, industrial or craft activity or practising a regulated profession. The following do not in themselves constitute commercial communications:

     (a)   information enabling direct access to the activity of the undertaking, organisation or person, including in particular a domain name or an electronic-mailing address;

     (b)   communications relating to the goods, services or image of the undertaking, organisation or person, compiled in an independent manner, particularly when provided for no financial consideration.

CHAPTER II

ADMINISTRATIVE SIMPLIFICATION

Article 5

Simplification of procedures

1   Member States shall examine the procedures and formalities applicable to access to a service activity and to the exercise thereof. Where procedures and formalities examined under this paragraph are not sufficiently simple, Member States shall simplify them.

2   The Commission may introduce harmonised forms at Community level, in accordance with the procedure referred to in Article 40(2). These forms shall be equivalent to certificates, attestations and any other documents required of a provider. L 376/52 EN Official Journal of the European Union 27.12.2006

3   Where Member States require a provider or recipient to supply a certificate, attestation or any other document proving that a requirement has been satisfied, they shall accept any document from another Member State which serves an equivalent purpose or from which it is clear that the requirement in question has been satisfied. They may not require a document from another Member State to be produced in its original form, or as a certified copy or as a certified translation, save in the cases provided for in other Community instruments or where such a requirement is justified by an overriding reason relating to the public interest, including public order and security. The first subparagraph shall not affect the right of Member States to require non-certified translations of documents in one of their official languages.

4   Paragraph 3 shall not apply to the documents referred to in Article 7(2) and 50 of Directive 2005/36/EC, in Articles 45(3), 46, 49 and 50 of Directive 2004/18/EC of the European Parliament and of the Council of 31 March 2004 on the coordination of procedures for the award of public works contracts, public supply contracts and public service contracts (1), in Article 3(2) of Directive 98/5/EC of the European Parliament and of the Council of 16 February 1998 to facilitate practice of the profession of lawyer on a permanent basis in a Member State other than that in which the qualification was obtained (2), in the First Council Directive 68/151/EEC of 9 March 1968 on coordination of safeguards which, for the protection of the interests of members and others, are required by Member States of companies within the meaning of the second paragraph of Article 58 of the Treaty, with a view to making such safeguards equivalent throughout the Community (3) and in the Eleventh Council Directive 89/666/EECof 21 December 1989 concerning disclosure requirements in respect of branches opened in a Member State by certain types of company governed by the law of another State (4).

Article 6

Points of single contact

1   Member States shall ensure that it is possible for providers to complete the following procedures and formalities through points of single contact:

(a) all procedures and formalities needed for access to his service activities, in particular, all declarations, notifications or applications necessary for authorisation from the competent authorities, including applications for inclusion in a register, a roll or a database, or for registration with a professional body or association;

(b) any applications for authorisation needed to exercise his service activities.

2   The establishment of points of single contact shall be without prejudice to the allocation of functions and powers among the authorities within national systems.

Article 7

Right to information

1   Member States shall ensure that the following information is easily accessible to providers and recipients through the points of single contact:

(a)   requirements applicable to providers established in their territory, in particular those requirements concerning the procedures and formalities to be completed in order to access and to exercise service activities;

(b)   the contact details of the competent authorities enabling the latter to be contacted directly, including the details of those authorities responsible for matters concerning the exercise of service activities;

(c)   the means of, and conditions for, accessing public registers and databases on providers and services;

(d)   the means of redress which are generally available in the event of dispute between the competent authorities and the provider or the recipient, or between a provider and a recipient or between providers;

(e)   the contact details of the associations or organisations, other than the competent authorities, from which providers or recipients may obtain practical assistance.

2   Member States shall ensure that it is possible for providers and recipients to receive, at their request, assistance from the competent authorities, consisting in information on the way in which the requirements referred to in point (a) of paragraph 1 are generally interpreted and applied. Where appropriate, such advice shall include a simple step-by-step guide. The information shall be provided in plain and intelligible language.

3   Member States shall ensure that the information and assistance referred to in paragraphs 1 and 2 are provided in a clear and unambiguous manner, that they are easily accessible at a distance and by electronic means and that they are kept up to date.

4   Member States shall ensure that the points of single contact and the competent authorities respond as quickly as possible to any request for information or assistance as referred to in paragraphs 1 and 2 and, in cases where the request is faulty or unfounded, inform the applicant accordingly without delay.

5   Member States and the Commission shall take accompanying measures in order to encourage points of single contact to make the information provided for in this Article available in other Community languages. This does not interfere with Member States' legislation on the use of languages.

6   The obligation for competent authorities to assist providers and recipients does not require those authorities to provide legal advice in individual cases but concerns only general information on the way in which requirements are usually interpreted or applied.

Article 8

Procedures by electronic means

1   Member States shall ensure that all procedures and formalities relating to access to a service activity and to the exercise thereof may be easily completed, at a distance and by electronic means, through the relevant point of single contact and with the relevant competent authorities.

2   Paragraph 1 shall not apply to the inspection of premises on which the service is provided or of equipment used by the provider or to physical examination of the capability or of the personal integrity of the provider or of his responsible staff.

3   The Commission shall, in accordance with the procedure referred to in Article 40(2), adopt detailed rules for the implementation of paragraph 1 of this Article with a view to facilitating the interoperability of information systems and use of procedures by electronic means between Member States, taking into account common standards developed at Community level.

CHAPTER III

FREEDOM OF ESTABLISHMENT FOR PROVIDERS

SECTION 1

Authorisations

Article 9

Authorisation schemes

1   Member States shall not make access to a service activity or the exercise thereof subject to an authorisation scheme unless the following conditions are satisfied:

    (a)   the authorisation scheme does not discriminate against the provider in question;

    (b)   the need for an authorisation scheme is justified by an overriding reason relating to the public interest;

    (c)   the objective pursued cannot be attained by means of a less restrictive measure, in particular because an a posteriori inspection would take place too late to be genuinely effective.

2   In the report referred to in Article 39(1), Member States shall identify their authorisation schemes and give reasons showing their compatibility with paragraph 1 of this Article.

3   This section shall not apply to those aspects of authorisation schemes which are governed directly or indirectly by other Community instruments.

Article 10

Condiations for the granting of authorisation

1   Authorisation schemes shall be based on criteria which preclude the competent authorities from exercising their power of assessment in an arbitrary manner.

2   The criteria referred to in paragraph 1 shall be:

(a)   non-discriminatory;

(b)   justified by an overriding reason relating to the public interest;

(c)   proportionate to that public interest objective;

(d)   clear and unambiguous;

(e)   objective;

(f)   made public in advance;

(g)   transparent and accessible.

3   The conditions for granting authorisation for a new establishment shall not duplicate requirements and controls which are equivalent or essentially comparable as regards their purpose to which the provider is already subject in another Member State or in the same Member State. The liaison points referred to in Article 28(2) and the provider shall assist the competent authority by providing any necessary information regarding those requirements.

4   The authorisation shall enable the provider to have access to the service activity, or to exercise that activity, throughout the national territory, including by means of setting up agencies, subsidiaries, branches or offices, except where an authorisation for each individual establishment or a limitation of the authorisation to a certain part of the territory is justified by an overriding reason relating to the public interest.

5   The authorisation shall be granted as soon as it is established, in the light of an appropriate examination, that the conditions for authorisation have been met. L 376/54 EN Official Journal of the European Union 27.12.2006

6   Except in the case of the granting of an authorisation, any decision from the competent authorities, including refusal or withdrawal of an authorisation, shall be fully reasoned and shall be open to challenge before the courts or other instances of appeal.

7   This Article shall not call into question the allocation of the competences, at local or regional level, of the Member States' authorities granting authorisations.

Article 11

Duration of authorisation

1   An authorisation granted to a provider shall not be for a limited period, except where:

(a)   the authorisation is being automatically renewed or is subject only to the continued fulfilment of requirements;

(b)   the number of available authorisations is limited by an overriding reason relating to the public interest; or

(c)   a limited authorisation period can be justified by an overriding reason relating to the public interest.

2 Paragraph 1 shall not concern the maximum period before the end of which the provider must actually commence his activity after receiving authorisation.

3 Member States shall require a provider to inform the relevant point of single contact provided for in Article 6 of the following changes:

(a) the creation of subsidiaries whose activities fall within the scope of the authorisation scheme;

(b) changes in his situation which result in the conditions for authorisation no longer being met.

4 This Article shall be without prejudice to the Member States' ability to revoke authorisations, when the conditions for authorisation are no longer met.

Article 12

Selection from among several candidates

1 Where the number of authorisations available for a given activity is limited because of the scarcity of available natural resources or technical capacity, Member States shall apply a selection procedure to potential candidates which provides full guarantees of impartiality and transparency, including, in particular, adequate publicity about the launch, conduct and completion of the procedure.

2 In the cases referred to in paragraph 1, authorisation shall be granted for an appropriate limited period and may not be open to automatic renewal nor confer any other advantage on the provider whose authorisation has just expired or on any person having any particular links with that provider.

3 Subject to paragraph 1 and to Articles 9 and 10, Member States may take into account, in establishing the rules for the selection procedure, considerations of public health, social policy objectives, the health and safety of employees or self-employed persons, the protection of the environment, the preservation of cultural heritage and other overriding reasons relating to the public interest, in conformity with Community law.

Article 13

Authorisation procedures

1 Authorisation procedures and formalities shall be clear, made public in advance and be such as to provide the applicants with a guarantee that their application will be dealt with objectively and impartially.

2 Authorisation procedures and formalities shall not be dissuasive and shall not unduly complicate or delay the provision of the service. They shall be easily accessible and any charges which the applicants may incur from their application shall be reasonable and proportionate to the cost of the authorisation procedures in question and shall not exceed the cost of the procedures.

3 Authorisation procedures and formalities shall provide applicants with a guarantee that their application will be processed as quickly as possible and, in any event, within a reasonable period which is fixed and made public in advance. The period shall run only from the time when all documentation has been submitted. When justified by the complexity of the issue, the time period may be extended once, by the competent authority, for a limited time. The extension and its duration shall be duly motivated and shall be notified to the applicant before the original period has expired.

4 Failing a response within the time period set or extended in accordance with paragraph 3, authorisation shall be deemed to have been granted. Different arrangements may nevertheless be put in place, where justified by overriding reasons relating to the public interest, including a legitimate interest of third parties.

5   All applications for authorisation shall be acknowledged as quickly as possible. The acknowledgement must specify the following:

    (a)   the period referred to in paragraph 3;

    (b)   the available means of redress; 27.12.2006 EN Official Journal of the European Union L 376/55

    (c)   where applicable, a statement that in the absence of a response within the period specified, the authorisation shall be deemed to have been granted.

6   In the case of an incomplete application, the applicant shall be informed as quickly as possible of the need to supply any additional documentation, as well as of any possible effects on the period referred to in paragraph 3.

7   When a request is rejected because it fails to comply with the required procedures or formalities, the applicant shall be informed of the rejection as quickly as possible.

SECTION 2

Requirements prohibited or subject to evaluation

Article 14

Prohibited requirements

Member States shall not make access to, or the exercise of, a service activity in their territory subject to compliance with any of the following:

1   discriminatory requirements based directly or indirectly on nationality or, in the case of companies, the location of the registered office, including in particular:

    (a)   nationality requirements for the provider, his staff, persons holding the share capital or members of the provider's management or supervisory bodies;

    (b)   a requirement that the provider, his staff, persons holding the share capital or members of the provider's management or supervisory bodies be resident within the territory;

2   a prohibition on having an establishment in more than one Member State or on being entered in the registers or enrolled with professional bodies or associations of more than one Member State;

3   restrictions on the freedom of a provider to choose between a principal or a secondary establishment, in particular an obligation on the provider to have its principal establishment in their territory, or restrictions on the freedom to choose between establishment in the form of an agency, branch or subsidiary;

4   conditions of reciprocity with the Member State in which the provider already has an establishment, save in the case of conditions of reciprocity provided for in Community instruments concerning energy;

5   the case-by-case application of an economic test making the granting of authorisation subject to proof of the existence of an economic need or market demand, an assessment of the potential or current economic effects of the activity or an assessment of the appropriateness of the activity in relation to the economic planning objectives set by the competent authority; this prohibition shall not concern planning requirements which do not pursue economic aims but serve overriding reasons relating to the public interest;

6   the direct or indirect involvement of competing operators, including within consultative bodies, in the granting of authorisations or in the adoption of other decisions of the competent authorities, with the exception of professional bodies and associations or other organisations acting as the competent

authority; this prohibition shall not concern the consultation of organisations, such as chambers of commerce or social partners, on matters other than individual applications for authorisation, or a consultation of the public at large;

7   an obligation to provide or participate in a financial guarantee or to take out insurance from a provider or body established in their territory. This shall not affect the possibility for Member States to require insurance or financial guarantees as such, nor shall it affect requirements relating to the participation in a collective compensation fund, for instance for members of professional bodies or organisations;

8   an obligation to have been pre-registered, for a given period, in the registers held in their territory or to have previously exercised the activity for a given period in their territory.

Article 15

Requirements to be evaluated

1   Member States shall examine whether, under their legal system, any of the requirements listed in paragraph 2 are imposed and shall ensure that any such requirements are compatible with the conditions laid down in paragraph 3. Member States shall adapt their laws, regulations or administrative provisions so as to make them compatible with those conditions.

2   Member States shall examine whether their legal system makes access to a service activity or the exercise of it subject to compliance with any of the following non-discriminatory requirements:

   (a)   quantitative or territorial restrictions, in particular in the form of limits fixed according to population or of a minimum geographical distance between providers;

   (b)   an obligation on a provider to take a specific legal form;

   (c)   requirements which relate to the shareholding of a company; L 376/56 EN Official Journal of the European Union 27.12.2006

   (d)   requirements, other than those concerning matters covered by Directive 2005/36/EC or provided for in other Community instruments, which reserve access to the service activity in question to particular providers by virtue of the specific nature of the activity;

   (e)   a ban on having more than one establishment in the territory of the same State;

   (f)   requirements fixing a minimum number of employees;

   (g)   fixed minimum and/or maximum tariffs with which the provider must comply;

   (h)   an obligation on the provider to supply other specific services jointly with his service.

3   Member States shall verify that the requirements referred to in paragraph 2 satisfy the following conditions:

   (a)   non-discrimination: requirements must be neither directly nor indirectly discriminatory according to nationality nor, with regard to companies, according to the location of the registered office;

   (b)   necessity: requirements must be justified by an overriding reason relating to the public interest;

   (c)   proportionality: requirements must be suitable for securing the attainment of the objective pursued; they must not go beyond what is necessary to attain that objective and it must not be possible to replace those requirements with other, less restrictive measures which attain the same result.

4   Paragraphs 1, 2 and 3 shall apply to legislation in the field of services of general economic interest only insofar as the application of these paragraphs does not obstruct the performance, in law or in fact, of the particular task assigned to them.

5   In the mutual evaluation report provided for in Article 39(1), Member States shall specify the following:

(a)   the requirements that they intend to maintain and the reasons why they consider that those requirements comply with the conditions set out in paragraph 3;

(b)   the requirements which have been abolished or made less stringent.

6   From 28 December 2006 Member States shall not introduce any new requirement of a kind listed in paragraph 2, unless that requirement satisfies the conditions laid down in paragraph 3.

7   Member States shall notify the Commission of any new laws, regulations or administrative provisions which set requirements as referred to in paragraph 6, together with the reasons for those requirements. The Commission shall communicate the provisions concerned to the other Member States. Such notification shall not prevent Member States from adopting the provisions in question. Within a period of 3 months from the date of receipt of the notification, the Commission shall examine the compatibility of any new requirements with Community law and, where appropriate, shall adopt a decision requesting the Member State in question to refrain from adopting them or to abolish them. The notification of a draft national law in accordance with Directive 98/34/EC shall fulfil the obligation of notification provided for in this Directive.

CHAPTER IV FREE MOVEMENT OF SERVICES

SECTION 1

Freedom to provide services and related derogations

Article 16

Freedom to provide services

1   Member States shall respect the right of providers to provide services in a Member State other than that in which they are established. The Member State in which the service is provided shall ensure free access to and free exercise of a service activity within its territory. Member States shall not make access to or exercise of a service activity in their territory subject to compliance with any requirements which do not respect the following principles:

(a)   non-discrimination: the requirement may be neither directly nor indirectly discriminatory with regard to nationality or, in the case of legal persons, with regard to the Member State in which they are established;

(b)   necessity: the requirement must be justified for reasons of public policy, public security, public health or the protection of the environment;

(c)   proportionality: the requirement must be suitable for attaining the objective pursued, and must not go beyond what is necessary to attain that objective. 27.12.2006 EN Official Journal of the European Union L 376/57

2   Member States may not restrict the freedom to provide services in the case of a provider established in another Member State by imposing any of the following requirements:

(a)   an obligation on the provider to have an establishment in their territory;

(b)   an obligation on the provider to obtain an authorisation from their competent authorities including entry in a register or registration with a professional body or association in their territory, except where provided for in this Directive or other instruments of Community law;

(c)   a ban on the provider setting up a certain form or type of infrastructure in their territory, including an office or chambers, which the provider needs in order to supply the services in question;

(d)   the application of specific contractual arrangements between the provider and the recipient which prevent or restrict service provision by the self-employed;

(e)   an obligation on the provider to possess an identity document issued by its competent authorities specific to the exercise of a service activity;

(f)   requirements, except for those necessary for health and safety at work, which affect the use of equipment and material which are an integral part of the service provided;

(g)   restrictions on the freedom to provide the services referred to in Article 19.

3   The Member State to which the provider moves shall not be prevented from imposing requirements with regard to the provision of a service activity, where they are justified for reasons of public policy, public security, public health or the protection of the environment and in accordance with paragraph 1. Nor shall that Member State be prevented from applying, in accordance with Community law, its rules on employment conditions, including those laid down in collective agreements.

4   By 28 December 2011 the Commission shall, after consultation of the Member States and the social partners at Community level, submit to the European Parliament and the Council a report on the application of this Article, in which it shall consider the need to propose harmonisation measures regarding service activities covered by this Directive.

Article 17

Additional derogations from the freedom to provide services

Article 16 shall not apply to:

1   services of general economic interest which are provided in another Member State, inter alia:

(a)   in the postal sector, services covered by Directive 97/67/EC of the European Parliament and of the Council of 15 December 1997 on common rules for the development of the internal market of Community postal services and the improvement of quality of service (1);

(b)   in the electricity sector, services covered by Directive 2003/54/EC (2) of the European Parliament and of the Council of 26 June 2003 concerning common rules for the internal market in electricity;

(c)   in the gas sector, services covered by Directive 2003/55/EC of the European Parliament and of the Council of 26 June 2003 concerning common rules for the internal market in natural gas (3);

(d)   water distribution and supply services and waste water services;

(e)   treatment of waste;

2   matters covered by Directive 96/71/EC;

3   matters covered by Directive 95/46/EC of the European Parliament and of the Council of 24 October 1995 on the protection of individuals with regard to the processing of personal data and on the free movement of such data (4);

4   matters covered by Council Directive 77/249/EEC of 22 March 1977 to facilitate the effective exercise by lawyers of freedom to provide services (5);

5   the activity of judicial recovery of debts;

(1)   OJ L 15, 21.1.1998, p. 14. Directive as last amended by Regulation (EC) No 1882/2003 (OJ L 284, 31.10.2003, p. 1).

(2) OJ L 176, 15.7.2003, p. 37. Directive as last amended by Commission Decision 2006/653/EC (OJ L 270, 29.9.2006, p. 72).

(3) OJ L 176, 15.7.2003, p. 57.

(4) OJ L 281, 23.11.1995, p. 31. Directive as amended by Regulation (EC) No 1882/2003.

(5) OJ L 78, 26.3.1977, p. 17. Directive as last amended by the 2003 Act of Accession. L 376/58 EN Official Journal of the European Union 27.12.2006

6   matters covered by Title II of Directive 2005/36/EC, as well as requirements in the Member State where the service is provided which reserve an activity to a particular profession;

7   matters covered by Regulation (EEC) No 1408/71;

8   as regards administrative formalities concerning the free movement of persons and their residence, matters covered by the provisions of Directive 2004/38/EC that lay down administrative formalities of the competent authorities of the Member Statewhere the service is provided with which beneficiaries must comply;

9   as regards third country nationals who move to another Member State in the context of the provision of a service, the possibility for Member States to require visa or residence permits for third country nationals who are not covered by the mutual recognition regime provided for in Article 21 of the Convention implementing the Schengen Agreement of 14 June 1985 on the gradual abolition of checks at the common borders (1) or the possibility to oblige third country nationals to report to the competent authorities of the Member State in which the service is provided on or after their entry;

10 as regards the shipment of waste, matters covered by Council Regulation (EEC) No 259/93 of 1 February 1993 on the supervision and control of shipments of waste within, into and out of the European Community (2);

11 copyright, neighbouring rights and rights covered by Council Directive 87/54/EEC of 16 December 1986 on the legal protection of topographies of semiconductor products (3) and by Directive 96/9/EC of the European Parliament and of the Council of 11 March 1996 on the legal protection of databases (4), as well as industrial property rights;

12 acts requiring by law the involvement of a notary;

13 matters covered by Directive 2006/43/EC of the European Parliament and of the Council of 17 May 2006 on statutory audit of annual accounts and consolidated accounts (5);

14 the registration of vehicles leased in another Member State;

15 provisions regarding contractual and non-contractual obligations, including the form of contracts, determined pursuant to the rules of private international law.

Article 18

Case-by-case derogations

1   By way of derogation from Article 16, and in exceptional circumstances only, a Member State may, in respect of a provider established in another Member State, take measures relating to the safety of services.

2   The measures provided for in paragraph 1 may be taken only if the mutual assistance procedure laid down in Article 35 is complied with and the following conditions are fulfilled:

(a) the national provisions in accordance with which the measure is taken have not been subject to Community harmonisation in the field of the safety of services;

(b) the measures provide for a higher level of protection of the recipient than would be the case in a measure taken by the Member State of establishment in accordance with its national provisions;

(c) the Member State of establishment has not taken any measures or has taken measures which are insufficient as compared with those referred to in Article 35(2);

(d) the measures are proportionate.

3 Paragraphs 1 and 2 shall be without prejudice to provisions, laid down in Community instruments, which guarantee the freedom to provide services or which allow derogations therefrom.

SECTION 2

Rights of recipients of services

Article 19

Prohibited restrictions

Member States may not impose on a recipient requirements which restrict the use of a service supplied by a provider established in another Member State, in particular the following requirements:

(a) an obligation to obtain authorisation from or to make a declaration to their competent authorities;

(b) discriminatory limits on the grant of financial assistance by reason of the fact that the provider is established in another Member State or by reason of the location of the place at which the service is provided.

Article 20

Non-discrimination

1 Member States shall ensure that the recipient is not made subject to discriminatory requirements based on his nationality or place of residence.

2 Member States shall ensure that the general conditions of access to a service, which are made available to the public at large by the provider, do not contain discriminatory provisions relating to the nationality or place of residence of the recipient, but without precluding the possibility of providing for differences in the conditions of access where those differences are directly justified by objective criteria.

Article 21

Assistance for recipients

1 Member States shall ensure that recipients can obtain, in their Member State of residence, the following information:

(a) general information on the requirements applicable in other Member States relating to access to, and exercise of, service activities, in particular those relating to consumer protection;

(b) general information on the means of redress available in the case of a dispute between a provider and a recipient;

(c) the contact details of associations or organisations, including the centres of the European Consumer Centres Network, from which providers or recipients may obtain practical assistance. Where appropriate, advice from the competent authorities shall include a simple step-by-step guide. Information and assistance shall be provided in a clear and unambiguous manner, shall be easily accessible at a distance, including by electronic means, and shall be kept up to date.

2   Member States may confer responsibility for the task referred to in paragraph 1 on points of single contact or on any other body, such as the centres of the European Consumer Centres Network, consumer associations or Euro Info Centres. Member States shall communicate to the Commission the names and contact details of the designated bodies. The Commission shall transmit them to all Member States.

3   In fulfilment of the requirements set out in paragraphs 1 and 2, the body approached by the recipient shall, if necessary, contact the relevant body for the Member State concerned. The latter shall send the information requested as soon as possible to the requesting body which shall forward the information to the recipient. Member States shall ensure that those bodies give each other mutual assistance and shall put in place all possible measures for effective cooperation. Together with the Commission, Member States shall put in place practical arrangements necessary for the implementation of paragraph 1.

4   The Commission shall, in accordance with the procedure referred to in Article 40(2), adopt measures for the implementation of paragraphs 1, 2 and 3 of this Article, specifying the technical mechanisms for the exchange of information between the bodies of the various Member States and, in particular, the interoperability of information systems, taking into account common standards.

CHAPTER V QUALITY OF SERVICES

Article 22

Information on providers and their services

1   Member States shall ensure that providers make the following information available to the recipient:

(a)   the name of the provider, his legal status and form, the geographic address at which he is established and details enabling him to be contacted rapidly and communicated with directly and, as the case may be, by electronic means;

(b)   where the provider is registered in a trade or other similar public register, the name of that register and the provider' s registration number, or equivalent means of identification in that register;

(c)   where the activity is subject to an authorisation scheme, the particulars of the relevant competent authority or the single point of contact;

(d)   where the provider exercises an activity which is subject to VAT, the identification number referred to in Article 22(1) of Sixth Council Directive 77/388/EEC of 17 May 1977 on the harmonisation of the laws of the Member States relating to turnover taxes - Common system of value added tax: uniform basis of assessment (1);

(1)   OJ L 145, 13.6.1977, p. 1. Directive as last amended by Directive 2006/18/EC (OJ L 51, 22.2.2006, p. 12). L 376/60 EN Official Journal of the European Union 27.12.2006

(e)   in the case of the regulated professions, any professional body or similar institution with which the provider is registered, the professional title and the Member State in which that title has been granted;

(f)   the general conditions and clauses, if any, used by the provider;

(g)   the existence of contractual clauses, if any, used by the provider concerning the law applicable to the contract and/or the competent courts;

(h)   the existence of an after-sales guarantee, if any, not imposed by law;

(i)   the price of the service, where a price is pre-determined by the provider for a given type of service;

(j)   the main features of the service, if not already apparent from the context;

(k)   the insurance or guarantees referred to in Article 23(1), and in particular the contact details of the insurer or guarantor and the territorial coverage.

2   Member States shall ensure that the information referred to in paragraph 1, according to the provider's preference:

    (a)   is supplied by the provider on his own initiative;

    (b)   is easily accessible to the recipient at the place where the service is provided or the contract concluded;

    (c)   can be easily accessed by the recipient electronically by means of an address supplied by the provider;

    (d)   appears in any information documents supplied to the recipient by the provider which set out a detailed description of the service he provides.

3   Member States shall ensure that, at the recipient's request, providers supply the following additional information:

    (a)   where the price is not pre-determined by the provider for a given type of service, the price of the service or, if an exact price cannot be given, the method for calculating the price so that it can be checked by the recipient, or a sufficiently detailed estimate;

    (b)   as regards the regulated professions, a reference to the professional rules applicable in the Member State of establishment and how to access them;

    (c)   information on their multidisciplinary activities and partnerships which are directly linked to the service in question and on the measures taken to avoid conflicts of interest. That information shall be included in any information document in which providers give a detailed description of their services;

    (d)   any codes of conduct to which the provider is subject and the address at which these codes may be consulted by electronic means, specifying the language version available;

    (e)   where a provider is subject to a code of conduct, or member of a trade association or professional body which provides for recourse to a non-judicial means of dispute settlement, information in this respect. The provider shall specify how to access detailed information on the characteristics of, and conditions for, the use of non-judicial means of dispute settlement.

4   Member States shall ensure that the information which a provider must supply in accordance with this Chapter is made available or communicated in a clear and unambiguous manner, and in good time before conclusion of the contract or, where there is no written contract, before the service is provided.

5   The information requirements laid down in this Chapter are in addition to requirements already provided for in Community law and do not prevent Member States from imposing additional information requirements applicable to providers established in their territory.

6   The Commission may, in accordance with the procedure referred to in Article 40(2), specify the content of the information provided for in paragraphs 1 and 3 of this Article according to the specific nature of certain activities and may specify the practical means of implementing paragraph 2 of this Article.

Article 23

Professional liability insurance and guarantees

1   Member States may ensure that providers whose services present a direct and particular risk to the health or safety of the recipient or a third person, or to the financial security of the recipient, subscribe to professional liability insurance appropriate to the nature and extent of the risk, or provide a guarantee or

similar arrangement which is equivalent or essentially comparable as regards its purpose. 27.12.2006 EN Official Journal of the European Union L 376/61

2   When a provider establishes himself in their territory, Member States may not require professional liability insurance or a guarantee from the provider where he is already covered by a guarantee which is equivalent, or essentially comparable as regards its purpose and the cover it provides in terms of the insured risk, the insured sum or a ceiling for the guarantee and possible exclusions from the cover, in another Member State in which the provider is already established. Where equivalence is only partial, Member States may require a supplementary guarantee to cover those aspects not already covered. When a Member State requires a provider established in its territory to subscribe to professional liability insurance or to provide another guarantee, that Member State shall accept as sufficient evidence attestations of such insurance cover issued by credit institutions and insurers established in other Member States.

3   Paragraphs 1 and 2 shall not affect professional insurance or guarantee arrangements provided for in other Community instruments.

4   For the implementation of paragraph 1, the Commission may, in accordance with the regulatory procedure referred to in Article 40(2), establish a list of services which exhibit the characteristics referred to in paragraph 1 of this Article. The Commission may also, in accordance with the procedure referred to in Article 40(3), adopt measures designed to amend non-essential elements of this Directive by supplementing it by establishing common criteria for defining, for the purposes of the insurance or guarantees referred to in paragraph 1 of this Article, what is appropriate to the nature and extent of the risk.

5   For the purpose of this Article

   –   'direct and particular risk' means a risk arising directly from the provision of the service,

   –   'health and safety' means, in relation to a recipient or a third person, the prevention of death or serious personal injury,

   –   'financial security' means, in relation to a recipient, the prevention of substantial losses of money or of value of property,

   –   'professional liability insurance' means insurance taken out by a provider in respect of potential liabilities to recipients and, where applicable, third parties arising out of the provision of the service.

Article 24

Commercial communications by the regulated professions

1   Member States shall remove all total prohibitions on commercial communications by the regulated professions.

2   Member States shall ensure that commercial communications by the regulated professions comply with professional rules, in conformity with Community law, which relate, in particular, to the independence, dignity and integrity of the profession, as well as to professional secrecy, in a manner consistent with the specific nature of each profession. Professional rules on commercial communications shall be non-discriminatory, justified by an overriding reason relating to the public interest and proportionate.

Article 25

Multidisciplinary activities

1   Member States shall ensure that providers are not made subject to requirements which oblige them to exercise a given specific activity exclusively or which restrict the exercise jointly or in partnership of different activities. However, the following providers may be made subject to such requirements:

(a)   the regulated professions, in so far as is justified in order to guarantee compliance with the rules governing professional ethics and conduct, which vary according to the specific nature of each profession, and is necessary in order to ensure their independence and impartiality;

(b)   providers of certification, accreditation, technical monitoring, test or trial services, in so far as is justified in order to ensure their independence and impartiality.

2   Where multidisciplinary activities between providers referred to in points (a) and (b) of paragraph 1 are authorised, Member States shall ensure the following:

(a)   that conflicts of interest and incompatibilities between certain activities are prevented;

(b)   that the independence and impartiality required for certain activities is secured;

(c)   that the rules governing professional ethics and conduct for different activities are compatible with one another, especially as regards matters of professional secrecy.

3   In the report referred to in Article 39(1), Member States shall indicate which providers are subject to the requirements laid down in paragraph 1 of this Article, the content of those requirements and the reasons for which they consider them to be justified. L 376/62 EN Official Journal of the European Union 27.12.2006

Article 26

Policy on quality of services

1   Member States shall, in cooperation with the Commission, take accompanying measures to encourage providers to take action on a voluntary basis in order to ensure the quality of service provision, in particular through use of one of the following methods:

(a)   certification or assessment of their activities by independent or accredited bodies;

(b)   drawing up their own quality charter or participation in quality charters or labels drawn up by professional bodies at Community level.

2   Member States shall ensure that information on the significance of certain labels and the criteria for applying labels and other quality marks relating to services can be easily accessed by providers and recipients.

3   Member States shall, in cooperation with the Commission, take accompanying measures to encourage professional bodies, as well as chambers of commerce and craft associationsand consumer associations, in their territory to cooperate at Community level in order to promote the quality of service provision, especially by making it easier to assess the competence of a provider.

4   Member States shall, in cooperation with the Commission, take accompanying measures to encourage the development of independent assessments, notably by consumer associations, in relation to the quality and defects of service provision, and, in particular, the development at Community level of comparative trials or testing and the communication of the results.

5   Member States, in cooperation with the Commission, shall encourage the development of voluntary European standards with the aim of facilitating compatibility between services supplied by providers in different Member States, information to the recipient and the quality of service provision.

Article 27

Settlement of disputes

1   Member States shall take the general measures necessary to ensure that providers supply contact details, in particular a postal address, fax number or e-mail addressand telephone number to which all recipients, including those resident in another Member State, can send a complaint or a request for information about the service provided. Providers shall supply their legal address if this is not their usual address for correspondence. Member States shall take the general measures necessary to ensure that providers respond to the complaints referred to in the first subparagraph in the shortest possible time and make their best efforts to find a satisfactory solution.

2   Member States shall take the general measures necessary to ensure that providers are obliged to demonstrate compliance with the obligations laid down in this Directive as to the provision of information and to demonstrate that the information is accurate.

3   Where a financial guarantee is required for compliance with a judicial decision, Member States shall recognise equivalent guarantees lodged with a credit institution or insurer established in another Member State. Such credit institutions must be authorised in a Member State in accordance with Directive 2006/48/EC and such insurers in accordance, as appropriate, with First Council Directive 73/239/EEC of 24 July 1973 on the coordination of laws, regulations and administrative provisions relating to the taking-up and pursuit of the business of direct insurance other than life assurance (1) and Directive 2002/83/EC of the European Parliament and of the Council of 5 November 2002 concerning life assurance (2).

4   Member States shall take the general measures necessary to ensure that providers who are subject to a code of conduct, or are members of a trade association or professional body, which provides for recourse to a non-judicial means of dispute settlement inform the recipient thereof and mention that fact in any document which presents their services in detail, specifying how to access detailed information on the characteristics of, and conditions for, the use of such a mechanism.

CHAPTER VI ADMINISTRATIVE COOPERATION

Article 28

Mutual assistance – general obligations

1   Member States shall give each other mutual assistance, and shall put in place measures for effective cooperation with one another, in order to ensure the supervision of providers and the services they provide.

2   For the purposes of this Chapter, Member States shall designate one or more liaison points, the contact details of which shall be communicated to the other Member States and the Commission. The Commission shall publish and regularly update the list of liaison points.

(1)   OJ L 228, 16.8.1973, p. 3. Directive as last amended by Directive 2005/68/EC of the European Parliament and of the Council (OJ L 323, 9.12.2005, p. 1).

(2)   OJ L 345, 19.12.2002, p. 1. Directive as last amended by Directive 2005/68/EC. 27.12.2006 EN Official Journal of the European Union L 376/63

3   Information requests and requests to carry out any checks, inspections and investigations under this Chapter shall be duly motivated, in particular by specifying the reason for the request. Information exchanged shall be used only in respect of the matter for which it was requested.

4   In the event of receiving a request for assistance from competent authorities in another Member State, Member States shall ensure that providers established in their territory supply their competent authorities with all the information necessary for supervising their activities in compliance with their national laws.

5   In the event of difficulty in meeting a request for information or in carrying out checks, inspections or investigations, the Member State in question shall rapidly inform the requesting Member State with a view to finding a solution.

6   Member States shall supply the information requested by other Member States or the Commission by electronic means and within the shortest possible period of time.

7   Member States shall ensure that registers in which providers have been entered, and which may be consulted by the competent authorities in their territory, may also be consulted, in accordance with the same conditions, by the equivalent competent authorities of the other Member States.

8   Member States shall communicate to the Commission information on cases where other Member States do not fulfil their obligation of mutual assistance. Where necessary, the Commission shall take appropriate steps, including proceedings provided for in Article 226 of the Treaty, in order to ensure that the Member States concerned comply with their obligation of mutual assistance. The Commission shall periodically inform Member States about the functioning of the mutual assistance provisions.

Article 29

Mutual assistance – general obligations for the Member State of establishment

1   With respect to providers providing services in another Member State, the Member State of establishment shall supply information on providers established in its territory when requested to do so by another Member State and, in particular, confirmation that a provider is established in its territory and, to its knowledge, is not exercising his activities in an unlawful manner.

2   The Member State of establishment shall undertake the checks, inspections and investigations requested by another Member State and shall inform the latter of the results and, as the case may be, of the measures taken. In so doing, the competent authorities shall act to the extent permitted by the powers vested in them in their Member State. The competent authorities can decide on the most appropriate measures to be taken in each individual case in order to meet the request by another Member State.

3   Upon gaining actual knowledge of any conduct or specific acts by a provider established in its territory which provides services in other Member States, that, to its knowledge, could cause serious damage to the health or safety of persons or to the environment, the Member State of establishment shall inform all other Member States and the Commission within the shortest possible period of time.

Article 30

Supervision by the Member State of establishment in the event of the temporary movement of a provider to another Member State

1   With respect to cases not covered by Article 31(1), the Member State of establishment shall ensure that compliance with its requirementsis supervised in conformity with the powers of supervision provided for in its national law, in particular through supervisory measures at the place of establishment of the provider.

2   The Member State of establishment shall not refrain from taking supervisory or enforcement measures in its territory on the grounds that the service has been provided or caused damage in another Member State.

3   The obligation laid down in paragraph 1 shall not entail a duty on the part of the Member State of establishment to carry out factual checks and controls in the territory of the Member State where the service is provided. Such checks and controls shall be carried out by the authorities of the Member State where the provider is temporarily operating at the request of the authorities of the Member State of establishment, in accordance with Article 31.

Article 31

Supervision by the Member State where the service is provided in the event of the temporary movement of the provider

1   With respect to national requirements which may be imposed pursuant to Articles 16 or 17, the Member State where the service is provided is responsible for the supervision of the activity of the provider in its territory. In conformity with Community law, the Member State where the service is provided:

    (a)   shall take all measures necessary to ensure the provider complies with those requirements as regards the access to and the exercise of the activity; L 376/64 EN Official Journal of the European Union 27.12.2006

    (b)   shall carry out the checks, inspections and investigations necessary to supervise the service provided.

2   With respect to requirements other than those referred to in paragraph 1, where a provider moves temporarily to another Member State in order to provide a service without being established there, the competent authorities of that Member State shall participate in the supervision of the provider in accordance with paragraphs 3 and 4.

3   At the request of the Member State of establishment, the competent authorities of the Member State where the service is provided shall carry out any checks, inspections and investigations necessary for ensuring the effective supervision by the Member State of establishment. In so doing, the competent authorities shall act to the extent permitted by the powers vested in them in their Member State. The competent authorities may decide on the most appropriate measures to be taken in each individual case in order to meet the request by the Member State of establishment.

4   On their own initiative, the competent authorities of the Member State where the service is provided may conduct checks, inspections and investigations on the spot, provided that those checks, inspections or investigations are not discriminatory, are not motivated by the fact that the provider is established in another Member State and are proportionate.

Article 32

Alert mechanism

1   Where a Member State becomes aware of serious specific acts or circumstances relating to a service activity that could cause serious damage to the health or safety of persons or to the environment in its territory or in the territory of other Member States, that Member State shall inform the Member State of establishment, the other Member States concerned and the Commission within the shortest possible period of time.

2   The Commission shall promote and take part in the operation of a European network of Member States' authorities in order to implement paragraph 1.

3   The Commission shall adopt and regularly update, in accordance with the procedure referred to in Article 40(2), detailed rules concerning the management of the network referred to in paragraph 2 of this Article.

Article 33

Information on the good repute of providers

1   Member States shall, at the request of a competent authority in another Member State, supply information, in conformity with their national law, on disciplinary or administrative actions or criminal sanctions and decisions concerning insolvency or bankruptcy involving fraud taken by their competent authorities in respect of the provider which are directly relevant to the provider's competence or professional reliability. The Member State which supplies the information shall inform the provider thereof. A request made pursuant to the first subparagraph must be duly substantiated, in particular as regards the reasons for the request for information.

2   Sanctions and actions referred to in paragraph 1 shall only be communicated if a final decision has been taken. With regard to other enforceable decisions referred to in paragraph 1, the Member State which supplies the information shall specify whether a particular decision is final or whether an appeal has been lodged in respect of it, in which case the Member State in question should provide an indication of the date when the decision on appeal is expected. Moreover, that Member State shall specify the provisions of national law pursuant to which the provider was found guilty or penalised.

3   Implementation of paragraphs 1 and 2 must comply with rules on the provision of personal data and with rights guaranteed to persons found guilty or penalised in the Member States concerned, including by professional bodies. Any information in question which is public shall be accessible to consumers.

Article 34

Accompanying measures

1   The Commission, in cooperation with Member States, shall establish an electronic system for the exchange of information between Member States, taking into account existing information systems.

2   Member States shall, with the assistance of the Commission, take accompanying measures to facilitate the exchange of officials in charge of the implementation of mutual assistance and training of such officials, including language and computer training.

3   The Commission shall assess the need to establish a multiannual programme in order to organise relevant exchanges of officials and training.

Article 35

Mutual assistance in the event of case-by-case derogations

1   Where a Member State intends to take a measure pursuant to Article 18, the procedure laid down in paragraphs 2 to 6 of this Article shall apply without prejudice to court proceedings, including preliminary proceedings and acts carried out in the framework of a criminal investigation. 27.12.2006 EN Official Journal of the European Union L 376/65

2   The Member State referred to in paragraph 1 shall ask the Member State of establishment to take measures with regard to the provider, supplying all relevant information on the service in question and the circumstances of the case. The Member State of establishment shall check, within the shortest possible period of time, whether the provider is operating lawfully and verify the facts underlying the request. It shall inform the requesting Member State within the shortest possible period of time of the measures taken or envisaged or, as the case may be, the reasons why it has not taken any measures.

3   Following communication by the Member State of establishment as provided for in the second subparagraph of paragraph 2, the requesting Member State shall notify the Commission and the Member State of establishment of its intention to take measures, stating the following:

(a) the reasons why it believes the measures taken or envisaged by the Member State of establishment are inadequate;

(b) the reasons why it believes the measures it intends to take fulfil the conditions laid down in Article 18.

4 The measures may not be taken until fifteen working days after the date of notification provided for in paragraph 3.

5 Without prejudice to the possibility for the requesting Member State to take the measures in question upon expiry of the period specified in paragraph 4, the Commission shall, within the shortest possible period of time, examine the compatibility with Community law of the measures notified. Where the Commission concludes that the measure is incompatible with Community law, it shall adopt a decision asking the Member State concerned to refrain from taking the proposed measures or to put an end to the measures in question as a matter of urgency.

6 In the case of urgency, a Member State which intends to take a measure may derogate from paragraphs 2, 3 and 4. In such cases, the measures shall be notified within the shortest possible period of time to the Commission and the Member State of establishment, stating the reasons for which the Member State considers that there is urgency.

Article 36

Implementing measures

In accordance with the procedure referred to in Article 40(3), the Commission shall adopt the implementing measures designed to amend non-essential elements of this Chapter by supplementing it by specifying the time-limits provided for in Articles 28 and 35. The Commission shall also adopt, in accordance with the procedure referred to in Article 40(2), the practical arrangements for the exchange of information by electronic means between Member States, and in particular the interoperability provisions for information systems.

CHAPTER VII CONVERGENCE PROGRAMME

Article 37

Codes of conduct at Community level

1 Member States shall, in cooperation with the Commission, take accompanying measures to encourage the drawing up at Community level, particularly by professional bodies, organisations and associations, of codes of conduct aimed at facilitating the provision of services or the establishment of a provider in another Member State, in conformity with Community law.

2 Member States shall ensure that the codes of conduct referred to in paragraph 1 are accessible at a distance, by electronic means.

Article 38

Additional harmonisation

The Commission shall assess, by 28 December 2010 the possibility of presenting proposals for harmonisation instruments on the following subjects:

(a) access to the activity of judicial recovery of debts;

(b) private security services and transport of cash and valuables.

Article 39

Mutual evaluation

1 By 28 December 2009 at the latest, Member States shall present a report to the Commission, containing the information specified in the following provisions:

 (a) Article 9(2), on authorisation schemes;

 (b) Article 15(5), on requirements to be evaluated;

 (c) Article 25(3), on multidisciplinary activities. L 376/66 EN Official Journal of the European Union 27.12.2006

2 The Commission shall forward the reports provided for in paragraph 1 to the Member States, which shall submit their observations on each of the reports within six months of receipt. Within the same period, the Commission shall consult interested parties on those reports.

3 The Commission shall present the reports and the Member States' observations to the Committee referred to in Article 40(1), which may make observations.

4 In the light of the observations provided for in paragraphs 2 and 3, the Commission shall, by 28 December 2010 at the latest, present a summary report to the European Parliament and to the Council, accompanied where appropriate by proposals for additional initiatives.

5 By 28 December 2009 at the latest, Member States shall present a report to the Commission on the national requirements whose application could fall under the third subparagraph of Article 16(1) and the first sentence of Article 16(3), providing reasons why they consider that the application of those requirements fulfil the criteria referred to in the third subparagraph of Article 16(1) and the first sentence of Article 16(3). Thereafter, Member States shall transmit to the Commission any changes in their requirements, including new requirements, as referred to above, together with the reasons for them. The Commission shall communicate the transmitted requirements to other Member States. Such transmission shall not prevent the adoption by Member States of the provisions in question. The Commission shall on an annual basis thereafter provide analyses and orientations on the application of these provisions in the context of this Directive.

Article 40

Committee procedure

1 The Commission shall be assisted by a Committee.

2 Where reference is made to this paragraph, Articles 5 and 7 of Decision 1999/468/EC shall apply, having regard to the provisions of Article 8 thereof. The period laid down in Article 5(6) of Decision 1999/468/EC shall be set at three months.

3 Where reference is made to this paragraph, Article 5a(1) to (4), and Article 7 of Decision 1999/468/EC shall apply, having regard to the provisions of Article 8 thereof.

Article 41

Review clause

The Commission, by 28 December 2011 and every three years thereafter, shall present to the European Parliament and to the Council a comprehensive report on the application of this Directive. This report shall, in accordance with Article 16(4), address in particular the application of Article 16. It shall also consider the need for additional measures for matters excluded from the scope of application of this Directive. It shall be accompanied, where appropriate, by proposals for amendment of this Directive with a view to completing the Internal Market for services.

Article 42

Amendment of Directive 98/27/EC

In the Annex to Directive 98/27/EC of the European Parliament and of the Council of 19 May 1998 on injunctions for the protection of consumers' interests (1), the following point shall be added:

'13. Directive 2006/123/EC of the European Parliament and of the Council of 12 December 2006 on services in the internal market (OJ L 376, 27.12.2006, p. 36)'.

Article 43

Protection of personal data The implementation and application of this Directive and, in particular, the provisions on supervision shall respect the rules on the protection of personal data as provided for in Directives 95/46/EC and 2002/58/EC.

CHAPTER VIII FINAL PROVISIONS

Article 44

Transposition

1   Member States shall bring into force the laws, regulations and administrative provisions necessary to comply with this Directive before 28 December 2009. They shall forthwith communicate to the Commission the text of those measures. When Member States adopt these measures, they shall contain a reference to this Directive or shall be accompanied by such a reference on the occasion of their official publication. The methods of making such reference shall be laid down by Member States.

(1)   OJ L 166, 11.6.1998, p. 51. Directive as last amended by Directive 2005/29/EC. 27.12.2006 EN Official Journal of the European Union L 376/67

2   Member States shall communicate to the Commission the text of the main provisions of national law which they adopt in the field covered by this Directive.

Notes

Notes